Extraterrestrial Sciences

"Any sufficiently advanced technology is indistinguishable from magic."
Arthur C. Clarke

by Joel A. Wendt

cover image: ***"Aschmunadai"***
an intelligence of the Zone Girdling the Earth ...
from Franz Bardon's "The Practice of Ceremonial Evocation"

Chronicles of the Mysteries

I. Introduction

II. The Idea of Mind – a Christian meditator considers the problem of consciousness – an early effort to raise questions about current thinking in the brain and psychological sciences.

III. The Quiet Suffering of Nature – The environmental movement is urged to find an I & Thou relationship with a conscious Living Planet.

IV. The Misconception of Cosmic Space as appears in the Ideas of modern astronomy - *and as contained in the understandably limited thinking embodied in the conceptions of the nature of parallax and redshift.*

V. Letters on Magic – a series of letters considers the relationship between the four classical elements of the ancient Egyptians (fire, air, water, earth) and the four fundamental forces/transformations of modern physics (gravity, electro-magnetic, and the strong and weak nuclear interactions.

VI. Some Reflections on the Truth Value of modern Theoretical Physics.

VII. I am not my brain: the map is not the territory – observations on the philosophical acumen of brain scientists, and their unjustified fantasies.

VIII. Cowboy Bebop and the Physics of Thought as Moral Art.

IX. Healing the Insanity of Psychiatric Medicines and Practices.

X. The Father at Rest – magical and mystical dark-matter physics in the Age of Technological Chaos

XI. A Shaman's Guide to the Covid Mystery

XII. Medicine's Einstein

XIII. Curious Ephemera - musings on the Steiner Ideas of the Eighth Sphere and the Third Force

Introduction

Poet
by

It is an essential thesis (theory) of this work that Nature is a self-aware sentient consciousness, which the ancient Greeks named "the Goddess Natura". As a consequence of this fact, the search for extraterrestrial life requires that we only need walk into the Woods with an open heart, and find that which we fancy must be billions of miles away, yet has always been right there in front of us.

For example, the ancient Hermetic Science of the Egyptians is also called "Magic". There exist three books, by Franz Bardon: "Initiation Into Hermetics", "The Practice of Ceremonial Evocation" and "The Key to the True Quabbalah" which illuminate the hows and whys and wherefores of the science of Magic.

There is also the Spiritual Science (sometimes erroneously also known as: Anthroposophy) presented to the world by Rudolf Steiner. His students are a bit confused, and believe those terms: Anthroposophy and Spiritual Science have the same meaning. Yet, these students ignore Steiner's frequent use of the term "anthroposophical spiritual science, which if they were an identity, logically comes down to something on the order of "grape flavored grape flavor", which is clearly nonsense.

Steiner did offer, in his first books, a Science of Knowing, whose principle works are: "A Theory of Knowledge Implicit in Goethe's World Conception" and "The Philosophy of Spiritual activity". The latter he describes as "some results of introspection (soul observation) following the methods of Natural Science" The former was called by Owen Barfield: "the least read most important book Steiner ever wrote".

Goethe's Theory of Color is well known to a few, and contradicts Newton's ideas about the nature of light. The story is told, that Goethe was interested in Newton's ideas, and had borrowed some prisms, but had net yet applied them. The owner wanted them back, so Goethe looked through a prism and declared: "Newton is wrong".

He had expected that the light that was to strike his eye would express the seven primary colors, and found this was not the case. Newton had in fact, not looked through a prism, but just shined light through it to get the effect on which his ideas were to rely. Although Goethe did observe that where there were shadows, the edges, those did express the division into seven colors. Following this experience he began a long series of experiments, which then formed the basis of experience out of which he later came assert that: "Colors are the deeds and suffering of light".

Steiner also inspired the creation of a Goethean Science, which uses as its primary means of operation the discipline of "phenomenology". If we just examine Nature in the right way, the phenomena themselves "speak", and there is no need for a theoretical construct behind the appearances. One of Barfield's principle works is called: "Saving the Appearances"; and, his wide ranging studies, of the changes in language over time, are entirely rooted in the phenomena.

I, myself, have made a decades long phenomenological study of human social and political life, and this ended up with me writing: "The Art of God – an actual theory of Everything". In that work, instead of pitting Science and Religion against each other, I resolved this riddle by first creating a theory of God, and offering it as giving us a better explanation of human experience then does the ideas of Big Bang cosmology, and Neo-Darwinian evolution.

We live today in a world dominated by the ideas of Scientific Materialism: all is matter, there is no spirit. I will next point to certain basic books of Goethean Science, after which I will offer my own studies of various riddles that arise if we are to come to know that we are not just matter, but also spirit.

It needs to be said, that the most students of Rudolf Steiner do not read Goethean Science works. Rather they mostly read his books and lectures, and have essentially created a religion, that I started calling Steinerism a few decades ago.

Among the significant works of this phenomenological approach, are a crucial set of works which are not in print, and not studied. These are the works of George Adams Kaufmann on advanced theoretical physics. "Space and the Light of Creation", which has three sections: 1) Radiation of Space; 2) Music of Number; and 3) Burden of Earth and the Sacrifice of Warmth.

In addition there is "Physical and Ethereal Spaces", which I describe as a yoga for the imagination. As well we have: "Universal Forces in Mechanics". These works are based upon the ideas of the new geometry: Projective Geometry.

Known to some Steiner students, we have then this: "Man or Matter – Introduction to a Spiritual Understanding of Nature on the Basis of Goethe's Method of Training Observation and Thought", by Ernst Lehrs, Ph. D. … which I call a gospel of physics.

This last idea needs some explication. A spiritual view of the present reveals that there is happening now a Second Becoming of Christ in the Realm of Living Thought. Those who practice Goethean Science encounter this spiritual aspect of thinking, via the disciplines authored by Goethe. Please note that I use the term "a", and not the term "the".

Another work is "The Nature of Substance – spirit and matter", which I call a gospel of organic chemistry, written by Dr. Rudolf Hauschka.

"Sensitive Chaos", by Theodor Schwenk, is a gospel of the nature of formation, through learning the sculpting effects of the laws governing movements in Water and Air.

"Man and Mammals – Toward a Biology of Form", by Wolfgang Schad, looks at form in the animal and human kingdom, in the light of Steiner's ideas of the threefold nature of form: the nerve-sense system, the heart and lung system, and the metabolic limb system – a gospel of form in the living organism. There is a group called: "The Nature Institute", which teaches these ways of observation.

Then there is the two volume studies of the Plant, by Gerbert Grohmann, which I designate as a gospel of the Green World.

As to geology, and the riddles of the layers of the Earth, we have: "The Mutual Evolution of Earth and Humanity – a Sketch of the Geology and Paleontology of the Living Earth", by Dankmar Bosse.

Given our modern ideas about the mystery of the starry world, I have written: "The Misconception of Cosmic Space as appears in the Ideas of Modern Astronomy", where instead of using Euclidean Geometry, we use the Ideas of Projective Geometry.

Also included below is my twelve part meditation on the relationship of the four fundamental forces and transformations in modern physics and the secrets of the ancient Idea of the Four Elements.

Also my writings on the "brain" and thinking are included; "I am not my brain – the map is not the territory"; "Cowboy Bebop and the Physics of Thought as Moral Art". I have also written the practical "Healing the Insanity of Psychiatric Medicines and Practices"

In addition my studies of "electricity" are included, which lead to the Idea of "The Father at Rest – magical and mystical dark matter physics in the Age of Technological Chaos",

We will begin, with my "The Quite Suffering of Nature", and "The Idea of Mind – a Christian meditator considers the problem of consciousness". These last two are where I begin over two decades ago.

A final work, for a kind of fun are: https://thecollectiveimagination.com/2023/05/22/musings-on-the-steiner-ideas-of-the-eighth-sphere-and-the-third-force/ .

~!~!~!~!~!~!~!~!~!~

The Idea of Mind

- a Christian meditator considers the problem of consciousness -

by

Joel A. Wendt

(originally written in the early '90's, then corrected slightly with
the addition of active URLs in the late fall of 2003)

For many people, having been raised in modern culture, mind is

thought to be something that exists in the brain, and as a byproduct of basically chemical and electrical processes in cells and nerves. This essay considers this problem quite directly and finds that, for all its inventiveness, science has yet to ask and seek the answer to the most important question - "what is mind to itself". When mind
considers itself directly, in its own inward environment, then the idea of mind, as a product of the biology of the brain, fails.

Introduction

If laymen were not intrigued by the mysteries of the world, there would be little interest in the constant flow of books and magazine articles explaining modern cosmology, anthropology, paleontology, and so forth. While such explanations are often fascinating, far too many science writers unnecessarily confuse the boundaries between fact and speculation. For the layman this distinction, between what scientists truly know and what they speculate might be true, is not understood and has engendered in the public mind a scientific appearing, yet somewhat mythological, world view.

For example, the once unanimous acceptance of natural selection as the guiding principle in evolutionary biology is slowly eroding in those circles where the problem is critically considered. Yet this idea, which is not supported by any of the geological facts, remains a staple of the modern view of our evolutionary past. It is used in countless places to explain and support other speculations, and will no doubt continue for some time to be one of the main beliefs we have of the world. Its truth is not proven, however. The known facts do not support it.

In this regard, when speaking of natural selection, or "Darwinism", I am basically referring to the general idea which modern humanity is taught, namely that the human being developed through millions of years as a result of accidental processes leading from a mineral ocean, through a biological soup, to single celled organisms, then to invertebrates, vertebrates, mammals and man. It is this general picture which is not sustainable in the face of the actual facts, and the genuine pursuit of the truth.

The fossil record reveals that between when a geological age begins and when it ends the plants and animals have remained the same. The paleontologist calls this "stasis" - over the whole of a geological age there is no observable evolutionary change, particularly no evidence whatsoever of one species being transmuted into another. Whatever change does occur, appears to happen in the interval between ages, which for unknown reasons remaining quite mysterious, and leaves no trace of its processes.

This is an objective instance where the theoretical speculations of science have not stood the test of time, yet our ideas of the world, once captured by this speculative conception, are unable to disentangle themselves. Natural selection is such a strongly held article of faith, both within and without the scientific community, that it will continue to be a dominant idea for many many years. In human psychology it has more kinship with myth then it does with truth.

It is this myth making capacity of scientifically authored speculations that concerns us. It is such a powerful force on the ideas we hold about the world, that we can fully expect, for example, that many readers will not believe what has been said here about natural selection. Dozens of books and articles supporting what is said could be cited, yet most people would rather dismiss these statements as the prejudices of perhaps a "creationist", then risk their own belief system and actually look into what is being discussed in those circles where this question is genuinely being considered. (See for example: Evolution: a Theory in Crisis, Michael Denton, (Adler & Adler, 1986); and <u>Dogma and Doubt</u>, by Ronald H. Brady.In a most recent popular critical examination of evolutionary biology, Darwin On Trial, Phillip E. Johnson, (1991, Regnery Gateway), the whole problem is carefully examined with an eye to aiding the layman in understanding the difficulties that "Darwinism" represents. The standard, however, is not to test modern evolutionary biology against some kind of competing theory, but rather to see whether it is good science. It is this which "Darwinism" fails at. It is simply bad science, and as a consequence results in two very serious and dangerous results.

The first is that it holds still the advancement of the biological sciences in that these might discover important facts upon which a more realistic theory could be advanced. As long as "Darwinism" is held to, biology is blind when it looks to the past, trapped in an illusion of its own creation.

The second danger is that this untestable theory is used to support other kinds of speculations in other realms, most significantly for our purposes, the investigation of human consciousness. Important questions, which otherwise would suggest alternative ways of thinking about consciousness, cannot be asked because "Darwinism" is already presumed to answer them. At various places, as we proceed with the text, we will encounter this danger. When this occurs, when we run into this speculative and myth creating impulse, I will endeavor to point it out.

The Idea of Mind

Recent advances in neurophysiology, in computer science, and in cognitive science and related disciplines, have produced numerous books, as well as major television series, on the workings of the mind. For the most part, when I read these books I find my morality, my heart-felt concerns, my idealism, my life of prayer, of meditation and contemplation - all these most precious, most subtle inner experiences - increasingly explained as mere electro-chemical phenomena, as products of brain activity in the most material sense, and nothing else. Here is the speculative myth making power of science in action. In saying this it should be noted that it is not so much that I am against science, but rather that science has only asked one-half of the essential question, namely what is consciousness viewed from the outside. The other half of the question is: What is consciousness viewed from the inside.

The views put forward by the vast majority of workers in these fields are materialistic, deterministic, and ultimately anti-religious, although often not consciously so. These questions of the ultimate truth of human nature, in so far as the mind sciences consider them, are being decided without really debating them in a forum in which the broader implications are considered. Neurophysiology, for example, really only asks certain limited kinds of questions (chemical happenings in brain cells, or how cells cooperate to apparently accomplish computation), yet appears to assume that inner states of consciousness are produced exclusively by these cell processes.

"It is old hat to say that the brain is responsible for mental activity. Such a claim may annoy the likes of Jerry Falwell or the Ayatollah, but it is more or less the common assumption of educated people in the twentieth century. Ever since the scientific revolution, the guiding view of most scientists has been that knowledge about the brain, its cells and its chemistry will explain mental states. However, believing that the brain supports behavior is the easy part: explaining how is quite another." (Mind Matters: How the Mind and Brain interact to Create Our Conscious Lives, Michael S. Grazzanica Ph.D. pp 1, Houghton Mifflin, Boston 1988).

We should perhaps note two things about the above quotation. First the words "common assumption" and "believing", by which Grazanica tacitly admits that we are not here dealing with proven facts, but rather with the "belief system" held in common by some unknown portion of the scientific community. Secondly, he clearly admits that moving from facts about brain chemistry and related phenomena to an explanation of consciousness, free will, morality etc. is a gigantic undertaking.

In that portion of the scientific community supportive of Grazzanica's "common assumption", brain and mind are considered a single phenomenon, and one popular science writer even goes so far as to say that the recent advances in neurosciences establish conclusively that there is no human spirit, and that all states of consciousness are caused electro-chemically. "There will of course be a certain sadness as the "human spirit" joins the flat earth, papal infallibility and creationism on the list of widely held but obviously erroneous convictions." (Molecules of the Mind, Jon Franklin, p 202, Atheneum, New York, 1987).

There can be no doubt that if a human being ingests certain chemical substances, whether for recreational purposes or as prescribed medicine, the state of consciousness is altered. Electrical stimulation of the brain also produces effects, whether it is simple stimulation of certain brain centers to cause pleasure or to bring out memories, or whether it is the more invasive electroshock therapy, still used routinely today for certain intractable mental disorders. In one part of our society we say free use of chemicals to alter mental states is a crime and in another part forced use is advocated in order to control deviant behaviors. (c.f. Deviance and Medicalization: from Badness to Sickness, Conrad and Schneider, Merrill Publishing Company, 1985).

The point of this is to realize that we are not only dealing with serious questions of truth, of whether scientists actually know what they claim to believe, but also with the social policy consequences of this knowledge. The central question remains, however: what is the relationship between mind and brain? As we proceed, I would like to show how to extend our knowledge of human consciousness by considering what one can come to know from what might be called: Christian meditative practice. In such a practice, what one can know about mind is quite different from what science knows. In such a practice, mind is explored from the inside rather than from the outside. Even though, unfortuanetly, those who have explored mind from the outside have pretty much concluded:

"...it has long been recognized that mind does not exist somehow apart from brain..." (The Mind, Richard M. Restak M.D. pp ll, Bantam Books, 1988);

"My fundamental premise about the brain is that its workings - what we sometimes call mind - are a consequence of it anatomy and physiology and nothing more." (The Dragons of Eden, Speculations of the Evolution of Human Intelligence, Carl Sagan, pp.7, Ballantine Books, 1977).

Quite other conclusions are possible, in fact, may be said to be mandated, if one takes the trouble to examine consciouness from the inside, as is possible for anyone with a more or less intact mental health, and the requisite good will.

At this point I would like to proceed in such a manner that it is provisionally allowed to use the words spirit and soul, but in a way that acknowledges the legitmate requirements of science for exact, emperical and logically rigorous consideration. These two words ar essential to understanding mind from a Christian contemplative view and can be put forward in a way free of metaphysical or mystical implications. The problem is in part confused by the fact that today, when we use the word mind in normal langague usage, we mean only the brain and as well confine this aspect of our nature within the boundaries of the skull. Mind (in modern usage) means brain, means within the head.

Soul and spirit, on the other hand, are not thought of this way, and while many people do not even think such entities exist in the same sense as mind and brain, at least these words have the advantage of being capable of a usage meaning something beyond the spacially limited confines of the cranium.

The problem is one of relating personal experience to langauge in a situation in which the practices of science have tended to already fix the meaning of certain words. For example, the poet will refer to heart with regard to the phenomenon of human feeling. Our whole language is filled with related expressions (heart-felt, warm-hearted etc.). On the other hand, the scientific community tends to see emotion (feeling) as a function of glandular and brain chemistry, and therefore as an aspect of the mind/brain/body nexus. Yet, an electo-chemical explanation seems to deny human experience, which has produced language implying that the center of our "feeling" life is not connected to the brain, not located specially in the head, but rather finds is primary locus in the chest. We say, "I have a gut feeling", or "my heart got caught in my throat".

The point of this is to notice the denial of this imagery (derived from human experience) by the processes of scientific thinking which have over the last few hundred years more and more confined the source of these experiences to the head and to material causes.

As a general trend in science this is called reductionism and involves a process which Eddington called earlier in this century: "Knowing more and more about less and less." Our body of knowledge about cell chemistry and neural networks in the brain grows, but often at a cost to genuine human understanding (I say this from direct experience, as one who has worked in a neuropsychiatric unit in a private hospital). Perhaps it is time to pause and consider whether or not it is necessary to go the other way for a while, to reintroduce the study of the soul, from the inside, as it appears to direct human experience.

This can, I am certain, be done with due regard for the demand of science for reproducibility. I recognize this is not the usual approach by religious thinkers, yet in this case our mutual respect for the truth seems to require it. This ethical demand of science for reproducibility, namely that whatever is asserted here concerning mind (soul/spirit) be discoverable by another who is willing to follow the procedures, the experimental protocols, as it were; this demand I believe is perfectly justified.

In "new age" circles one hears frequently about mind, body and spirit, meaning, I suppose, that these are three distinguishable human characteristics. In modern mind sciences we hear of mind and brain. Are these differing perspectives talking about the same things at all? It will be useful to note in passing that when Freud's works were translated from German into English the words "geistes" (spirit) and "seele" (soul) were both translated as mind (c.f: Bruno Bettelheim's Freud and man's soul, A.A.Knopf, 1983), even though English did have the correct dictionary terms. This really only shows that for the English consciousness the inner life was already thought of as mind even though Europe had had a long tradition of referring to inner life in terms of soul and spirit (Freud thought and wrote out of that tradition).

Modern American English still uses these terms as in: soul power, soul brother, soul music, or in noting the distinction between the spirit and the letter of the law. Yet such usage's are more metaphorical, more imaginative, than the exact language usage which science demands, in fact depends upon. Even so, while brain has a very concrete physical existence, mind does not; it is much more ephemeral. It can't be touched, nor can consciousness, or inner life, or feeling, or even idea. Yet, these apparently non - sense perceptible - phenomena are all recognized intuitively. We accept loss of consciousness in sleep and in certain conditions of trauma or illness. We moderns are in love with feelings and their expression, about which have recently been written more books than one can read. The practice of science would get nowhere without ideas and in fact the principle foundation of science's logical rigor is mathematics, which has no sense perceptible existence at all, and is nowhere observable in nature, even with instruments.

Imagine that Descarte invented calculus while high on dopamine (a neurotransmitter identified as a factor in drug use and satisfaction). How are we to relate the chemical state of the brain and the simultaneous ideas? Is one producer and one product? And, if the productive cause is then questionable, can we accept the product?

Descarte has recently joined the (illustrious?) group of historic personalities to be diagnosed has having a psychiatric disorder (depression in his case) by a psychiatrist who never personally met him. If true would this make calculus a dubious discovery, or a hallucination (i.e. unreal)? Our electrical technology is impossible without calculus (and its relative differential equations), so there is something very different about this non - sense perceptible - phenomena called mathematics. It is somehow part of the world yet only knowable through mind.

It is clear that accepted scientific ideas are not being disputed because their producer has been at one time categorized as having been either physically or mentally ill. Yet, one can find in the literature (in the brain sciences) the idea that so-called mystic states and other kinds of religious experiences represent, or are caused by, unusual chemical states; i.e. are not what their experiencers say they are: experiences of God. But, how can this be, how can one make such a distinction that the discovery of a mathematical truth is different from the discovery of a religious truth, merely on the basis of the possibility that chemical happenings in the brain can induce hallucinatory states of consciousness?

Now the working scientist should have an argument here, which is, at first blush, quite reasonable. That nature conforms to mathematically oriented models at least establishes (I won't say proves) that this formal relation exists. Granted calculus can't be seen, but it does allow prediction of physical phenomena. Nature acts in conformance with mathematical principles. Where is the evidence it acts according to the principle God - this the working scientist should ask. After all, this is the habit of mind of the scientist to form such questions. Or, perhaps to put it another way, what predicted observation would permit the logical inference of the entity God?

Even so, such a response has not really appreciated the problem as I have been trying to state it. All the ideas of science are first and foremost mental phenomena. They appear in mind as a product of mind, not in sensible nature. I don't see gravity or even light. I see falling objects and colors. I infer the law of gravity and the existence of light from these experiences and, if I am a scientist, I make rigorous my observations through experimentation and precise instrumentation. But natural selection and the big bang are in each case mental creations, they proceed from the act of thinking, not from sense perceptible nature.

What this means to me is that if I am going to prefer one kind of mental phenomena over another (e.g. the idea of accident in the creation of life versus the idea of God) then I'd better be clear as to why I have such a preference. Yet, before I can make such choices, I need to understand mind, to understand the act which makes such a choice. But to understand mind don't I first need to understand understanding, to think about thinking?

To the philosophically sophisticated reader this may seem to be running backward in time. Modern academic philosophy (linguistic analysis), from Quine to Ayer to Wittgenstein is no longer thinking about thinking, at least in the way someone such as Frichte or some other 19th century German philosopher approached the problem. For the lay person the question might be put this way. How can I look to current work in linguistic analysis, in neurophysiology, in cognitive psychology, in order to build up my idea of mind, when these systems are already products of mind? Is not the cart before the horse? Don't I first have to have clearly before me what thinking is to my own experience of it, before I apply it in practice? I have mind directly before me. What might I understand if I investigate the nature of my own experience first?

This is a crucial point. If we were to examine each of these disciplines we would find some idea of mind, either being assumed or derived from the particular work. In some cases very explicit statements are being made about what thinking is, how it is caused, how it proceeds, what its potential is and so forth. Yet, it is thinking which is producing these ideas. How might such investigations evolve if first it was clearly before the thinker, just what thinking was to his own experience?

There are other reasons for making such a question the foundational step. Earlier in this century, the physicist/novelist C.P. Snow pointed out the existence of two cultures, the cultures of science and of literature (or the humanities). These cultures did not speak the same language and did not consider the same problems. Moreover the scientists seemed to believe that only their method produced objective truth, and that the humanities only produced subjective truths. Alan Bloom (in his The Closing of the American Mind) recently observed how the distribution of assets in the university reveals the domination of the sciences today, at least to governments and businesses, who provide most of the funds for research. When was the last time a President convened a panel of poets to help him define a problem? (This is not to say that this is a bad idea by the way. I suspect in many instances our poets and troubadours would give much wiser advice). My own view is that Snow did not go far enough, although his being a scientist/novelist makes this limitation understandable. There are, I believe, three cultures (or three constituent spheres to Culture): a culture of science or Reason, a culture of humanities or Imagination and a culture of religion or Devotion. Reason, Imagination and Devotion are related to the older ideas of Truth, Beauty and Goodness, in that the former are human capacities of the soul and the latter are the outer expressions of those capacities. Reason engenders truth, Imagination engenders beauty, and Devotion engenders goodness.

In reality this is a complex relationship. On a certain level, or from a particular viewpoint, these soul capacities are also capable of being called powers. The romantic poet S.T. Coleridge called imagination the "esemplastic power" and felt it was not just an aspect of human consciousness, but was a force of Nature as well. Reason, for example, could be called Truth, as that appears in the soul as a hunger first, then a question, and finally an answer. Reason is then a dynamic process which is intimately connect to Truth. In a way they are a mirror of each other.

The difficulty for both Snow and Bloom is that they have no practical experience at devotion; they didn't really understand it or appreciate its role in their own soul, or in the world. Most Christian contemplatives are cloistered and are not encouraged to either prove their claims (in fact they make no "claims") or to exhibit works. Certainly no science curriculum, and few humanities curriculums teach the works of St. John of the Cross, or St. Teresa of Avila. Our secular age is filled with writings and teachers who believe religion is superstition, but who have never tested it on its own terms. When Christ Jesus says "No one comes to the Father except by me." it doesn't seem to occur to people that knowledge of God might depend upon method just as much as science does. Perhaps the reason the scientist doesn't find God behind creation is because he looked in the wrong place. God being ephemeral (spiritual), perhaps God can only be observed (known) by the ephemeral in man. Perhaps only to mind in a pure state is the supra-sensible, the Invisible, apparent.

I have written briefly here of reason, imagination and devotion because I wanted us to remember that mind (soul/spirit) produces much else besides technical wonders. So that when we think about thinking we will remember all the kinds of things which flow from mind and appreciate that skill and effort are as much involved in the discovery of truth as in the creation of beauty or in traveling on the stony path to goodness. Moreover, there seems to be evidence that our greatest geniuses are often active in such a way that combines these qualities. Are not the true scientists and artists devoted to their calling? Einstein was mathematical, musical and faithful. Michael Faraday, who was the founding theoretician of electrical and magnetic phenomena, was a man of special religious devotion. Teilhard de Chardin is a very obvious case in point, and so is Goethe, whose scientific work was impeccable, although today much under appreciated. Here is what Roger Penrose, a major thinker on the problem of mind and science, had to say in his The Emperor's New Mind, pp. 421, Oxford University Press, 1989:

"It seems clear to me that the importance of aesthetic criteria applies not only to the instantaneous judgments of inspiration, but also to the much more frequent judgments we make all the time in mathematical (or scientific work) Rigorous argument is usually the last step! Before that, one has to make many guesses, and for these, aesthetic convictions are enormously important…"

And here is Karl Popper, whose work on scientific method sets the standard (for many at least), in his Realism and the Aim of Science, pp. 8, Rowan and Littlefield, 1956:

"…I think that there is only one way to science - or to philosophy, for that matter: to meet a problem, to see its beauty and to fall in love with it;…".\

Or as we might add to Mr. Popper's thought: "...to meet a problem (reason), to see its beauty (imagination) and to fall in love with it (devotion);...

I'd like now to introduce the ideas of Thomas Taylor, as expressed in the introduction to his early 18th century book: The Theoretic Arithmetic of the Pythagoreans. He observes there an interesting fact and draws from it an intriguing conclusion. He starts by deploring the increasing emphasis in education on the practical side of mathematics instead of the theoretical side, i.e. teaching math only with the idea of enabling people to be good accountants or engineers. The theoretic side has special characteristics for Taylor, which should not be lost to the process of education. In Nature, says Taylor, we do not find the perfect circle or the straight line. All the beautiful (or elegant in modern mathematical parlance) characteristics of mathematics arise not from the contemplation of Nature, which is imperfect, but rather are products of the soul which thereby reveals its perfection.

Or to restate Taylor's observation in our terms: mind (soul/spirit) in showing its capacity to think the idea of the perfect, the elegant, the beautiful, as that appears in mathematics, reveals its own nature. Mind could not produce the quality of these ideas except as that reflects the quality of its own condition. Yet, we know that the brain is a physical organ, and is no less imperfect that any other aspect of material nature. How then does this electro-chemical machine come to the ideas which are clearly beyond its own structure? While you might say that God is an illusion, and therefore some kind of mental dream or hallucination, I don't think you can get very far arguing the same way about the circle, or other geometric, and algebraic formulations without making a complete mockery of the scientific and technological achievements which depend upon these ideas.

Taylor's observation, which I make my own as well, is simply this. What the human being produces, through his soul capacities of reason, imagination and devotion, namely truth, beauty and goodness, necessarily reveals that the human spirit possesses a reality clearly transcendent of a mere brain bound existence.

With this background then I would like to return to the question of what is thinking, and what the answer to that question can reveal for us about the nature of mind. I don't expect to answer this question here in the way it must ultimately be answered. No written work ever convinces, even scientific papers. The reader must make his own investigation and draw his own conclusions. This is fundamentally what truly constitutes proof, even in science. My obligation to reason is to state clearly my conclusions and observations and to explain adequately my methodology in order that another can test my results. My reader's obligation is to honestly carry out the instructions, otherwise there can be no scientific validation or invalidation. This will not be easy, and few will even try for the truth is that years of effort have gone into the understanding I presently have of mind. In fact it is not the point of this essay to establish or prove the idea of mind that might be held by a Christian contemplative, but rather to expose it, to make it known, and to do so in a way which accepts as authentic and justifiable the scientific requirement for reproducibility. That the effort at replication may well be beyond the will power of those who agree or disagree is a situation over which I have no control.

This is not a cop out, by the way. That it takes years of study and development to be able to understand "Hilbert space", in no way lessens its mathematical truth. Likewise, do we have to be able to paint the Mona Lisa in order to appreciate its beauty? So, as well, we can marvel at the goodness of the idea of mind as a moral/spiritual act, even though we may lack the ability to completely engender a full understanding of such a condition ourselves.

On the other hand, and if we are willing, we can learn fundamental mathematical and scientific truths, without just having faith in the scientist's teachings. We can, as well, take up artistic activity and discover our own creative potential; and certainly we might devote ourselves to prayer and contemplative thinking in order that we learn to encounter the threshold between the visible and moral (invisible) worlds.

For my own purposes I now want to put aside (for the most part) the word mind and use instead just the terms soul and spirit. These two words are to mean no more and no less than what the reader experiences in his own inner life. Such a process is called introspection or looking within. It is a most ancient discipline; the meaning of the Greek admonition: "Know thyself ". This does not mean, by the way, to know one's subjective individual character traits as is often thought, but rather to discover the universals of human nature as they appear inside our own being.

Earlier in this century there was briefly a psychological "school" which sought to discover truths about the psyche (soul) through introspection, but this work did not make much headway, did not seem to contribute scientifically. and was abandoned. Its flaw was to pretend there was no tradition, no previous exploration of inner life, of psyche (soul) which might offer some experienced insight into the problems involved. The pretense is understandable in that invariably those disciplines which actually know something practical about inner life are spiritual disciplines and the general trend of scientific thought has been to view spiritual ideas about the Earth,

Cosmos and Man, as mere superstition. It is no wonder then that, when science seeks to investigate inner life, its anti-spiritual assumptions and preconceptions become an impediment to the discovery of just those facts sought after.

Every human being experiences consciousness, which includes sense experience (sight, hearing, touch, taste and smell), varying degrees of well being (health, vitality and illness), thoughts, dreams, feelings, impulses of will, desires, sympathies, antipathies, and so forth. Our language is full of a variety of words for different inner experiences, or states of consciousness, and these usages can often be very instructive. For example, why do we call someone "bright" or speak of "flashes of insight" or draw cartoons in which having a "bright idea" is depicted by a light bulb going on over someone's head? We do this because we instinctively know that certain kinds of thought activity (intuitions) are accompanied by phenomena of inner light. This is not light as seen by the physical eye, but light experienced by the "mind's eye", the individual human spirit.

In our ordinary state of soul (consciousness) this experience is not paid attention to because we are focused outwardly on the problem, whose solution the "flash of insight" represents. Moreover, the activity by which we produce the "in-sight", lies below the level of consciousness. It is unconscious. Now the fact is that within many spiritual disciplines exists the knowledge by which this unconscious can be made conscious, the inner eye strengthened and intuitions can be produced more or less at will. Even so, not all spiritual disciplines are the same, have the same world view, or the same purposes. It becomes necessary then to say a few words about this, in particular the differences between Buddhist and Christian depth meditation practices, the principle paths of Eastern and Western forms of spiritual life.

Buddhism today enjoys a certain ascendancy in America.

\"The Buddhist movement has become a regional phenomenon. It is pervasive. And it is quietly transforming our North American culture. This is the golden age of Buddhism. Right here. Right now. " (Don Morreale, quoted in Masters of the Universe, Pamela Weintraub, Omni, March 1990.)

Examine, for example, the book by William Irwin Thompson, Imaginary Landscape. This is a book straining to realize ideas about man and the world by combining reason, imagination and devotion. Thompson is a cultural historian fascinated with the cutting edge of the new sciences such as chaos research and cognitive science. Thompson has clearly been influenced by Buddhism (apparently the Tibetan Llama Choygam Trungpa), and this reveals itself in the ethereally vague, almost ungrounded character of Thompson's prose. If you were to follow reading Thompson's book by reading Speakers Meaning by Owen Barfield, who is a student of the Western spiritual teacher, Rudolf Steiner, the different effect of the style of meditation and related practices on the thinking of the two writers is clear. There is a mystery here concerning the effect of meditation styles on cultural life.

I do not say this because I am opposed to Buddhism as a spiritual path, but rather as an observer of culture and the ebbs and flows in the dynamics of a civilization's cultural existence. Years ago I had a profound experience of Buddhism, for which I am ever thankful, yet I believe there must arise an effort on the part of the leaders of both Western and Eastern cultural life to work together, in mutually supportive ways. There is, I believe, hidden in the mysteries behind both Christianity and Buddhism, a higher unity, which ought to sought for; all the while remaining mindful of the different effects on the soul life of the individual which are due to the different practices, and the natural consequences these must have in the life of a culture. Just like political leaders, humanities spiritual leaders owe the individual certain responsibilities.

The orientation of Buddhist and Christian inner disciplines toward the act of thinking is quite different. The reader who begins to take an objective look at his inner life, at his soul (which includes all that appears inwardly, both conscious and unconscious), will find that there is an actor, a self, an egoicity. To this we refer when we think or say "I". Buddhist meditation takes the view that this "I" is the cause of suffering, the cause of life's difficulties and that it (the "I") needs to be abandoned, eventually to disappear into an experience of self within Self.

Christian meditation sees the "I" as the point of creation, as the image of God, which can be redeemed from its fallen nature, so as to produce the mysterious and paradoxical Pauline dictum: "Not I, but Christ in me."

The Buddhist leaves the act of thinking, the "I"'s spiritual activity, to take its own course, believing that this activity only produces illusions. Christian meditation sees the act of thinking as capable of being metamorphosed, altered through discipline, into a new organ of perception, an organ which can then perceive deeper into the mysteries of creation.

Lest one believe this is an inconsequential matter, just consider the following as reported in the Boston Globe newspaper in December of 1990. The story reveals that a Carthusian priest, a monk in a Catholic contemplative order, has just completed seven years training in the meditation practices of Vipassana Buddhism. This priest, Rev. Denys Rackley, is quoted as saying: "What Western Christians need...is practical knowledge...of preparing the mind for the spiritual experience, something almost entirely unknown in the West." It is understandable why he believes this, but it is not true. The depth meditative practices with Christian understanding are not unknown, but one does have to look for them, rather then look to the East.

Father Denys is also quoted as saying: '...as long as you're functioning at the level of the rational thinking mind, you're not really into the heart of the spiritual life". This is the Buddhist view, but one of the purposes of this essay is to suggest that thinking can in fact lead to direct spiritual experience. And that for the Christian, to abandon his cognitive capacities in the manner of Eastern meditative practices is to miss developing "Not I, but Christ in me."

This short consideration hardly exhausts what would be a proper examination of these differences, nor does it deal with the complex and difficult relation between modern depth Christianity and the current theological beliefs of many Christian churches. I did feel it necessary, however, to note briefly these themes as part of giving as rounded out a picture of mind (soul/spirit), as that exists for the Christian meditative practitioner.

The reader may then consider the soul to be all that appears before him inwardly as his consciousness, including as well sense experience. While we feel, and have been taught, that sense experience is caused by outer nature, the actual experiencing of these so-called stimuli occurs within the soul or conscious awareness. For example, if one whose normal environment is urban were to be transported suddenly to a grand vista of nature they would experience the soul's expansive movement deeper into the senses. Normally in urban life the soul withdraws as far as possible from its sense experiences which are so chaotic and immoderate. We tend to hear, see, smell, taste, feel (as in touch) with less sensitivity while we lead an urban existence. The opposite is also true. If an urban dweller, who has spent a month or so in raw nature were to suddenly return to downtown Manhattan, they would experience a sudden contraction of the soul, a rapid withdrawal from the senses, and a constriction of the diaphragm (so as to breathe less deeply the toxic air).

Soul includes as well that which exists in the unconscious, and which manifests over time, such as mood, character, temperament and other like phenomena. Within the field of soul, within the totality of psychic life, the "I" or spirit appears as the experiencer, the actor, and the creative or initiating cause.

Now please remember that this way of describing soul life comes from the process of active objective introspection. It does not try to infer from outer perception as do the sciences, but seeks to objectify the direct experiences of the observer of his own self. Just as science then points to technological products to validate its views, so can these practices point to reproducible effects in the inner life brought about by the disciplined activity of the "I" through self development exercises, such as concentration, meditation, contemplation and prayer. I would like to put forward a model here, just as science does, but in this case I want it to be clear it is only a device by which to convey an idea, a mental representation of a real process, which can be known, but which can't be described by the concepts we are used to.

Imagine if you will that you are holding a "stick" between the palms of your hands. If you move your left hand in such a way as to push the "stick", your right hand will move as well. Move the right hand and the "stick" will push the left. This then is the idea I want to suggest for the brain-mind relationship, or the body/soul/spirit relationship. Brain chemistry can cause changes in consciousness, but as well the "I", the spirit, can cause changes in brain chemistry. In Mind Matters, Grazzanica, having already likened brain to a mechanism, then says paradoxically: "A thought can change brain chemistry, just as a physical event in the brain can change a thought". My question for Grazanica is: what does he think causes the thought which changes the brain chemistry?

If I ingest substances, food or chemical, I alter my state of soul, of consciousness. There is no ignoring the fact that brain chemistry effects states of mind (soul). However, the opposite is also true. My active spirit can also effect states of soul, and in some circumstances brain and body chemistry as well (c.f. the capacities of Jack Schwartz who is able to control consciously a number of so-called involuntary bodily processes including blood flow.). Moreover, any conscious physical movement is initiated by my spirit which first imagines it. Ordinarily we are not aware of how our "I"'s will brings about this physical movement. The "stick", as it were, is hidden deep in the unconscious.

With regard to the act of thinking, however, the whole activity lies within the reach of my self conscious spirit. Thinking takes place in the conscious parts of the soul and with training one can become aware of and be active in the whole process.

Ordinarily we experience thinking as an inner dialogue, a flow of words. This talking to ourselves (don't we say, "I can't hear myself think") is the end product of unconscious processes. In this instance it is the spirit which intitiates the silent wording and the soul which hears. This act of thinking (which is unconscious) produces thoughts or trains of thought (the flow of words) of which we are conscious. The training disciplines of a specific spiritual practice can, stage by stage, uncover and make open to experience, and will activity, what remains otherwise hidden in the unconscious.

I will now describe some of the consequences of such a discipline in terms of capacities and experiences. This is not meant to be exhaustive, only indicative. Later we will discuss certain books which have much more to offer in this line, books which I have used (tested) myself. The stream of "words" can be brought to a halt. The act of thinking can then be focused on a single concept. The discovery here is that concept and word are two different experiences. This is another crucial matter, but its main difficulty for the reader's understanding is that it cannot be put into words. It is completely a function of experience.

Now ordinarily we think of concept and idea as the same as the word which we experience in our inner dialogue. The true experience of the concept is beyond language. It can ultimately be experienced in a way analogous to that in which a sense object is experienced. The difference is that I am in an unusual state of consciousness, which can be described as "sense free". Only to my mind's eye, my spiritual eye, does the concept appear. Moreover, as an experience it is more vivid, more intense, than sense experience. It touches, as it were, my whole soul, filling the soul with "sensation", with image, sound, tactility, engagement (I am pulled toward it, it seems to rush toward me). In addition the experience can only be sustained if my "I" is active in a certain way. In the face of sense experience I can be passive. In the face of the supra-sensible experience of the pure concept, I must remain active inwardly.

Roger Penrose in his The Emperor's New Mind relates how as a mathematician (recall what has been said previously about mathematics by Taylor) he is beginrung to think mathematical truths have their own independent existence. "...I cannot help feeling that, with mathematics the case for believing in some kind of ethereal, eternal existence, at least for the more profound mathematical concepts, is a good deal stronger..." (pp. 97). Mathematical thinking is a very concentrated activity, is good practice for meditation and contemplation and can easily evolve into the contemplation of the pure concept.

When we think, then, in the ordinary way (stream of words), our unconscious thought-creative activity is within the realm of the pure concept, but our conscious awareness is only of the words which fall out, as it were, like autumn leaves blown free of the living tree of our mind.

As with mathematics, so with music. Consider the poetic intuition out of the imagination of the writer Kim Stanley Robinson in his novel: The Memory of Whiteness:

"A music leads the mind through the starry night and the brain must expand to contain the flight like a tree growing branches at the speed of light."

Thinking cannot only focus on the single concept, it may also suspend itself just before the act which produces the awareness of the concept. Thinking can take up a question, but not proceed all the way to an answer. We can live in the question, in a condition of heightened anticipation. A great deal can be learned from appreciating the qualitative difference of the "I"'s activities of "focus" and "question".

Up to now little has been said here of the Christian nature of such practices. Consider then that the Christian contemplative's practice is to think in a concentrated and focused way ever and ever again on the Being of God. If Penrose has begun to suspect that mathematics is derived from an experience of something that is "there already", are we to be surprised when the contemplative finds God as an experience in his consciousness (soul) and as a consequence (in part, we will have to avoid complicating things with the problem of Grace) of the activity of his thinking (spirit)? Prayer is another form of question, and by combining question and focus, or prayer and contemplation, the contemplative proceeds in an exact, disciplined and rigorous fashion.

The summa of my own investigations (which is not by any means to be considered more than the work of a beginner) is the discipline of sacrifice of thoughts. I have found it especially important to learn to give up any tendency to fixed ideas. Always it is necessary to approach the situation ignorant, to sacrifice all previous ideas. "Blessed are the poor in spirit. " is the Beatitude. Only in a condition of humility, of not knowing, can I come to the more subtle, more intimate inner experiences. One of my favorite teachers calls sacrifice of thoughts: "...learning to think on your knees...".

This leads us to the consideration of the core problem, that of morality and conscience.

Many people today think of education and character development as having to do with pouring something into an otherwise empty soul. To my experience this is mistaken. Rather it is always a question of development, of unfolding. A human being becomes. True morality then involves the development of a capacity, and is not merely a matter of instruction. You can get people to conform, but real morality comes from the inside out and is not a response to expectations of right behavior. (This appears to be a new condition for mankind. Previously, in human development, morality, to a great extent, was set for the individual by the outside social structure, through codes of behavior, traditions, and other socially enforced expectations.

Depth introspection of the act of thinking will discover that the outcome of thinking is significantly affected by the moral intention of the thinker. Just as the act of thinking needs to be made conscious, so the moral intention connected to the object (or the why) of the thinking needs to be fully conscious. If, for example, I am a business man looking for a solution to a certain problem, the answers I get will vary according to the moral intention. Ultimately the practitioner of such thinking will come to an appreciation of the activity of conscience within his own soul life.

This is a special experience. The "voice" of conscience needs to be carefully distinguished from the more subjectively incorporated authority figures. The conscience, for example, never endlessly nags us, does not make us feel inferior. Conscience is the experience of the higher element of our nature, which is normally in the unconscious. In the awakening and the development of conscience we begin to develop within us this higher element (What St. Paul calls: "Not I, but Christ.in me."). The conscience does cause pain, "pricks of conscience", because it forces us to recognize the true moral consequences of our actions. The truth hurts and our voice of conscience reminds us of the truth. The conscience, however, loves us, which is why it makes us conscious of the truth, but does not seek to destroy our self image or impair our self esteem.

Now just as one can evoke certain kinds of inner experiences through various types of thinking disciplines, so can one evoke the voice of conscience and thereby come to certain moral knowledge. This understanding of the life of the soul and the activity of the spirit, this part of the idea of mind, involves the most subtle inner discrimination; and, since it places morality within the realm of individual knowledge, it represents a threat to authoritarian organizations, religious or otherwise. No one, who eventually learns this fine discrimination, will ever assert to another that they possess a more perfect moral knowledge. Each individual must make his own experiences.

This does not mean that morality is subjective, or that it is relative and changeable. The problem is more subtle and more complicated. The conscience is an organ of knowledge - of understanding the true moral qualities underlying human action. Two individuals with the same choices, the same life questions to balance, if they strive for the same depth of understanding, they will arrive at the same knowledge of what is right. However, the reality is that, in life, two individuals seldom have to face the same choice. Our lives are very individual, regardless of superficial similarities. What needs to be weighed and balanced is unlikely to be the same. So when the individual problem is presented to the organ of conscience, we often get an individual result.

This can be very confusing. In part the confusion is due to our usually thinking of morality as a set of immutable principles, and the teaching of most religious authorities of quite definite rules and codes. For example, to many murder and abortion are absolutely prohibited. In these instances, to suggest, as the above seems to suggest, that the individual has some kind of free choice, is to appear to go against these most obvious and traditional moral restrictions. Such thinking, however, misses the point.

First we should remember that most of us, in many situations, do not follow the indications of our conscience, to the extent we become aware of them. Conscience gives us knowledge; we choose to act, or not, upon that knowledge. That we often choose to ignore conscience in no way takes away the power of conscience to know what is moral. Secondly, what is often forgotten, is that one of the most common ways we ignore conscience is in judging other people. If we put to conscience whether we should judge another's morality, what answer do you think conscience will give? "He who is without sin, let him cast the first stone.".

In the process of coming to this understanding of the role of conscience, or moral intention, and the consequences of these acts upon the activity of thinking, we also come to a practical understanding of many of the lessons of the Gospels. The teachings of Christ Jesus, in that they have a practical psychological effect, in that they concern matters of "mind", conform exactly to all that has been said above. In spite of what religious dogma might say, this knowledge, which is derived from the direct experience of a Christian meditant,and which is also representative of a community of such meditation practitioners, in no way conflicts with true Christianity.

Certain implications flow from this idea of mind. We might ask the question: where is the "there" where the "already there" is? When the mathematician Penrose proposes that mathematical ideas are "already there", where is this "there"? Inside the physical space of my skull? This is our habit of thought, but does that "habit" have to be true?

It will help to consider a parallel problem/question. Which comes first in evolution/creation, mind or matter? We assume matter, or at least such is the fundamental assumption current in science today. The basic belief is that at some point in evolution the complexity of the nervous system reaches a point where consciousness arises and ultimately what we know as mind (soul/spirit to the Christian meditative expenence). We have no proof of this. It really hasn't even been seriously investigated, if it can be investigated at all. That mind arises spontaneously, out of some accidental physical condition is an axiom (unproven assumption) of many mainstream scientists.

Such a supposed event, lying as it does in the distant past, cannot even be the subject of an experiment, or any other direct observation. This alleged event must be inferred, but from what? The fossil record only gives us bones, hardened substances. The soft tissues are always dissolved. And as to the thoughts?

We do have a picture of stages of development, one that we have been indoctrinated in from our earliest years in school: single cell plant, to multi-cell, to invertebrate, to vertebrate, to mammal, to man. We have an idea of mind (soul/spirit) as solely reason, and therefore connect mind and tool making. This picture itself is an inference. Are we justified in building inference upon inference. The fact that the majority of scientists believe this to be the case is of no moment whatsoever. We don't vote facts into existence, and at the very least the history of science itself reveals, not an unbroken advance, but rather a series of "beliefs", a series of substitutions of ideas often quite at odds with each other (c.f. T. Khun, The Structure of Scientific Revolutions).

Is there any reason for inferring the opposite? Is there something which suggests mind preceded matter? As a matter of fact there is. The discipline of philology, the study of language as developed by the mind (soul/spirit) of Owen Barfield reveals that what we call thinking was experienced by certain ancient peoples as outside them. The whole way they used language, their references to muses and to genii, shows that they experienced thoughts as coming into them from the outside. (c.� Owen Barfield's Speaker's Meaning, also his Poetic Diction, History in English

Words, and Saving the Appearances: a Study in Idolatry). Barfield's investigations, which represent deeply profound and scientific studies of the history of meaning and the meaning of history, suggest unequivocally that modern assumptions regarding the nature of consciousness, both historical and prehistorical, must certainly be rethought; and if that is done, the inferred idea of matter proceeding mind in evolution will be replaced with its opposite, that mind is prior. Moreover, this philological research shows that mind (soul/spirit) has over the course of history (that is the period of man's evolution for which we have records) only just finished a long period of contraction; thinking, having first been outside the human entelechy, is now inside.

This is not the place in which to give a full recapitulation of the relevant trains of thought (arguments) which Barfield makes, nor to go into the supporting evidence that can be found in the field of art history (c.f. Art and Human Consciousness, Gottfried Richter, Anthroposophic Press, 1985). Rather I wanted to point out the question and as well to point to work which finds a satisfactory answer. Where is the "there" where one finds ideas already? It is in the great field of Mind (Soul/Spirit) which encompasses all of Nature (sense perceptible as well as supra-sensible), to which our individuality, our "I", has access through its own disciplined inner activity. Just as it is quite unreasonable to expect the imperfect to conceive the perfect (the material brain to imagine the immaterial and elegant truths of projective geometry), so it is non-reason to assume that mind (soul/spirit) is not born out of its own likeness. Matter cannot have given birth to consciousness, to thinking, or to certain moral knowledge (conscience). Our inwardness (soul/spirit) can only be the progeny of the Universe's Inwardness.

How do I know this? Because I have explored my own inwardness, and found there much more than I had been lead to assume was "there" by the scientifically oriented education of my youth. It has become a matter of experience, an empiricism of inwardness. In fact, such is the nature of this experience that the idea of mind as solely a product of brain electro-chemistry cannot be sustained. Moreover, there is a community of practitioners which replicates (repeats) this experience, the whole activity being conducted with the rigor and discipline justifiably required in this scientific age.

I would like to remind the reader, as we draw this exploration to a close, that the intention has never been to prove an opposite idea of the mind/brain nexus to that one currently held in science, but rather to give as clear as possible a picture of the idea of mind which can be held by a Christian meditation practitioner. Further, to do this in a way which at least offers the reader the opportunity of testing for him or herself the truth of this idea.

Ultimately, I believe it will be most healthy for our culture and our civilization, if what is understood as the powers of reason, be supplemented by the faculties of imagination and devotion, as well. What is offered then, in this theme, is not adisagreement with present day mind sciences, but rather an attempt to extend them, to evolve them by adding to their considerations what can be discovered about the nature of mind from a disciplined investigation which proceeds from the inside, from what appears to our direct experience of mind.

We need to remember that these questions are fundamental to the future course of our civilization. It is crucial, both for the health of our social order, and the meaning we attribute to our existence, that we have a true idea of human nature. Our culture is deeply psychologically split, in a quite unhealthy way, by the confused idea we have of human nature which raises Reason above the capacities of Imagination and Devotion, and which makes so-called scientific knowledge the only truth worth considering. This is a prejudice which grants an illegitimate power to what is really far too often only another belief system.

In the hospital where I worked for over seven years, powerful drugs are routinely administered to individuals, without sufficient consideration for these individuals spiritual nature or needs. That their "depression" might instead by caused by a life crisis with moral and self definitional (spiritual meaning) dynamics, is not really considered. At the same time, just down the hall, in the chemical dependency units, where the alcoholics anonymous model is practiced, meetings frequently end with the Lord's Prayer, and spiritual self transformation is considered an absolute necessity in order to deal with the relevant problems.

What a picture this gives us of the deep inconsistencies that exist in our culture!

We can do no better than to begin to end our considerations of this theme with these remarks by a spirit (individual) in whom reason, imagination and devotion were maintained in the soul in a remarkable balance. From Emerson's essay Nature: "Nature is the incarnation of a thought, and turns to a thought again, as ice becomes water and gas. The world is mind precipitated, and the volatile essence is forever escaping again into the state of free thought. "

Here, with remarkable intuitive powers, Emerson sees to the heart of what we have been attempting to suggest. Contrary to the assumptions of the scientific age, namely, that there is no correlation between human thought and the world, the world itself is a product of Thought, and the human being, in that he or she thinks, has directly before him, in the experience of his own mind, the like, but rudimentary, capacity. We were Thought into being, and we also can think.

In the preceding, I attempted to show how one could begin that exploration which will validate, in a scientifically acceptable way, the proposition that human consciousness and the act of thinking are not the product of material happenings in a physical brain, but the products of acts of soul and spirit. Whether critics of such an idea will be willing to struggle with the difficult work of replication, I cannot say. At the same time I will insist that, without such an effort, any argument to the contrary need not be listened to or heeded.

For those who will wish to take this challenge seriously, I recommend the following two books: The Philosophy of Freedom, Rudolf Steiner, Anthroposophical Press; and Meditations on the Tarot: a journey into Christian Hemeticism, author anonymous, Amity House.

~!~!~!~!~!~!~!~!~!~

The Quiet Suffering of Nature

"And while they were eating, Jesus took bread, and blessing it, he broke and gave it to them and said, "Take; this is my body." And taking a cup and giving thanks, he gave it to them, and they all drank of it; and he said to them "This is my blood of the new covenant, which is being shed for many..." Mark 14: 22-23

Where is humanity without the Earth? Without air, water or food we die. What then is the true name of that extraordinary Earth-Being whose nature it is to sacrifice itself for us, and in whose own living substance we are nurtured from birth until death?

*

For many people today, within the environmental movement and without, the treatment of the Earth, by much of humanity, is understood to be a terrible tragedy. The destruction of the rain forest, the over fishing of the oceans, the casual production of toxic wastes, the continuation of atomic testing - the list is almost endless of the crimes committed against the natural world and not coincidentally, also against humanity.

More recently we have had to face the possibility of even worse as the arguments over global warming and climate change of taken center stage in our political life. Unfortunately, passion is insufficient and real knowledge is needed. Below I will address those issues more carefully.

A central thesis of those concerned is that these excessive activities are unnecessary; those who carry them out have alternatives. Yet, if we honestly look at what is being done, and especially at the conceptual context in which these deeds are carried out, in most cases we will have to admit, that from the point of view of the apparent destroyers, their acts are necessary. The truth is that the conflict is over what these acts mean, not over the acts themselves.

Most of the time those, who seem to be abusing the natural environment, are acting in pursuit of their self interest. They are business people, whose obligation to their corporate stockholders is to maximize profits. If they don't act, they lose their jobs, their livelihood and all that that implies. For example, loggers and tree lovers collide over national forest policy. One wants to use in order to continue an existence already set on a certain course, the other wants to preserve out of an appreciation of what will be lost when it all is gone. In an odd kind of way both are conservationists. One wants to conserve and existing way of life, the other, a rapidly disappearing kind of life. Both are expect-able moral and human responses to a situation where no agreement is possible, because the contexts of meaning, in which the situation is viewed, are opposed. Each, given the quite different assumptions under which life is pursued, acts forthrightly. At the human level both sides are right.

This is not to say that there are not individuals and/or companies who act immorally or criminally, who take what they want in defiance of convention or good sense. But these aberrations are the exception. For the most part, the conflict over environmental policies owes its existence to opposing life paths and world conceptions, and not to any intrinsic or objective truth about what is right and what is wrong. Both sides, being human, can be understood.

However, there is something missing. While one can understand the human elements - how each view is appropriate to its adherents - there is something that is not understood. **Nature** is not understood, because neither side grants to the natural world the same effort at understanding they could grant to each other.

It is the thesis of this essay that the environmental movement, for all its passion and good intentions, is simply not radical enough in its understanding of the natural world. Concepts, like ecology and preservation and save this and save that, are impotent before the truth of Nature. What Nature truly is, is quite beyond such an incomplete idea as "save the rain forest", or "stop global warming".

Nature is more than a living environment which we find necessary for our survival as just another species. In solemn and sacred truth, Nature has consciousness and being. As a consequence, the environmental movement will only begin to do that which is needed, in the face of the terrible tragedy befalling the natural world, when those who would lead it realize that the Nature they wish to save is filled with just as much will and intention as a human being, and is just as much deserving of being treated with personal dignity and respect. Environmentalists need to find a new way of approaching Nature; namely to come to Nature as someone, rather then something. The only relationship which will be effective for achieving the quite worthy goals of the environmental movement, is the relationship of I and Thou. For there is an immense unasked question: what does Nature want? And no human being has the right to impose their personal point of view over that of Nature Herself.

We must again learn to approach Nature as someone with whom one can communicate, and who is better able to advise us about what to do than we can imagine. We need to begin to recognize how trapped we are in the confines of the lifeless and materialistic mental images (conceptions) provided by the one-sided scientific education of Western culture. Even the Indians, the aboriginals, the original peoples still living within the bosom of Nature, have lost, for the most part, that intimate connection and conversation by which the Spirit of the Natural world is perceived, appreciated, understood and listened to. What is left, namely tradition, although quite wonderful in its wise conception of the Earth as our Mother, as a conscious being, this tradition is itself inadequate for the tasks which need to be done.

Moreover, this consciousness, this being of Nature is not singular, is not simple. The being of Nature is multiple and complicated, diverse and specialized. What has been conveyed to us out of the deep past is not superstition. Stories and tales of the elemental beings, of undines and gnomes and fairies and sprites, all this seemingly legendary material owes its existence to the fact that in the past human beings did in fact experience more directly the world of the spirit, the world which lies presently separated from humankind by a kind of veil. And recognition of these Nature beings is just a beginning, for the world of the spirit extends quite beyond that realm of mere earthly Nature, but to cosmic Nature as well.

Even so, this bold assertion of the consciousness and being of Nature in itself is insufficient. The reader of this essay is entitled to more. It becomes necessary, then, to explore not only the sterile quality of the conceptions of the natural world provided us by the processes of Western science, but also to suggest the means by which these ideas can be overcome and a true communion with the Spirit of Nature reestablished.

The reader should be cautioned that in this single essay there will no proof of what is asserted. Such a task would be impossible. What can be done, however, is to show briefly how it is that science came to such a narrow view of the natural world, what personalities resisted this process, and how then that resistance matured so that today one can find once again a way toward an intimate conversation with Nature, yet remain fully within the rational. There is already existing much work about Nature by those who have begun this difficult and much needed task.

Even though this essay will endeavor to show that the conceptions of modern science have failed to find their way to the truth of the natural world, this is not to be seen as a criticism of that science. In the main, scientists follow quite rigorously and with great diligence a path of seeking which shows every chance of leading them to the truth. Science stands upon an excellent moral foundation when it says: anyone who asserts the truth of a thing, must be able to show others that means necessary for them to find this truth for themselves. Experiments must be reproducible. Theories must be testable.

It is also necessary to be brief, so to the extent the reader may wish for more the author at once apologizes. Many books and certain websites will be referred to, however, which if read and appreciated will more than satisfy the questing human spirit.

We all will perhaps remember from school, at least somewhat, what has been called the "Copernican revolution", the early struggles of science against the doctrines of the Catholic Church. This often resulted in various practitioners of the new discipline called natural philosophy (eventually to be called science) being excommunicated, and in some instances burned at the stake. We may think we are past this now, but anyone with an ear for these things is aware that even today those who espouse views sufficiently outside main-stream science (the Church of our time) are rebuked by their peers, shunned in the communities of their specialization, and at risk for having their funding, i.e. their livelihood, taken away. Some of these "arguments" are more public, e.g. "cold fusion", creationism vs. Darwinism, climate change and so forth. Less perceivable to the general public is what can happen to someone who looks today for the spirit in nature, or otherwise seems to think that some "superstitions" may have been based upon the truth.

In the beginnings of science the problematic philosophic problems were more out in the open. But since the materialistic ideas won the day, theirs are the views in the histories of science in which the ordinary person is educated. As in politics and war, so in science: the winners write the histories. Several of the "romantics" and the "transcendentalists" had grave problems with the course science was taking. The poet Goethe was a vigorous opponent of Newtonian optics (Newton, oddly enough, was an alchemist). The poet Coleridge had a much different approach to early biology. Emerson wrote in his essay Nature: "Nature is a thought incarnate, and turns to a thought again as ice becomes water and gas. The world is mind precipitated, and the volatile essence is forever escaping again into the state of free thought." Kepler, who gave us the fundamental laws of planetary dynamics was also an astrologer, and warned repeatedly about the danger of "throwing out the baby with the bath water", i.e. abandoning whole-sale all the hard won wisdom of the previous ages in the rush to make everything "scientific".

One could go on...Ruskin, Howard, Faraday, the list is long of those who opposed a completely mechanistic view of Nature.

For an excellent examination of the whole flow introduced into scientific thinking with the idea of Nature of a mechanism, and related problems, the reader of this essay should become acquainted with Evolution and the New Gnosis: Anti-establishment Essays on Knowledge, Science, Religion and Causal Logic, by Don Cruse, with Robert Zimmer. See also Cruse's website.

The essential thing to realize here, is that, as this "war" over what was the true picture of Nature was in its beginning stages, there were few "pure" scientists. That Goethe is remembered mainly as a poet is true only because the winners wrote the histories. He was in fact an extraordinary scientist, as anyone will realize who studies his Theory of Color. That Kepler and Faraday had a lot more to say then what is taught in school today is a simple fact. Faraday gave us the fundamental laws of electricity and magnetism, but he did so in the context of observations which lead him to consider that a distinction between "ponderables" and "imponderables" in Nature, i.e. between matter and spirit, was essential. Both were present, both were necessary.

Clearly one view won the day. The "why" of this is not simple, and cannot be found in the idea that one was true and one was false. We can perhaps get a slight feel for the underlying dynamics by realizing that at the time when all this was happening, the whole of Europe was emerging from a world view dominated by the ideas of the Roman Church. Thus, for many, to strive for a spirit-free view of nature was to also strive for freedom from a no longer desired authority which had for centuries been telling people what was true and what was not. To find spirit in Nature would have been to grant power back to an institution many were violently struggling to leave behind.

More crucially, scientists were lead in directions that were determined by the yet unknown nature of what they discovered. Ultimately, with the discovery of electricity, scientists, understandably following carefully the trail as it appeared before them, were lead rapidly into what one author has called "a country that is not ours". As part of this process a concept concerning "force" arose, which was very different from the way past ages looked at the problem of causation. This new concept of force was abstract, and completely divorced from any idea of being or consciousness. No longer were the happenings in the natural world the product of the activity of beings, the product of intended activity. Thus more and more the possibility, that Nature may have a spiritual foundation, disappeared. For depth of historical detail, read Ernst Lehr's remarkable Man or Matter.

As everyone is aware, it is pretty much assumed today that older conceptions of Nature are purely superstitious; that a Nature with being and consciousness is an impossibility. With the arrival of DNA research and genetic engineering, the difficult problems in biology are believed to be mostly solved, and few new conceptions are needed. Physicists routinely act as if the mind of modern man has little problem forming true concepts of events billions of years in the past. Zoologists accept Darwinian evolution as a settled matter, and resent deeply the struggles of the "creationists" to suggest otherwise. Nero-physiologists are convinced that the secrets of the mind are shortly to be theirs. While the clockwork is complicated, Nature is clearly a mechanism, made up of very small parts acting in understandable ways leading from a remote "big bang" through a long period of evolution to the arrival of life, and ultimately consciousness (mind). Unfortunately, they've probably got it mostly wrong.

It would be possible to make an argument about this "wrongness" solely from the history of science itself. In Thomas Kuhn's The Structure of Scientific Revolutions, it is established that science, rather then being a carefully built up structure, erected on a sure foundation, is instead a succession of points of view, the newest one substituting for the preceding, rather then being built out of it. Science is somewhat like a rat in a maze, convinced at every point it has solved the puzzle only to discover another dead end which has to be abandoned. Based merely on behavior one would have to assume that what is believed to be true now about these great questions (what is life and consciousness, where did they come from, how did the universe begin) will, in its own time, be found false and replaced by other views.

Or to take another tack, one could argue that most of what is said, about these big questions (does Nature have consciousness or mind, and which comes first in evolution, mind or matter), by modern day science, is itself pseudo-science, i.e. a modern form of superstition, because the theories are not testable. See in this regard, Karl Popper's Realism and the Aim of Science; also, Natural Selection, and the Criteria by which a Theory is Judged, (now called Dogma and Doubt) by Ronald H. Brady, Systematic Zoology, 28:600-621, 1979), and Darwin on Trial, Phillip E. Johnson, (Regnery Gateway, 1991).

While the above discussion has been unnecessarily brief, it should have hints enough so that the reader wanting more can find his own way. In any event, the work of the Nature Institute should be taken into account.

It remains then to find some process by which these questions can be answered in ways which satisfies our human desire for testable and reliable truths. What can be said about this, as briefly as possible, will be related next.

We can perhaps begin by asking what kind of an approach to the spirit would be necessary, what pathway to finding out the truth about Nature and Spirit, will meet the quite reasonable demands of science for reproducibility and testability. In a sense we need a science of the spirit, or perhaps to put it another way, a spiritual science.

Those who know the foundations of science are aware that science stands basically upon two touchstones, one being a philosophical point of view, which at one time was called logical positivism, and the other being mathematics, which provides a rigor and discipline to the practice of science which is very beneficial. So we can anticipate as well that our spiritual science needs a testable philosophic basis, and a reproducible mathematical structure (or perhaps better said, skeleton).

Another aspect of modern science which supports its reliability is the technology which proceeds from it. This suggests then that our spiritual science will have to show some results, will need to have produced observable effects, somehow people will have to have been able to take from this spiritual science and acted upon and changed the world.

Well, that is quite a lot, and I believe enough. We should now, perhaps, cut this spiritual science a little slack, and not expect some other things. We ought to allow it to be different in certain ways, after all that is exactly what it has to be given the basic assumptions. Certainly we can't expect it to be widely known or popular; for mainstream science has to have been constantly resistant to such ideas. Therefore, we ought to allow it to be young. How could it be otherwise, or wouldn't we already know of it?

Certainly we have to allow for some controversy, after all the ideas it produces will be different from the mainstream. As well, we should not expect to understand it immediately, nor expect that we will come to the necessary understanding without some, in fact perhaps, a great deal of effort. After all we have been educated into the mainstream. We think those ideas automatically, and most of our words take their meaning from this quite dominate way of thinking about the natural world. Let us take a sample problem, and see if it can help us better appreciate what a spiritual science will need, how it will be different and the kinds of struggles necessary to understanding what it might be able to communicate to us about the natural world. With this problem, by the way, I am not attempting to do something definitive, but rather to use it to give us a more concrete sense of what such a science needs to be, and how it might be different.

Consider for the moment the idea of space. When we think this idea on a very large scale we usually think of the great universe of stars; and, having been influenced by television and films we will have an image of movement between stars, as if we were a starship traveling at light speed across the cosmic spaces. While the "spacial" world is three dimensional, and seemingly endless, for the modern physicist, there are certain problems. Was there "empty space" before the "big bang", before matter erupted from its supposed birth point and exploded into the evolving universe? Or to put it another way, was space "created"?

For all of humanities history, up until the last four or five hundred years, very different ideas of cosmic space existed. To the naked eye the starry heaven is a remarkable vista; a place we cannot go, a place of mystery whose rhythms and movements seemed to announce great and small events in the lives of peoples and kingdoms. Our ancestors did not have the idea of endless three dimensionality; for them the heavens were the abode of the Gods. But the early natural philosophers thought otherwise, and with the new tools, first the telescope, and then later the spectrometer, the computer, and so on almost endlessly, the old vision was shattered. The theory of parallax gave us distance, red shift gave us velocity, the universe was expanding and enormous. And we? We were small and insignificant. The Earth as the Center of the Universe? Hogwash!

Who would dare doubt this? To suggest otherwise, to some, would be evidence of an unstable mind. To believe that this endless emptiness might have consciousness and being...get a life, better yet, go see a psychiatrist.

One hesitates to bring bad news...but... First off, most of astronomical-physics, or what is sometimes called cosmology, is not testable by the ordinary means we have and use, say in geology or zoology. We can't go to the nearest star and see if it is in fact made up the way spectrometry suggests. We can't go there in such a way that confirms whether the distance we develop from parallax is accurate, nor can we go off to the side, so to speak, and measure in some other way the velocity to confirm what we think the red shift tells us.

Our methods are limited. What certainty of belief there is comes in large part from the fact that each step has been rigorously examined by many scientists, and carefully repeated over and over again, and whenever possible each part was worked upon in such a way that it could, if possible, be used as a double check against any other part. If it isn't true, it isn't because our best efforts haven't been spent working it out. If it isn't true it's because we missed something, or haven't yet discovered something or maybe assumed something was a certainty that will later turn out not to be so.

The point to note is this: our idea of space, even to the extent developed by modern cosmology, does contain speculation (although as sound as humanly possible) and elements that can't be confirmed directly, but which have to be inferred. Anybody got a better one?

At this point we should perhaps examine a particular aspect of this discussion a little more closely. By and large for the ordinary person, that cosmic space is a three dimensional endlessness is an idea, or better yet an imagination created through education and further developed through the experience of films and television. We don't have a direct personal experience of this seeming fact. Our whole culture believes it. We are raised to think it. For a detailed examination of this question, go to: <u>The Misconception of Cosmic Space as Appears in the Ideas of Modern Astronomy.</u>

In this, it (the idea) bears an odd relationship to an older idea, that of the flat earth. For the naive consciousness of the time in which people believed in a flat earth it was an obvious fact. The earth was observably flat. Yet the time came when people became convinced the earth was round, and thus a different belief was taught and became part of the general cultural imagination of what was real. Only after this did humanity receive the gift of seeing from space the beautiful blue-white globe of the world.

Now what we are trying to notice here is not the particular fact of the three dimensionality of cosmic space, but rather that we know it as an idea, as part of the general cultural imagination of the world's reality. We do not know it as an experience, but rather as one part of a very complex system of ideas in which we are indoctrinated through education. This complex of ideas, of which large parts are believed to be absolutely true, constitutes for modern educated humanity a new myth. Just like the ancients, whose myths we now call superstitions, we have our world view, our socially indoctrinated concepts of what the world is, how it is organized, what fundamental principles caused it to be, and how those principles cause it to behave in the present. The most comprehensive name for this myth is scientific materialism, and even though many scientists understand the limitations of their work and ideas, for the ordinary person, these ideas are reality.

To say that the modern scientist is similar to the old priests of the ancients is not to overstate the case. For the ordinary person the protocols and methodologies of science are a protected mystery. Only after long preparation and education is one admitted to the sanctuaries of modern science as a co-worker. And there are secrets, things kept hidden from the general public. For example, Darwinian evolution (i.e. natural selection) is in serious trouble, but the "priests" don't want the creationists to know it. The physicists studying quantum theory are beginning to use the word "intention" in describing the quantum behavior of certain kinds of small "particles". No one should be surprised if scientific materialism is slowly coming apart, because as long as the scientist is rigorous in his pursuit of the truth he is bound to discover the role of spirit in Nature. It's there and thus it must be eventually found.

Hopefully we will now have sufficient preparation to look at what exists today of another point of view, another "imagination" of the world that again finds mystery in the processes of the natural world. Again, this caution. At best all this essay can do is expose this approach to the natural world to the reader. Its fundamental works can be cited, its relationship to the general trends of science noted, and its basic ideas and principles briefly referred to. Beyond that one cannot go. It remains for the reader to investigate this ongoing work with an unprejudiced eye and an open mind, for its is a certainty that nothing new will be discovered if one already knows the questions and the answers.

I am going to approach the following more in the form of a narrative story then as an expository essay. This personality lived and did this, this other personality did that. The pictures conveyed will necessarily only be partial. Our problem is not unlike that of the five blind wise men who chanced to meet an elephant. One, who touched the tail, thought of it as like a twig. The one, who touched the ear, believed it was a large leaf. To the one, who touched the leg, it was a tree, to the one, who touched the side, it was a rock and to the, one who touched the trunk, it was a...well I can't remember all the story, but I think you get the point. If you draw instant conclusions from this article you will not get the understanding you otherwise might if you instead investigate carefully and directly for yourself.

I would also like to add a special contextual fact, one which many in the environmental movement will have some awareness of. Many today look to aboriginal peoples for an example of a healthy relationship to the natural world. Among such peoples are a number of prophecies, and I would like to direct the attention of the reader to a particular one: that of the Hopi Indians of America's Southwest. Part of the Hopi Prophecy is an expectation that there will arrive someday among them someone or some group which they call the Pahana, or the True White Brother. This individual or group is to bring purification, to inaugurate the Day of Purification, and to provide the "life plan for the future".

Mankind's loss of conscious knowledge of the being of nature, as that has occurred over the course of our history, is also the descent of a kind of darkness. It should surprise no one, who bothers to think carefully about it, that the return of such an understanding, a kind of broad social enlightenment, must necessarily be accompanied by an extended, and cultural-wide rite of passage - quite aptly named by the Hopi: the Day of Purification.". Without going into the very complicated details, I would like to suggest that the following will eventually be understood to be part of the fulfillment of this ancient prophecy.

In 1861, while the American Civil War was just beginning, in Kraljevec, a village on the border between Hungary and Croatia, a man by the name of Ruldolf Steiner was born. By the time he had died in 1925, he had laid securely the foundations for just that spiritual science we have imagined must need to exist, if we are to find our way again to the being of Nature in a modern scientific fashion*. Among the several biographies of Dr. Steiner can be found this one, written by A.P. Shepard: Scientist of the Invisible, Rudolf Steiner, a biography. To those who know and clearly understand his work, this is a most apt title.

*[Obviously this is not the only way. Here we are looking at science, while other Ways are possible and the internet is full of them, for example Robert John Stewart and Stephen Clarke, both of whom, in related ways, approach the Realm of the Divine Mother in more traditional, and less scientific, ways. Both seek to know the truths of the Natural World as Spirit, and both also seek to do this without leaving behind the rational aspect of our own being.]

We can get an early measure of Steiner's genius by noting that at the age of 23, he was invited to edit and write the introduction to Goethe's scientific writings. For those of us raised in the cultural West, it is difficult to realize what a remarkable honor this was, because Goethe has not the same significance for us that he has for Central European culture. To appreciate this, just imagine a 23 year old being asked to edit Einstein's writings. During the course of this work, Steiner realized that Goethe's views of nature depended upon a philosophical position quite different from that of main stream science, and one which Goethe himself had never articulated. Steiner therefore undertook to remedy this situation and produced in 1886 a remarkable philosophic text: A Theory of Knowledge Implicit in Goethe's World Conception.

In 1894, in a more formal way, and also fully cognizant of the philosophical ideas and temper of the time, Steiner produced a deeper philosophic text, which was an expression of his own personal work and not just the elaboration of something implied in Goethe's scientific books and papers. Called The Philosophy of Spiritual Activity, it also carried the intriguing subtitle, "some results of introspective observation following the methods of natural science".

What is expressed in these two books it would be quite impossible to even summarize. In one sense they approach the same fundamental question: how do we know what is true? The basic difference between modern philosophy and Steiner's may be broadly painted this way: For the mainstream, the activity of human consciousness, of the mind, is subjective in nature and, in combination with our senses, is not a reliable way to the truth of the world. For Steiner, as for Goethe, the opposite is true. The human being is so designed that our senses, when properly trained, can give us all of Natures secrets as long as the mind is disciplined as well. For the human being is of nature, and what appears inwardly to a properly trained human thinking is the essence of Nature Herself. Here are Steiner's own words from Theory of Knowledge:

"It is really the genuine, and indeed the truest, form of Nature, which comes to manifestation in the human mind, whereas for a mere sense-being only Nature's external aspect would exist. Knowledge plays here a role of world significance. It is the conclusion of a work of creation. What takes place in human consciousness is the interpretation of Nature to itself. Thought is the last member in a series of processes whereby Nature is formed.".

The central question, these books pose and proceed to answer in a quite empirical way, is: what do we make of human thought? The approach, while expository, if read carefully, reveals that the reader is challenged at each step to observe in his own mind those universal processes leading to the production of thoughts, so that by an empiricism of thinking and observation about thinking the human being finds that in the activity of thinking one stands upon the threshold to a yet unknown world. An internal process, which once stood in darkness, and which went on without any thought given to its nature or meaning, now begins to unfold new possibilities. When this is pursued fully one comes to realize that the Inside of the human being is a thing much greater and more significant that the outside of things as these appear to the senses.

Let us try to work with an analogy. Imagine opening up the hood of an automobile. There before one is a mass of complicated wires, hoses, machines and other strange and unknown devices. That is for most of us. For the master mechanic, the view is something else altogether. We both see the same thing, but the ideas we bring to what we see are quite different. The master mechanic's understanding and experience allows him to identify and see relationships where to most of us there would just be chaos. The reality and significance of those man made objects is not in what appears to the senses at all. Only to the mind does the essential arise.

It was Goethe's insight to realize that something similar was true of our relationship to Nature. With this very significant difference. Man made objects are created according to our intentions; we give them purpose. This can itself be taught. But what is the purpose of a flower; who is to teach us that?

Over many years of work Goethe came to realize that one could trust the senses if one did not add ideas to what was observed. Rather one observed all the manifestations of the object of study (for example the world of plants), until one could recreate in ones own imagination the observed processes. For example, over the course of its birth from seed to its flowering end, a bush will produce a variety of types of leaves. The early ones quite often different from the last. What Goethe did was to recreate in his imagination this process of movement, from the earliest form of the leaf to the latest. (This is very much an oversimplification of his work, by the way.) Over time, Goethe began to experience something which seemed to stand behind the transformations from one form of leaf to the next, but which did not arise from his own activity. In a way his mind became a sense organ into another realm. Through the discipline of his thought life, and the devotion to what came to him through the senses, Goethe began to experience inwardly what he called the Ur-Plant, the spiritual Archetype from which all plants are formed.

In a like manner Goethe examined the animal kingdom in addition to the kingdom of the plants. He found his way of working there to be successful as well. He called his activity: "learning to read in the Book of Nature". What Nature presents to the senses, if appreciated in a disciplined way, "spoke". Even so, the history of science passed this work by, and other ways of thinking became the established methodology.

It remained then for Rudolf Steiner to rescue this overlooked work and restore it to its deserved place in the history of human thought. As a consequence of Steiner's activity there has come to be born: Goethean Science. Its practitioners are few, and the number of its published works also small. But in their own way these works offer the beginning of a whole new way of understanding, and teaching, about Nature. And when Goethean Science is put into relationship with Steiner's more mature work, Spiritual Science, the means to commune with Nature emerges as well.

Let us at this point simply become aware of a few of the published works of Goethean Science. Many readers of the various versions of the Whole Earth Catalog will be aware of the book: Sensitive Chaos, (The Creation of Flowing Forms in Water & Air), by Theodor Schwenk, Anthroposophic Press. Here, with beautiful text, pictures and drawings, some of the basic laws by which form arises in Nature are uncovered, simply through the careful exploration of how water and air move. I will say no more here, for those who genuinely want to investigate Goethean Science will trouble themselves to become acquainted with its basic works.

About the realm of the animals can be found this: Man and Mammals, Toward a Biology of Form, by Wolfgang Schad, Waldorf Press. Here is expressed one of the most profound ideas, first put forward by Steiner, yet consistent with Goethe's studies, about the relationship between function and form which appears everywhere as a threefoldness, a remarkable law of organization of both the organic and the ideal according to laws of polarity.

With the idea of polarity we brush up against one of the things we noted above as a precondition for a new, yet spiritual, science, namely an appropriate mathematics. The Goethean Science movement and its more spiritually complex relative, the Anthroposophical Movement, have produced many works exploring a remarkable form of mathematics called Projective Geometry. Here are just a few of the available texts: Physical and Ethereal Spaces, George Adams, Rudolf Steiner Press. Projective Geometry, Creative Polarities in Space and Time, Olive Whicher, Rudolf Steiner Press. The Plant Between Sun and Earth, George Adams and Olive Whicher, Rudolf Steiner Press. The Field of Form, Lawrence Edwards, Floris Books.

With these and other related texts, as well as with the two philosophic texts of Steiner noted above, our new science stands upon all the necessary foundation it needs, as we indicated earlier - that is an appropriate mathematics and philosophy of knowledge.

For those who legitimately may need to understand how main-stream science took the path it did, and what can be done about it, there is: Man or Matter, Ernst Lehrs, Anthroposophic Press (already mentioned above). The description, in the Anthroposophic Press Catalog about this book, reads as follows: "Now a classic, this is the fundamental text for those seeking a spiritual understanding of nature on the basis of Goethe's method of training observation and thought. Working out of a detailed history of science, Lehrs reveals to the reader not only how science has been inescapably lead to the illusions it holds today, but more importantly, how the reader may correct in himself these misconceptions brought into his world view through modern education."

It remains for us then to link up Goethean Science, and Rudolf Steiner's Anthroposophy, or Spiritual Science. This, however, is not so simple, for in really considering the spiritual we run also into the religious, which for many is either a grave difficulty or a profound and untouchable belief. If we proceed carefully, we can nevertheless walk through this potential mine-field without too much harm. Hopefully these guidelines will help.

It is not the intention of this essay to argue for or against any religious belief, including, broadly speaking, agnosticism or atheism. The point is to remain true to the principles of modern science which require reproducible experiments and testable hypotheses. However, when we approach the spiritual we have to be realistic about what is involved in "reproducing" and "testing". In the realm of the spirit such matters a more difficult because in large part they require of the individual a far greater effort and self-mastery than ordinary experimental science.

Consider this analogy. If I were to attempt to reproduce current work in particle physics, in a scientific way, I would need access to the appropriate devices (regardless of how complex and costly). Further I would need an appropriate education and familiarity with the current work and theories. These are all a given. So it is with research in the realm of the spirit. One needs to develop the inner capacities and to have mastery of the ongoing work. Thus, to attempt to dispute or criticize spiritual science without such effort is to defy the scientific spirit of the age, and to make a mockery of reasonable human discourse.

With this needed understanding in mind let us begin to enter more deeply into the realms of a modern spiritual science.

A personality not mentioned so far, and, in the view of many, certainly Steiner's peer in the science of the invisible (spiritual research), is one Valentin Tomberg. In his remarkable lectures published under the title: The Four Sacrifices of Christ and the Appearance of Christ in the Etheric, (Candeur Manuscripts), given in Rotterdam in the turn of the year 1938 to 1939, we can find the following:

"You see, the transition from all that is most prosaic produced by the nineteenth century to what the future holds is offered by the spiritual manifestation of Goetheanism - Goetheanism is, in fact, a bridge on which the transition can be made from the quantitative thinking of the nineteenth century to a qualitative, characterizing thinking. Now, where this transition leads is to Spiritual Science. Here it is not only a matter of being able to think qualitatively, but of placing the moral element in the thinking into the foreground. And by way of comparison, one could say that Goetheanism is related to Anthroposophy, to Spiritual Science, in the same way as the organic world is related to the soul world. The organic calls for qualitative thinking; the soul world, for the formation of moral concepts*." (emphasis in the original).

*[See my: Living Thinking in Action, for certain details: http://ipwebdev.com/hermit/liveT.html]

For some readers, right at this point there will be a difficulty. Having used the word "moral" at once we encounter all kinds of preconceptions about what that means. If there is anything which seems to lie outside of the realm of the scientific, of the objective, it would be the question of what is moral. (Although, interestingly enough, there are some who think there can be an objective "ethics".)

However, in the understanding of Steiner and Tomberg and their many students, the core need of modern humanity is freedom. And not just political liberty, but more importantly freedom in thought, freedom of spirit. Steiner's The Philosophy of Spiritual Activity is sometimes called The Philosophy of Freedom, the problem being how to translate from the German, Die Philosophie der Freiheit. One translator invented a new English word to stand in for Freiheit: namely Freehood, which is obviously very clumsy and unattractive. My poet-self leans toward a freer translation, namely The Philosophy of Free Becoming.

The key to this problem lies in a general confusion of our time regarding human inner life and the role of conscience. An objective introspection of human consciousness comes to realize that there is an equally objective experience which is the "voice of conscience". Just as the darkness, which inhibits us from truly understanding the production of our own thoughts, can be lifted, so can the darkness which makes dim the "voice of conscience" be eliminated. "Conscience" is an aspect of our spirit, and it is this higher element of our nature which knows what in any given situation it means to be moral. This places morality outside the realm of doctrine, dogma or rules or anything other then our own higher judgment. Steiner's The Philosophy of Spiritual Activity calls this part of human potential: ethical individualism. Morality then becomes as much an act of freedom as any other.

There can be difficulties here. Freedom, Steiner pointed out, is something different from license. Of course we can do anything, but whether we should or not is a whole other question. In the past the problem has been who is to make the judgment of what we should or should not do. In Goetheanism and in Spiritual Science, it is the individual himself who makes that judgment. Given the gift of "conscience" we have a capacity for certain moral knowledge. The difficulty is whether we pay attention or not, not whether we can know what is moral or not. Conscience can be ignored and often is. But that is a whole other issue.

Hopefully this discussion will have helped some regarding the confusion that can arise when one suggests that with Goetheanism we leave behind quantitative thinking for qualitative thinking, and that with Spiritual Science we go onward to moral thinking. In each case it is a question of what is to be the object of our search for knowledge. With quantitative thinking we gain a mastery of the material-mechanical aspects of existence, thus our civilizations technological successes. With qualitative thinking we gain a mastery of the living aspects of existence and with moral thinking we gain a master of the invisible aspects, the aspects of soul and spirit. In each case we can have an "objective" knowledge, because we chose a method appropriate to the purpose we pursued, and because we acted in a disciplined way, so that our investigations remained "empirical", reproducible and testable.

It is then with Spiritual Science that we enter on that path that can lead to a real knowledge of the being and consciousness of Nature, to a communion with that which lies behind the veil of the sense world. From one point of view, anthroposophy or spiritual science, as founded by Steiner, has two main themes. The first theme is how to attain knowledge of what aboriginal peoples might call the world of the invisibles. The second theme is the results of that research. In the literature of both goetheanism and spiritual science one finds both these themes well elaborated. Yet, when criticism of these disciplines is presented, it is usually made by ignoring the how and arguing instead with the what, the results. This is rather easy, because the results very often contradict what is already thought by the main streams of both science and religion.

A good way to appreciate this problem is to imagine that what is being experienced today, by the arrival of these disciplines, goetheanism and spiritual science, is the way of thought of the future making its first beginning appearances in our present. Think what it would have been like to have been a contemporary of Galileo. What he taught directly contradicted the views of the time. Think what it is like to change our habits, say ways of writing and speaking, for example. For most of Galileo's contemporaries to change their habits of thought is impossible. And not just because they are habits, but also because of the social pressure. The habits of our way of thinking and the social dynamic which supports them are extremely powerful forces. No one, therefore, should expect these new disciplines, Goetheanism and spiritual science, to overcome the modern version of this mental and social inertia very easily.

These problems are made all the more complex by the fact that even within those groups which struggle with spiritual science (such as the Anthroposophical Society) in an attempt to learn it, there is not a uniform approach. The groups which support and practice these new disciplines are made up of human beings and there are many difficulties, disagreements and confusions. I point this all out, so that those, who might choose to investigate more closely these disciplines, will approach Goetheanism and spiritual science with a certain carefulness.

If what has been written so far, especially as regards the possibility of learning to commune with the spiritual realities behind the natural world, has meant anything for the reader, then I will close with these words of guidance.

Be methodical and patient. Face the challenge of the philosophical problem contained in the books mentioned concerning it. Do not fear encountering the mathematical aspect, projective geometry. It is usually presented in ways far easier then we can imagine - not by abstract algebraic formulation, but through drawing and visualization. At the same time become acquainted with the practitioners, the people carrying out the various fruits of this work. Remember what was said regarding the need for a new science, a spiritual science, to have produced results, just as materialistic main-stream science has? Have you heard of Waldorf Schools, biodynamic agriculture, Camphill Communities, Eurythmy, anthroposophical medicine, curative education, the Christian Community, astrosophy, psychosophy, rhythmic massage, Werbeck singing, anthroposophical nursing?

Beware skipping past Goetheanism. That way leads to an illness. Thinking must go through a transformation, from the quantitative, to the qualitative and then to the moral. It is a process of inner metamorphosis. Each stage is essential. The goal is spiritual science, which stands upon the philosophic work and the mathematical work. Out of this disciplining of the thought life, then can be grown a disciplining of the sense life, the life of perception.

Expect obstacles. The moral thinking depends upon that moral training which only arises from the life we live, the immediate moral challenges of our own personal existence. There is nothing abstract here. It is all too painfully real.

Do not become confused by and in love solely with the results of spiritual research. It is much more important to master the how. With the how we are then free to choose just what we will think about. If we become too involved in the what, the results, it is possible to become captured by the rich conceptual world there unveiled, and then to lose sight of the necessity of making all concepts our own work product. Those, who encounter the Anthroposophical Society in their search, will meet many who have fallen into this error. Remember, the only ground on which we can stand as a free spiritual being in the world of the material and the immaterial is those qualities of being that arise from The Philosophy of Free Becoming.

Let me sum up with a brief look at global warming in a new way.

Everywhere we see what appears to be environmental degradation. Loss of species, shrinking of glaciers and so forth. A kind of war has broken out in science itself, and certainly politically, as various interests vie for dominance. There is a lot of undisciplined and superficial thinking. Some examples:

When we have extreme winter weather conditions, some will say this proves there is no warming, for in their superficial thinking and the elaboration of their political ideologies, they look for any evidence that supports the already assumed bias. Factually, we have to step back from the idea of global warming, and appreciate better the idea of climate change. The former is not necessarily a consequence of the latter.

The idea of global warming suggests a process which continues to the point of grave consequences, but the evidence for it may in fact be an indirect effect of climate change. When complex systems undergo basic changes in the nature of their given present state of equilibrium, they oscillate wildly for a time, before acquiring the new steady state. To have the idea of long term continuous warming, we have to make assumptions that are not really justified. What happens if we consider the possibility that the Being of Nature is in a kind of dialog with the human beings.

Some people think that human beings are a kind of virus, and that Nature would continue in a better way if we were all gone. But aboriginal peoples have all understood that the Earth is our Mother, and we are Her children. Our Mother is not out to kill us - challenge us yes, but not kill us.

We are immortal spirits, whose very existence is the point of the Creation. But like a true Mother, the Earth will not tolerate our laziness or insolence. The Hopi Prophecy considers this problem in detail, and in advising us of the coming time of the True White Brother, this Prophecy lets us know that in such times as these, where grave consequences arrive to our immature actions, we will still be loved by the appearance of new wisdom - new revelation - to go with the challenges of the time. The Mother speaks to us even now.

Yet the thesis of many in the global warming point of view is that environmental degradation is human caused and can by human beings be corrected. This is itself a grave arrogance. This view still finds itself unable to form and I and Thou relationship with Nature. We are not listening, but instead interpreting all according to our own biases, wants and desires. Opposing corporate choices, and thinking our judgment superior to that, it does not occur to us the our shared Mother loves all, the environmentalist and the polluting destroyer.

If we read (see the meaning of) ordinary motherhood, we will see a manifestation of the Divine Mother as well. All that is great in the Cosmos, exists in a small way also in the individual human being. Mothers give away their being to their children, willingly. She will let die in the body of Her Son (the physical Earth), but both will endure in the Spirit, just as we do.

In reality, the climate change crisis is designed to slow civilization down, and to put the breaks on our tendencies to excess and a too fast - too immoderate - way of life. Climate change is a gift.

~!~!~!~!~!~!~!~

The purpose of this essay has been to introduce a question into the environmental movement (What does Nature want?). The secondary purpose has been to point out an ongoing work which is laying the foundation (Goetheanism and spiritual science) for answering just that question - a foundation which does not require the abandoning of the principles of science. To those who may wish to travel this path, I add this: You will not travel it alone. Many there are who seek to reunite the Circle and the Cross. See The Mystery of the True White Brother, and The Songs of a True White Brother on these pages.

Then, as a free spirit among other spirits we will come to that communion with Nature, which we seek and desire, a silent Eucharist of the Invisible.

(Here are some essays on the website of someone
who has fully realized this new way of working with Nature,
and
here is a link to Adonis Press, which specializes in books
concerned with this new way of looking at Nature.)

~!~!~!~!~!~!~!~!~

The Misconception of Cosmic Space As Appears In the Ideas of Modern Astronomy

*- and as contained in the understandably limited thinking embodied
in the conceptions of the nature of parallax and redshift -*

by Joel A. Wendt
- introduction -

Before entering on to the main body of this essay, we should consider briefly the nature of thinking and of the imagination. In this little book there are a number of different comments on thinking and on the imagination, coming from different directions, but here I want to point out some basic facts as a foundation for the coming work.

The first is that human beings think, and that there is no science without the activity of human *thinking.* Thinking determines which questions the scientist asks, what experiments he conducts, and then ultimately how the data provided by the experiments is interpreted - that is what does this scientific activity **mean.** For this essay we are confronted with the scientific meaning created by human thinking in relationship to some considerable portions of the data accumulated by scientific work centered on questions concerning the stellar world. We are asking here in this essay whether what science thinks today of the meaning and significance of the stars is what we ought to continue to think, in the future, or even today to assume is still a reasonable understanding.

As scientists all possibilities need to be on the table ... anything less is a fraud ... still, if you are afraid of the dark, or of the mysterious, then maybe this place is not for you, ... but if you want to adventure, and still be scientific: The Fermi Paradox Resolved *discusses generalities, here we get to nuts and bolts. Just keep in mind there have been astronomers since there where eyes to see stars ...*

As part of the process of examining the underlying questions, we will be using a particular capacity of the mind, which might be called the imagination, or picture-forming capacity. We make all manner of mental pictures in the normal course of ordinary thinking, and in scientific thinking we carry out this activity in quite specific directions. Certain astronomical ideas, for example the idea of parallax, are specifically grounded in the picture-thinking connected to Euclidean geometry. While we sometimes use a pencil and paper to work out the details of this geometric picture thinking, the fact that should not be ignored (but often is) is that it is the mind of the human being that contributes the fundamental activity from which our modern astronomical conceptions arise. In fact, our interpretation of the meaning of astronomical data is entirely a result of mental processes, a number of which are expressly born in the imagination.

Yes, we carefully observe the stellar world with all kinds of remarkable instruments. We also use a great deal of mathematics in how this material is interpreted, but mwe must never, in the process of unfolding this scientific investigation of the world of the stars, forget the centrality of thinking and of the imagination to the whole process. If we take thinking and the imagination away, there is no science of astronomy. Why this is so important will hopefully become more clear as this essay unfolds.

- main body -

"Our Father in the skies..." are the first words of the Lord's Prayer, as translated by Andy Gaus in his book **The Unvarnished Gospels**. I start here to point out the fact that the *people living in ancient Palestine, at the time of the Incarnation of Christ, had a different kind of consciousness than we do today.* When they looked at the heavens, they understood (and were taught by their wise elders) that the sky was the abode of the Divine Mystery. In fact, they understood the whole of Creation to be en-souled with *Being* and *Consciousness*. Since that time a different conception of the heavens and of the earth has come into existence for large portions of humanity. How did that original conception change and what can we learn by observing carefully the nature of that change?

Everyone understands that if we make even the slightest error in the aim of the bow and arrow, by the time the arrow reaches the end of its journey, it doesn't take much of an original error to cause the arrow to have completely missed the target. Human beings are flawed, and science is the activity of human beings. In the following essay I am going to concern myself with clearly amateur* researches and thinking into the problems of parallax and red shift, as these ideas are used to create for us a conception of the world of the Stars.

Johannes Kepler thought we were in danger of throwing out the baby with the bathwater, in our wholesale rejection of the ancient understanding/knowledge of the starry world.

The best of ancient lore on the stellar world is here: Practical Astrology by, Comte C. de Saint-Germain ... no other book on the ancient stellar wisdom combines into a single system: astrology, tarot, and numerology - want to know why? Study that book...

[While I am not a member of the priesthood of the religion of Natural Science, I do know how to observe carefully and how to think objectively, so just because astronomy isn't my profession, the reader should not automatically anticipate they will be misled. The reader should, however, themselves test the themes outlined below in their own careful picture-thinking. The tendency of scientific thinking has been toward too much analysis, and not enough synthesis, while the return of a focus on the imagination will help us move forward in the future toward a needed balance between these two basic gestures in thinking.]

The fundamental question is this: the current generally understood idea of cosmic space is that it is essentially a three dimensional endlessness - a very big box, which while it must have some unusual properties as a container, it is nevertheless organized such that everywhere inside it one can expect that the same rules of physics we observe in the laboratory on the Earth, will be true all that way out there...one upon a time in a galaxy far far away. Is this conception of endless three-dimensional space true?

Let us consider a rather simple geometric thought experiment, which everyone (trained mathematician or otherwise) can do.

Make a picture of a small perfect sphere in your mind. It has a center and a periphery. That is the nature of the bubble in physical space, where individualizing consciousness exists. A machine can't write this stuff, given that only a human being reads-into words what we do ... also individually. We are point centers of consciousness, wandering troubling seas ... We are love&magic, ... or not <shrug> ... Sense8 sentience - all minds connected - best scale is local, and to music - dancing ...

One can use the terms radius, circumference and diameter with respect to this sphere, but they really don't have any exact meaning unless we define one of these characteristics by giving it first an exact measure. For example, if we said the radius of our mental sphere was one meter, well understood rules of the geometry of a perfect sphere would give us diameter and circumference (as well as other related characteristics, such as the degree of arc of the curvature of the surface, the area of the surface, etc.).

The inner geometry of center and periphery - my ~!~ experience. Every object, inert or otherwise, has existence certainly. Why deny/pretend that all the ITS&THINGS also have consciousness and will? The "smartphone" robs our ability to remember, saving all kinds of data reducible to code. Aladdin's Lamp, with a dash of Dick Tracy's wristwatch radio - dangerous waters as we borg ourselves and pretend that the stuff ... well, a tool is only as good as the tool user. The best tools are hand crafted from scratch, and given ceremonial rites - everything is sacred - even hell >"Shamans" 0ogle images here>

... every object, every surface, every place where we see, light-is-with-darkness, or there is no color ...

Now keep in mind that we don't have to conceive of this sphere in terms of measure. It can just exist in our mind as a measureless perfect geometric form.

Next, we imagine the radius line, from the center of the sphere to the periphery, increasing. We again don't have to measure it, we just make the picture in our thinking of this imaginary sphere as something that is slowly growing through an elongating radius line. The radius line grows. As that line grows all the other characteristics of the sphere grow as well.

We could also mentally cause the same effect by changing any other properties. For example, if we cause with our picture-thinking the area of the surface to increase, we change at the same time all the other relationships.

Now lets return to the increasing of the radius line. In your imagination now picture that intersection between the radius line and the periphery of the sphere. At this intersection there is a degree of curvature of the arc of the sphere. We can notice as we do this thought experiment that as the radius line grows, the tightness of the curvature of the surface lessens.

To help this, lets imagine the radius line decreasing. We shrink it, and as we do this the curvature of the periphery of the sphere gets tighter and tighter, until we make the radius line zero. When we make the radius line zero we have lost the sphere, and it has disappeared into a dimensionless point.

Yet, since we are working without any need for measure, a zero radius sphere is simply a point. Once we give measure of any amount to the radius line of a zero radius line sphere (a point), the sphere returns. A radius line of a nanometer takes a point and makes it a sphere.

Seeing this clearly with our geometrical imagination (which is quite exact and precise, by the way), we now do the opposite and complete the earlier exercise by increasing the radius line to infinite length. Instead of a radius line of zero, it is now infinite. What then happens to the curvature of the sphere when the radius becomes infinitely elongated? [For a delicious discussion of "infinity" see David Foster Wallace's: Everything and More: A Compact History of Infinity.]

Well, if we carefully follow out our precise and exact geometrical imagination, we will be able to observe this process unfold. As the radius line increases in length the original tightness of the curvature of the surface of the sphere lessens, until at the moment the radius line is infinite there will be no curvature at all. The sphere has disappeared, and undergone a metamorphosis into a plane. If we think carefully about what we have learned here, we will see then that any sphere of any measure of radius line is always an intermediate geometric form arising in between a dimensionless point and a plane at infinity.

This fact is already well known in the profound mathematical science of projective geometry, and we have now ourselves discovered what is called there: the Plane at Infinity. The sphere then is geometrically in between the infinitely large and the infinitesimally small, or in between the plane at infinity and a geometric point (which has no measure at all, unless we put it into relationship with something else). A point by itself is just that - nothing else. It occupies no space at all.
Well then, what is the *point* of this exercise?

There are several. First it is crucial to realize that we can think geometrically without using any measure at all. If one is lucky enough to come upon a copy of **Projective Geometry** : creative polarities in space and time*, one has the possibility to study this wonderful geometry using only a pencil, a straight edge and some paper (large sheets are easier for some constructions). Measure has been done away with, and the creators (or discoverers) of this mathematics describe it is *all geometry* - meaning by this that every single other geometry is a special case of projective geometry. Also George Adam's Physical and Ethereal Spaces.

*[check Waldorf Schools or other Rudolf Steiner institutions for copies of this book. It is often tragically out of print.]

The difficulty for Natural Scientists has been how to apply this beautifully symmetric, measure free geometry, to the natural world. Science is rooted in measure, and while the ideas of this geometry are recognized as significant, what could they mean in a world that is already hopelessly entangled in a science which has to use measure for everything?

With this riddle in the background, let us now examine the history of ideas by which the old view of the heavens as an abode of the Divine Mystery came to be supplanted by a view in which space is conceived as a near endless three dimensional container, punctuated with mass caused curvatures (the space-time gravity ideas following after Einstein, using the Reinman geometry - again a special case of the more general projective geometry).

Giordano Bruno, who was burned at the stake as a heretic in 1600, is credited with having first suggested the idea that a star might be like the sun. Would that our histories were more accurate, because what we think of as the sun today, and how he thought about such matters (he was, among other disciplines, a deeply thoughtful meta-physician*) is not quite grasped by believing his idea, that a star and our sun were relatives, in fact mirrors in anyway our modern conceptions. For Bruno, the idea that a star and our sun were related, was a completely different idea than we hold today. The details of that, however, is a whole other matter.

*[Meta-physics, contrary to modern views that it is not a science at all, was really always seen as a product of a *synthesis* of ones total understanding. Modern physics comes from taking things apart,

from *analysis*. Meta-physics always had the task of make the parts of all human knowledge into a single whole. For a good example of modern thinking that is "holistic", as regards astrophysics, read Georg Blattmann's The Sun: the ancient mysteries and the new physics.]

Bruno did agree to a degree with Copernicus, and so in those years the ideas being produced by natural philosophers (the grandfathers of natural science) came to be at odds with the dogmas of the Roman Catholic Church. While the previous age of careful thinkers (the Scholastics), would have understood (keeping to Aristotle) that there was a difference between *quantities* and *qualities*, the scientific impulse coming to the fore in those years more and more felt it could only deal with that which could be counted or measured - that is *quantities*.

The various categorical *qualities* of Aristotelian meta-physics more and more dropped away from consideration (although this was a long term process and many thinkers (Kepler and Faraday, for example) thought this was an error of thought to do so.
In any event, pure astronomy slowly freed itself from the meta-physics connected to astrology and related disciplines, by a process in which the *qualitative* problems were left aside and everything was more and more rooted in only what could be counted (and measured). Kepler, it has been forgotten, was an astrologer as well as the discoverer of the three fundamental laws of planetary motion*. Not only that, but Newton was an alchemist. The tendency has been to frame the history of these thinkers as if they thought as we do today, when anyone who actually reads what they wrote discovers they did not. (For a comprehensive examination of this overlooked history of science, read Ernst Lehrs' **Man or Matter**: *Introduction to a Spiritual Understanding of Nature on the Basis of Goethe's Method of Training Observation and Thought*. Also read the physicist Arthur Zajonc's **Catching the Light**: *the entwined history of Light and Mind*.

*[Kepler believed, for example, that his formula and ideas regarding the Third Law of Planetary Motion was a rediscovery of the ancient's idea of the Harmony of the Spheres]

As this process matures, it reaches a kind of high point in the 19th Century, and two important ideas are given birth out of the context of this leaving aside of the problem of *qualities*, and resting all theories of the starry world only on what can be counted and measured. These ideas are parallax and Redshift. Such concepts don't emerge on their own, so we have to work carefully with them, still keeping in mind how dependent they are upon measure alone.

The idea of Redshift doesn't come by itself, for example, for it is really based upon spectroscopy. This science is itself not based initially on stellar observation, but on work in the laboratory where various fundamental elements are combusted (burned) in such a way that they produce "light". This "light" is measured according to the quantitative ideas of Newtonian Optics, and so we get the "spectral" lines for such basic elements as hydrogen.

As a result stellar light phenomena, including light phenomena from our sun, are used in such a way that it is assumed that this light from the stars, and our sun, is produced in those places by a burning process similar in kind (but not degree) to what was done in the laboratory. If the light from a star, or our sun, has a certain mathematically accurate vibration (frequency), that is like or essentially similar to the hydrogen line obtained in the laboratory, this light frequency is then seen as showing us that in that star, or our sun, hydrogen is being burned up, which combustion process gives off that particular light frequency.

This is so important a fact (actually assumed to be universal) that in the movie **Contact**, the frequency used to send the message to Earth from the fictional stellar civilization is the hydrogen light frequency times pi. That is, it is a material constant multiplied by a geometric constant.

All the same, there was a problem with the hydrogen light frequency, for example, from the stars. The observed light frequency in the normal range for hydrogen (assumed to be an exact universal constant) isn't actually quite so exact to observation. Various stars' hydrogen lines are discovered to be a bit off center, so to speak, such that they can be described (in the assumptions of physical astronomy) to be either red shifted or blue shifted. The greatest number of stellar objects are red shifted (only a very very few are blue shifted).
Following Newton, color is a spectrum of light frequencies, with a red end point, where beyond which it becomes invisible to the eye, or a blue end point (actually violet, but convention names that end of the spectrum the blue end) where beyond this end it also becomes invisible to the eye. We see with our eyes a normal color Newtonian spectrum (so it is assumed) and at the edges of this visible spectrum the light is no longer visible, although it still can be observed and measured with instruments (the red end becomes infrared or heat, and the blue end becomes ultraviolet, leading then to such as x-rays). The wavelength of the frequency at the red end is longer and longer (elongation), and the wavelength of the frequency at the blue end is shorter and shorter (compaction).

These questions arise: what does it mean that light from the stars is not exactly showing us the precise hydrogen line we came to know in the laboratory, and what do we make of the fact that this shift toward the red (the dominant types of shift) itself varies? Some stellar objects show small Redshift and other's quite large Redshift.

The original dominating idea for the meaning of the phenomena of the redshift (elongation) of such as the hydrogen line frequency was arrived at by creating an analogy between light waves and sound waves, in 1842. We all know (or experience at least) the so-called Doppler effect - the shift in sound of a train horn as it comes toward us or away from us. This *movement* toward or away produces a change in the pitch (auditory frequency), even though we know that the actual pitch the horn is making never changes. The change in pitch is heard because of the *movement* of the source of the sound (which compacts or elongates the frequency, as *perceived* by the ear, which is relatively stationary).

By analogy then, Redshift was thought to give evidence of the movement of the object away from the observer on the Earth. Whatever was going on, most of the stellar objects had this Redshift phenomena (in varying degrees) and from this analogy was born the idea that the Universe is expanding (which then later is supposed to logically give us the Big Bang - an explosion which creates an expanding

Universe). I point out this last to urge the reader to notice how interwoven are all the ideas we have today about the physical universe, such that if, for example, redshift doesn't really mean what we think it means, then this idea of the expansion of the Universe loses one of its main supports. (See link at end of essay for current thinking on this problem in conventional astronomy.)

The first problem to arise after the more or less universal acceptance of this *theory*, was the recognition that while light was superficially a wave phenomena (a movement propagating in a medium), similar to sound, the analogy didn't really hold, so a lot of thought went into how to revisit the redshift phenomena and appreciate it better. Unfortunately, while many scientists feel certain older kinds of ideas ought to get dropped away from any current point of view, some ideas seem quite unwilling to be abandoned, so the Doppler analogy remains, even though contemporary physics sometimes sees light as both particle and wave simultaneously (depending on what questions you ask, and which experiments you do).

One of the newer *theories* as regards Redshift (moving away from the Doppler analogy) is that it is partially a consequence of the temperature in the star. Another sees some Redshift phenomena as reflecting the influence of gravity wells.

I point this out only to suggest that theories themselves are in constant motion (a kind of social Brownian-motion among different minds). I am not so much interested in the current theory here, because it is my view that the resolution to the fundamental question lies in a quite different direction.

Let us now leave Redshift behind, and go on to the idea parallax, which arose a few years before Redshift historically (1838, so it says on-line).

The basic idea of parallax is that it enables us to measure (remember what was said above about measure) how far a star (or other stellar phenomena) is from the Earth. Basically this is done by coming up with an observational angle, that can be measured on the Earth, and is made possible in large part by the orbit of the Earth around the sun. Since I can't put in a drawing here (the reader can go on-line if they desire) I'll try to do this with words.

Place on the grass of a football field, in your imagination, two poles. One pole is at the center of the goal line, and the next at the center of the 10 yard line nearest that goal line. Now go down to the goal line at the other end of the field, and set up a transit (a device for taking the measure of an angle of changes in a sight line). Move the transit from one side of the field to the other, stopping every yard, and make observations of the angle of observation between the two poles obtained by viewing them from the moving transit.

As we do this the angle we are measuring changes. This angle is widest at one side of the field, and then contracts, until we are right opposite the two poles (at which occurrence the near pole occults the other, or stands in front of it), and then the angle expands again as we move toward the opposite side of the field.

Now imagine such an activity taking place with respect to the light phenomena of stellar objects. The transit is actually the earth, which moves constantly, changing the observational "angle" with respect to distant objects. As this earth-transit moves, some of the distant objects seem to occult each other, as if one was in front, and the other behind.

However, since these objects are so far away (apparently), the angles that are measured are very very very small (small fractions of seconds of degree of arc). One writer suggested that if you took a quarter, and looked at it from a distance of three miles, measuring the angle between a transit observation of one side of the quarter, and then the other side - this picture suggests how small an angle is actually being measured by this method (parallax) with regard to the nearest star to the earth (for stars believed to be further away, the "angle" is progressively smaller).

Using this data (the angle measurements coupled with our knowledge of the diameter of the Earth's orbit) we can use the basic rules of Euclidean geometry to determine the length of the sides of the resultant triangle. This information (with a couple of other geometric ideas rooted in measure) then gives what we think to be the distance of the stellar object from the Earth.

Now since redshift is _believed_ to tell us that most stellar objects are moving away from us, these distances change over time, which then appears to give us a kind of confirmation of the parallax. The problem is that some of these observations came in conflict (an inconsistency between Redshift and parallax). One of the most obvious of these was discovered by the astronomer Hal Arp, who as a result for a time found himself to be seen as a heretic by his fellows, and was temporarily shunned (couldn't get telescope time to continue his research (see his book, **_Quasars, Redshifts, and Controversies_**).

Basically what he observed (using conventional astronomical ideas and methods), was that Quasars (quasi-stellar objects), while they had a very high Redshift (suggesting they were traveling very fast away from us, and since they were _thought_ to have been doing this for some time - no changes in rate of velocity and/or acceleration were assumed, they were also _thought_ to be quite far away, while the parallax measurement seemed to imply they were much nearer. Quasars seemed to occult (get in front of) much slower (less Redshifted) stellar objects). The two phenomena could not be reconciled. Were Quasars near or far?
I'll not go into what were the conventional adjustments made (its all very complicated, and unnecessarily so in my view) in order to preserve the basic set of ideas of modern astronomy, but we can (with justification) simply step past these ideas. Why?

Because fundamentally the problem is due to the fact that phenomena of redshift and parallax is organized in accord with Euclidean geometry and the need in science to measure. In effect, at every point in the development of these ideas (though scientific thinking and imagination), we exported to Cosmic Space those conceptions that were true here in the center (the Earth), and further, we _assumed_* that these conditions were an invariable constant.

*[There is no *empirical* evidence for this whatsoever - it is 95% theoretical.]

For example, the distance we measure using the idea of parallax can't actually be tested empirically. In essence, we export from our Earth reality the concept of Euclidean three-dimensional space to the apparently farthest reaches of the starry world, but at the same time have no way of testing the set of assumptions behind the activity of exportation of such an idea. We can't go off to the side of the *container* in which all stars are held, and measure from another quarter whether in fact the distance the parallax formulation gives us is correct.

For another example, we find the hydrogen frequency line by a laboratory experiment here on the surface of the Earth, and then assume that nothing of physics changes at cosmic distances, and that the universe will obey the same laws way out there that it obeys here. Under the influence of these assumptions we export our earthly picture to cosmic spaces, something that really isn't justified if science wishes to remain properly empirical.

All our observations are made on the Earth or from near-earth space. It is really only in our mind that we go outward toward cosmic space. If that is the case, then we must be very very careful in how we let one thought grow from the other.   Clearly if there is an error in thought (remember our arrow to the target analogy at the beginning of this essay), then the *further out* in space our imagination, of the picture of the meaning of the data we collect *here* goes, the more a small error in our thought will produce a quite large miss in our understanding of the truth.

While there were many small mistakes made (such as the assumptions observed regarding the hydrogen line), there is one single idea that saves the situation as it were. We set aside Euclidean geometry and substitute for it Projective Geometry - the fundamental geometry of which all other geometries (including Euclidean) are a special case. Let us next then try to apply this geometry to the image creation aspect of our thinking, because after all it is the image we are making of cosmic space that is important. It is the mind that travels to cosmic space, riding the ideas we have created from the data only empirically observed here. We, who live today, have traveled far down the historical path of one kind of mind-created image, and now it is time to perhaps deconstruct it and create something new. Lets recall the older (or current) image first, namely of a three dimensional emptiness, filled with stars which are like our sun, some surrounded by planets like our planet. It is a powerful image. Science fiction, books and films, tell all kinds of tales. If one were to suggest that this might not be correct, most people would think you were crazy.

Return now to our earlier work in which we expanded the radius line of the sphere to infinity and observed how the sphere became a plane at infinity (or the reverse, where if we contract the radius line the sphere disappears into a dimensionless point). Also keep in mind that the geometric form never changes its basic nature - it just *transforms* at the different extremes (the infinitely large and the infinitesimally small radius aspect).

A lot of people should have some trouble here, because they conceive of infinity as something much larger than say the multiple light years of measure we have applied to the distance between the Earth and the stellar objects. In this regard, lets look at some apparent facts so far developed under the old methodology.

For example, the so-called nearest star, Proxima Centuri is thought to be 4.2 light years away (its degree of arc in parallax is .77233 seconds of arc - which is by the way the largest degree of arc using parallax measures, for every more distant object will have a smaller degree of arc). 4.2 light years (this next is an amateur calculation) is 24 billion miles (that's 24,000,000,000, or 24 thousand million). The farthest distance objects are high multiples of that. We'll return to this a bit later.

Remember, we have exported an idea to cosmic space which we can't empirically test. Science, tied to the idea of counting and measure, has exported to cosmic space a measure (huge light year distances), which idea can't be checked by any other means. As a result, we are quite right to challenge this exportation of measure to test whether it is a thought that is properly rigorous. Since we cannot empirically test the assumed measure, we are left with the quite definite necessity to even more carefully and rigorously subject that *idea* to the tests of logic.

Here is a very important question. If at the center of our infinitely small sphere, the point, there is no actual space, once we have created any measure of radius distance (a nanometer, for example), we now have three dimensional space, then what happens at the infinite radius, when the sphere disappears and becomes the plane at infinity? Is this transition as apparently sudden as the one from the point to the very very small sphere? [Again, for a delicious discussion of "infinity" see David Foster Wallace's: Everything and More: A Compact History of Infinity.]

If we actually think very carefully about this we will notice (using our geometric imagination) that even the transition to the very very small is not sudden. There is a lot of work on theses themes in mathematics, and you can Google it by starting with Zeno's paradoxes. In any event, at the infinitesimally small end of the transition, from the sphere to the point, the *process itself* is likewise smaller and smaller in nature, while the transition from the very large sphere to the plane at infinity must, by virtue of laws of symmetry common to projective geometry, be larger and larger in nature. Keep in mind we are thinking here of the *transformational process*, from one geometric state or form to another state or form.

The plane at infinity doesn't appear suddenly out of nowhere, but as we approach it the nature of three-dimensional space is slowly undergoing a metamorphosis. Three-dimensional space is becoming plane-like in its fundamental nature, but not all of a sudden. Space itself is changing, and the rules of physics applicable to a purely three-dimensional sphere (Earth conditions) will no longer, at these extremely large distances, apply.

What are huge light year imagined measures then (such as the 78 billion light years assumed for diameter the visible universe - there being thought to exist a greater universe we cannot yet see even with our instruments)? They are simply a fantasy or myth, born in the assumptions of the scientific imagination. Since we cannot conceive of anything as knowable scientifically, without measure and counting, we presently are unable to conceive of the universe without measure either. Again, an assumption that causes the arrow to miss the mark. The question right here then is whether the current limits of our imagination and thinking reflect the actual limits of reality. Confined for a time in the limited box of Euclidean Geometry, we stand on the cusp of transcending those limits by applying the more universal Projective Geometry.

This should not surprise anyone, for we already know that in particle physics, where the transition of matter endowed space becomes infinitesimally small (remember the sphere collapsing into the point - which has led us into all the paradoxes of quantum physics) the conditions there are suggestive of all kinds of alterations of the rules observed at a more (relatively) macro scale of matter. At very small dimensions, the rules of physics change, so why would we be surprised that at very large dimensions, the rules of physics will also change.

In fact, in the wonderful movie **Mindwalk**, the character of the physicist describes matter as a huge emptiness, punctuated with geometric points, where fields of force intersect. In effect, there is nothing there at all in terms of substance (or what we call matter) but this organism of intersections of fields of force in various kinds of pure geometric points (no space). No space at the infinite periphery, and no space in the infinitesimal point. In between, the perfect geometric sphere mediates between the greatest and the smallest. "*Think on it: how the point becomes a sphere and yet remains itself. Hast thou understood how the infinite sphere may be only a point, and then come again, for then the Infinite will shine forth for thee in the finite.*" Rudolf Steiner.

Now if this is true, then as macro cosmic space becomes more plane-like and less like the normal physical conditions of the Earth, we ought to be able to observe phenomena (just as we do in the very smallest dimensions revealed by quantum experiments) that reveal to us that this <u>condition of space</u> itself has altered. Space, being no longer three dimensional at the plane at infinity, must become something else.

Before we believe this is a poor idea, recall that already we have been taught about the so-called *gravity wells* (especially near such objects as our Sun). Many of us have seen images, either on TV or in a page in a magazine, which suggests that near a massive object, space itself is *distorted*. Light, we are told, traveling near this imagined state of a gravity well, can't travel in a straight line. This is thought to have been proved by Einstein's predictions regarding light from Mercury as it passes toward us from the other side of the sun (when Mercury's orbit causes it to hide (be occulted) behind the Sun. Using the Reinman geometry (a special case of projective geometry) Einstein was able to calculate exactly the amount of the bending of light by the gravity well our our Sun.

Since we already know how to imagine a *distorted* near space around a massive object like our Sun (recall that Bruno thought our Sun and stars were of a similar nature) it is not too great a leap to imagine a fully *transformed* space at the transition from the very large sphere to the Plane at Infinity. In a sense, the image of gravity wells is already a transformation of our ideas of space itself, although not going so far as to free itself fully of the need to measure. What I am suggesting is that we take our spacial imagination faculty all the way, and also bring projective geometry itself all the way into play as descriptive of the natural world.

Keep in mind that in current theoretical astronomy, scientists are unable to explain stellar motion without adding to their assumptions about the total visible mass of stellar objects, 9 times more mass in the form of the so-called Dark Matter. Estimates of the total mass of visible objects can't explain apparent stellar motion (using conventional ideas), so, in order to save the theory, _invisible_ mass - Dark Matter - has been invented.

But this invention is unnecessary if we use projective instead of Euclidean geometry. Which is of course exactly what our observations of light, and other phenomena of the stellar world, can tells us if we let them. Once we overcome the one-sided Euclidean geometry previously applied in parallax, and substitute Projective Geometry principles, then all the anomalous problems of redshift and other mass-centered problems are resolved.

The reason the hydrogen line of stellar objects is different is because it (the light) originates in a kind of _space_ which itself is different). A star isn't a sun (unless we change our ideas of our near sun-space - going back to Bruno, which is entirely justified but a whole other problem). Those stellar objects with large Redshift characteristics (such as Quasars) are deeper (a presently necessary poor choice of words, for it implies a continuation of three dimensions) within the transformed plane-like space. In fact, if we make a picture only of the Redshift (disregarding Euclidean parallax) phenomena by itself (and related other astronomical facts of stellar radiation and mass phenomena), a new kind of picture emerges.

Think for a moment on all the pictures we have been graced with of the starry world from the Hubble telescope. Everyone has seen these. Rich colors, but not empirical [See "How Do Space Pictures Get So Pretty - Photoshop of course"]. Marvelous shapes and forms. Just looking at the Redshift characteristics we can make a picture of an object that is remarkably active. It is not static or at rest in relationship to the Earth, but dynamic. Its relationship to other stellar objects is more fixed (perhaps musically harmonious, because there is a dance of such objects - including our solar system - all based on the projected geometric form of the vortex*), but the light phenomena, which our instruments observe, suggests (since we observe this variation of Redshifts, x-ray stars etc) that stellar objects have dynamic properties. The various kinds of radiation, pouring toward the earth from the cosmic periphery, are not constant, but rather always changing and dynamic.

*[A vortex is, in terms of projective geometry, a _dynamic_ form. That is, it is, in its actual nature, in movement. A tornado funnel cloud is a vortex, and we see a vortex every time we flush a toilet. A vortex is also a relative of the cone of light, which is how we think of what light does when it enters the eye through the lens. These cones of light are well described in all their geometric properties by the rules of projective geometry; and, a vortex is simply a dynamic (moving) cone-like form in nature. [See the amazing visual art of DjSadhu]

Many stellar objects are extremely dramatic (x-ray and neutron stars, for example). Keep in mind that these pictures are created by a thinking which has removed all *qualities*, remaining only in *quantities*. To better appreciate this lets make a little analogy.

Consider a flower garden in full late summer bloom. Vivid colors, lots of insect life and birds dancing and playing. For some almost violent growth (how fast does a sun flower grow, on its way to a height of 12 to 14 feet in three months time). Of course, to the gardener it makes no sense to disregard the way such a garden makes us feel (its qualities), but if astronomical thinking were applied to a flower garden, all that would disappear. We'd end up with a bunch of numbers (how many, of which kinds, what frequency of light were the colors, what was the speed of growth etc. etc. etc.). Our actual *experience* of the garden is washed away by the process of limiting our thinking only to the quantitative.

Now think (if you can remember) of a time when you were deep in Nature, away from city lights, and lay on your back in a meadow looking up at midnight at the night sky. Thousands upon thousands of stars, and your mind naturally saw everywhere patterns. Moreover, we feel awe. The starry night touches something deep inside us, that can only respond with marvel and wonder. We forget this living in our cities, and we have also forgotten (and losing) even the ability to have such a view because the atmosphere itself is becoming so polluted that less and less of the stellar light passes through it to our eye. [For a more careful discussion of the nature of consciousness as regards qualities and quantities, go here: "I am not my brain; the map is not the territory" .]

This is what we observe - what we experience. What we think - what is our mental image or picture - having been formed by modern astronomical ideas, is that this endless emptiness is filled with objects like our own planet and solar system. But now we are discovering in this essay the possibility that deep space is not three dimensional at all. Cosmic space is a peripheral plane of light, alive with dynamic processes creating what? What is this new kind of space - the plane at infinity - from which stellar light pours down upon the Earth, and then becomes captured by our photographic processes? The light from the stellar world is dynamic, and when we make an image (Hubble stares at certain regions of space for 10 or 11 days at a time), we have eliminated that dynamism, and made the picture static or fixed.

Lets take a small side trip here, to consider light itself. The book mentioned above, **Catching the Light**: *the entwined history of light and mind*, goes into remarkable detail and history. Keeping our projective geometry idea in mind, we might then make a relationship between the sphere that has collapsed into a point, and what is now called light quanta or photons. As mentioned above, these quanta exhibit all kinds of properties that normally spacial (in a three dimensional sense) objects do not.

For example, the world we see of trees and clouds does not reveal the micro world of light quanta and the other many strange particles known to modern high energy physics. The scientist doesn't see much of this either, except with his instruments and the image making powers of his mind.

We could say (from our more naive point of view - which has a special validity) that it is as if light quanta have stepped outside of time and space (this is one way of viewing what the experiments with light show to us today through quantum physics). To help here, let me add another idea from projective geometry.

We know in Euclidean geometry this general rule: parallel lines never meet. In projective geometry (of which, remember, Euclidean geometry is a special case) parallel lines meet at infinity. To appreciate this better we need to practice another imagination, for we can with our picture thinking follow quite easily in thought the wonderful paradox expressed here.

Picture two parallel lines (I can do this here):

$$\underline{\hspace{2in}}\cdot\underline{\hspace{2in}}$$
$$\underline{\hspace{4in}}$$

Now imagine the top line, in the center of which is a point, rotating around that point. Picture, for example, the top line crossing the bottom line at about a 45 degree angle toward the left side of the page. As we rotate this line further to the left, the angle of crossing gets smaller and smaller, until at infinity it no longer crosses the line. Yet, if we keep rotating the line in the same direction of rotation, as soon as it goes the smallest possible distance further, the top line starts to cross the bottom line at the farthest distance to the right.

When we couple this idea with our appreciation of the plane at infinity, we can with our geometric imagination feel (picturing it is hard, but logically we can feel this is right - and all these ideas have been proved by those working with the rules of projective geometry using algebraic-like formulas and calculations) that these two lines, which could be seen as parallel lines contained in a sphere, will at infinity arrive at the same point on the plane at infinity, because as we saw before, when the radius line of the sphere is infinite it is no longer a three-dimensional space. The rounded sphere has become a plane, an all encompassing plane to be sure, surrounding from the infinite periphery (the unseen universe imagined by cosmologists) all that was at one time interior. The surrounding geometric *quality* remains, but since space itself is transformed, it accomplishes a kind of paradoxical miracle.

To travel to infinity in one direction (in terms of the spherical three-dimensional nature of ordinary space) means to return from the opposite direction, for once *within* the plane at infinity, the line that intersected the ever flattening arc of the sphere is now simultaneously a point that is everywhere. The point, in the center dimensionless, expands, first becoming a growing measureless sphere until it ultimately becomes a plane. Our geometric imagination never has to leave the proper and logical train of geometrical thought. Once more: "*Think on it: how the point becomes a sphere and yet remains itself. Hast thou understood how the infinite sphere may be only a point, and then come again, for then the Infinite will shine forth for thee in the finite.*" Rudolf Steiner.

If we then appreciate that the night sky is the plane at infinity, and that the measure we exported from our earthly perspective is not valid out there in cosmic space, then the light quanta, existing there outside of time and space, radiates toward us from this cosmic periphery, only becoming *space-bound* when within three-dimensional space. At the periphery, light quanta are not limited by the so-called speed of light, but are everywhere at the same time, yet somehow differentiated, for that is what we see, not just with the eye but with all our instruments as well. This violation of the previous limiting idea of the speed of light has now been disproved in certain quantum physics experiments (Google: Alain Aspect 1982).

Light comes towards us from the stellar reality. If that reality is not spacial in the sense that we previously assumed (rooted in three-dimensionally matter based bodies like suns and planets), then what is it? What can exist in the transitional space in between a true three-dimensional sphere, and the pure plane at infinity? If *out there* is not an empty space in which three dimensional matter arises, what does arise there in that space that, like the infinitesimally small, will not allow itself to conform to Earth-like physical laws?

These are the questions that have to be faced if we apply projective geometry to the relationship between our Earth center, and the peripheral plane at infinity. If we look at the stellar phenomena, such as Redshift, then what meaning can be attributed to that kind of existence which creates light that violates the rules we know at the Earth center?

Perhaps it would be better (disregarding the word "deeper" above) to think of these objects as more filled with Life. The plane at infinity, as *transformed space,* reveals a high level of dynamic properties in all its light radiations. Could that dynamism be Life? Why could we think that and remain within reason?
Something is happening out there that comes here. Light is created out there and comes here. Our science has made all kinds of pictures for us of what is happening out there, yet these pictures are not empirical, but entirely theoretical. Moreover, they are entirely material and assume that the laws of physics at cosmic distances will be the same as they are on the Earth, which already we have noticed is not justified for the very very small.

If we work from the idea of the plane at infinity first (for which projective geometry grants us every right), then we might ask whether or not *space itself* is created out there. We see the light coming toward us from the cosmos, and we notice its dynamic properties (all the various intensities of redshift, among others - Quasars, neutron stars etc). If we discard measure (which projective geometry doesn't need), then the plane at infinity, with its inward radiating light is perhaps creating space itself, not from a point center (such as the Big Bang), but from the cosmic periphery.

The plane at infinity (transcendent of matter oriented three dimensionality) *creates* three dimensional space and time, by radiating light inwardly from the cosmic periphery. Redshift is not old light receding, but its opposite - new light becoming space and time. This is exactly the idea of a student of Rudolf Steiner's, George Adams Kaufmann, in his 1933 essay on cosmic theory (rooted in projective geometry): ***Space and the Light of Creation***, which essay's first chapter is *Radiation of Space* (the second chapter is *Music of Number,* and the third and last chapter is *Burden of Earth and the Sacrifice of Warmth*). [This book small book on cosmic theory is quite difficult to find, although connecting to a Rudolf Steiner library may help.]

What kind of power could create Space itself? Our point centered assumptions, working from only quantities, have only been able to think of a spiritless matter filled Universe, born in a Big Bang. Certainly, working inwardly from the cosmic periphery (the plane at infinity) which the new geometry gives us every right to do, what is that which can be *out there* that rays inwardly the creation of Space itself?

"*...and in it was life and the life was the light of the world...*" The *power* (fiat lux - let there be light) surrounding the Universe, is Life, and the Life creates the Light, and the Light rays inwardly creating Space and Time, in the center of which the Earth of living matter and substance arises, itself a narrow spherical band, for Earth life is only on the surface - go too deep and it is fire and there is no life, go too high and it is airless and again no life.
From the plane at infinity, through the inward plane-ward sculpted spheres of light, resting for a moment at the Earth periphery, where humanity unfolds its evolution, then eventually still collapsing to smaller and smaller spheres, ultimately disappearing into pure point centered geometric intersections of fields of force and the mysterious light quanta we discover in our laboratory experiments in quantum physics. But is it light quanta that is born first in the cosmic periphery, and then flies inward ultimately dying into very very tiny points from out which are built living matter and substance?

Should not, according to the laws of symmetry so essential to projective geometry, there be both a similarity and a difference between the infinitely large and the infinitesimally small? If life is created at the cosmic periphery, does it die into the very very small, only to be reborn instantaneously once more in the cosmic periphery? Recall our imaginative experiment with the parallel lines. If time and space rules don't apply to light quanta (photons), this will be true both at their point of first appearance and then again at their point of disappearance.

Yet, something not quite right here. The measureless sphere exists in between the infinitely large and the infinitesimally small. Appearance and disappearance are the same process in a way. Here again is Rudolf Steiner: "*Think on it: how the point becomes a sphere and yet remains itself. Hast thou understood how the infinite sphere may be only a point, and then come again, for then the Infinite will shine forth for thee in the finite.*"

Created out of the uncreated and formless, generating space and time, falling then inward toward the center from the periphery until collapsing into the nothingness once more of timeless and space-less point centers, before returning instantaneously again to the cosmic infinite plane of life.

And, the simultaneously opposite: Arising out of the uncreated and formless nature of the mysterious light quanta, radiating outward from an infinite number of point centers, spreading out toward the cosmic periphery, there to disappear into the remarkable spaceless and timeless plane at infinity. A mystery aptly caught in the image of a mobile imagination of the gesture in space that creates the form we know as the lemniscate - the symbol for infinity.

Moreover, of all the mysterious facts quantum mechanics has discovered, it seems that it is the mind itself that determines the nature of the collapse from potential becoming (probability) into manifestation. Consciousness is crucial. Without consciousness there is no manifestation, only probability. Could not a Larger more Infinite Consciousness exist at the Periphery, where time and space themselves are first manifested? Then too, if the Great Mind can do that, what then is involved in the small mind, when it thinks and acts so as to unfold its own creative imagination and exact picture formation in learning of and practicing the measureless beauty of projective geometry?

In the Beginning was the Word, and the Word was toward God, and God was what the Word was. It was with God in the Beginning. All things happened through it, and not one thing that happened happened without out it. In it was life, and the life was the light of the world....*

So Christ advises us to pray: "*Our Father in the skies...*"
*translation from the Greek of a part of the prologue to the John Gospel, from the book, **The Unvarnished Gospels** by Andy Gaus.

Of course, currently Natural Science hasn't the capacity to appreciate such a change in their understanding of the Cosmos. But this book isn't written for scientists, its written for those Christians, who might like to have a sense that one can still be deeply religious and not abandon the rational.

What we have done, by the way, is look at the image building processes of the fine minds at work in natural science, which have created a kind of myth regarding the stellar world - a myth quite different from that held by more ancient minds in ages long ago. We have not returned to those ancient myths so much, as taken up, out of the advancing progress of natural science itself, a particular discipline (projective or synthetic geometry - all geometry), and applied it to move past the current astronomical myth to what perhaps might well be the kind of truth the physicist pursues when he chases his holy grail of the so-called: Theory of Everything. (See my latest book: **_The Art of God: an actual theory of Everything_**)

Most versions of the Theory of Everything rely on highly abstract mathematical complexities - a kind of near-secret symbolic language only useful to the priests of Natural Science. Would it be possible to construct a Theory of Everything using ordinary language? Can the symbols of words on a page and simple concepts, understandable by ordinary consciousness, produce a better Theory of Everything? May it not be necessary in fact to reintroduce qualities and mix those with quantities, if we are actually going to have a true Theory of Everything? Doesn't such a Theory not only have to explain consciousness, but our form of consciousness - why we live in the world in between the very very large and the very very small?

We have constructed this essay in a way that makes it possible for the naive consciousness to behold in their own minds something that so far has been presented to the world as a secret mystery only knowable to the mathematical adepts of the religion of natural science.

We live in a time when there are to be no more priests, of the religious or the scientific kind. No more claims that the ordinary and naive mind has to be dependent on another for their understanding of the world and of the universe.
The Universe wants to be known, just as we want to be known. *"You see, for now we look as if in a mirror, shrouded in mystery; but then we will see face to face. Now I partly discern; but then I will perceive the same way that I was perceived all along. And so we will have faith, hope and love, these three: but the greatest of these is love."**
*[Andy Gaus, **Unvarnished New Testament** - end of chapter 13, of St. Paul's First Letter to the Corinthians.]

addendum
- many questions remain -

No reader should consider that the above has exhausted all the remarkable possibilities of projective geometry in advancing our understanding of the Nature World as it appears to both our senses and our scientific instruments. All I have really done is try bring to *light* aspects of thinking and the imagination that many don't yet appreciate.

Nor is the above perfect by any means, for it is clearly the work of an amateur. That fact, however, should not stop us from going onward and asking all the many questions that still need to be asked. [As an aside: in my considerations of the nature of electricity and its relationship to Nature, I discuss how space itself needs to be carefully rethought in order to appreciate that "space" itself needs to be re-conceived even as regards electrical and magnetic phenomena: "Electricity and the Spirit in Nature - a tale of certain considerations of the present state of science, in the light of a modern practical understanding of the nature of mind".]

For example, does the plane at infinity collapse into one point, or into all points? We can think of the very smallest, as we observe them in the local conditions of the earth in our laboratory experiments, as a very huge number of such point centers. All matter and substance seems to be built up out of light quanta, and other oddly named particles.

Now a plane, which has no measure, is infinite in all directions. It can also be constructed, under the well known rules of projective geometry, of points. There is, in this geometry, a plane of points, a plane of lines, a point of lines, a point of planes, and a line of points and a line of planes. If we recognize that the Plane at Infinity is made up of all possible points, then what keeps it from radiating toward our Earth-Center that which becomes all the many point centers from which matter and substance arise. Once there, in this infinite number of point centers, that which has first radiated inward, returns once more to the periphery. This our geometric imagination can experience.

A deep study of projective geometry reveals several kinds of processes which arise according to the basic relationships of plane, line and point; or, the source or origin of light (the plane at infinity), light becoming space and time (radiation of space) and light dying into the source once more through its collapse into the infinite number of point centers quantum physics discovers. To this we add the process of that which radiates out from point centers towards the periphery. In the *light of understanding* this, we can come to quite new conceptions of how crystals grow, and what is happening at the growing point of a plant. Such work has been done, in fact, by the Goethean Scientists pointed out in the above essays.

In addition to these questions then we are right to ask another: what is the nature of the *space* occupied by the *imagination* itself? We know this exists, and not only that it exists, but that we *create* it. We consciously create imaginative space ourselves. What are we that we can do something that has such kinship with the space and time creating activity of the Mystery at the Plane at Infinity? "*Imagination is more important than knowledge. For knowledge is limited to all we now know and understand, while imagination embraces the entire world, and all there ever will be to know and understand.*" Albert Einstein [emphasis added, ed.]

- healing materialism -

The human being possesses a remarkable power in that he (or she) is able to make images and share them with others. *Meaning* streams from one to another upon this product of the picture-thinking imagination. We are taught science out of this image creation capacity. We tell the wonderful stories of our ancestors out of this same image creation capacity. What we frequently don't do well, is find a way to be scientific about this image creating capacity itself.

Of all the scientific disciplines that will enhance this image building capacity, in a logically rigorous fashion, it is the discipline of projective geometry (as taught by such as Whicher above) that will be the most fruitful. At the same time, the human being is more than rationality - much more.

That human culture produces art and religion, as well as science, ought to give us a significant clue. Whicher's book takes account of this, to a degree, by including a number of pictures of art, including religious art. What is less appreciated is the role of human intention, of human will, in all this (the *will* is the point-of-meaning center of the same consciousness which the quantum physicist recognizes is needed for the potential to collapse into the real).

At the end of the main body of the essay above, I tried to remind the reader that we are part of reality. Quantum mechanics has seen this, for the potential of quantum events only collapses into actual space and time when our consciousness participates. The genius of Owen Barfield discusses *participation* in detail, in his book **Saving the Appearances: a study in idolatry**.

In this book, through a wonderful examination of what the deeper study of human languages can reveal, Barfield shows us how there is an evolution of *consciousness*, to go along side the physical evolution so far discovered. For Barfield, the quite ancient times could be called: *original participation*. This was a time when the human consciousness was instinctively one with reality, thus giving birth to all the ancient myths.

This original participation eventually faded away, giving us an intermediate state, called by Barfield (and others): the *on-looker separation*. Humanity is pushed out of the condition of original participation by the Gods themselves, so that we can by this independence learn to experience our freedom and our ego (self) consciousness. The on-looker separation is itself marked by special changes in language, in art and also gives rise to natural science. It is as on-lookers (forgetting our role as thinking observers) that we build the images of the natural world, both earthly and cosmic, as only matter and never spirit.

But the natural world will not submit for long to that false view, and so quantum mechanics finds that it must reinsert human consciousness into its concepts of the basic physics of the world. With this now well established basic scientific knowledge, to which we can add the discipline of projective geometry (especially with its understanding of visual cones of light), the path is laid out of science itself toward what Barfield called then: *final participation*.

Quantum mechanics tells us that our consciousness is needed for the *potential* to be able to collapse into the *real*. Projective Geometry tells us not just rules about the light cone of physical space, but as well the light cone of internal imaginative space. Rudolf Steiner's introspective science (outlined in **A Theory of Knowledge Implicit in Goethe's World Conception** and **The Philosophy of Freedom**) shows us how to experience the world of image building (organic form) and concept creation (pure thinking) in a fully mature *participatory* way.

At the same time, I don't participate solely as a rational being, but as a being to whom art and the sacred have meaning. In a certain sense, given the often raw nature of emotions, the human being is often simultaneously: irrational (overly emotional), rational (mentally disciplined) and Transrational (capable of huge leaps of non-logical intuitional insight). If I add these dimensions of my being to my imaging building and conceptual formulations, what kind of picture of the world will I paint? Given this question, I will end with a couple of stories as a kind of demonstration.

In the mid-seventies I was traveling with some friends in Northern California. We were a group of adults and children, and during the day a few of the adults were designated camp-parents, while the others were free to wander farther. Thus I found myself, on the evening of the Summer Solstice, sitting on a beach in Northern California watching the Sun set over the Pacific Ocean.

As the Sun set, the sky slowly grew darker and stars slowly appeared. This is what I observed as I continued to watch the point on the horizon where the Sun had set. Together, as a group, at the precisely same degree of arc of the edge of the ocean, there appeared three stars in a somewhat vertical line. The Sun goes down, and soon thereafter where it went down a vertical line of three stars appears. Now the reader should realize that I was at that time quite convinced of the spiritual reality of things, out of my own direct experience. As a consequence, when I observed our natural world I perceived it as a *teaching*. For example, we can observe that of all the many inorganic and organic beings that appear in visual space, there are a variety of forms. Of this variety of forms, only one form, one shape, has hands that have been so creatively freed by our ability to be able to stand upright.

Moreover, this *human* being changes his living environment in profound ways. We act upon the creation, as if it was within us that the creative power itself was slowly incarnating. To my thinking then, there existed a kind of dialog between the world of the senses and my own inner being (the *teaching*). Here I was on a beach watching the Sun, itself a very special form (we receive light and heat from it that are necessary for life - without the Sun we do not live). As this form set on the Summer Solstice, the first stars to appear (the *night teachers*), were three.
This then is what the teaching sang to me on that beach: one becomes three. So the Mystery of the Trinity was written right there in the most simple events of the world of the senses. One becomes Three.

The ambient light became slightly dimmer, and not too soon thereafter, above the three was four, in the shape of a kind of box, standing on one of its corners above the last star of the three. The One becomes Three and then Four is added to become Seven. Those who know what is sometimes called the occult significance of Numbers will recognize here all manner of analogies, about which nothing more need be said. (for the more traditionally fixed of mind, the Sun set and in the order described, the constellation of the Great Bear emerged, standing on its tail above the same place on the horizon the Sun had set on the night of that particular Summer Solstice - yet this constellation did not appear all at once, but in a very definite sequence as the day light faded and the night lights manifested themselves).

In this way I was initiated more deeply into the Mystery of the Night Teachers, and while I wished my life would have allowed me to study over many decades this teaching by which we noted not just the starry sky, but when and <u>in what order</u> the stars emerged, I did then realize that those who observed from such as Stonehenge saw a world of wonder we have still yet to fully appreciate.

One more similar picture. If the shape of the sense world is from a Creator, and this Creator is such profound Mystery that we have hardly yet begun to appreciate all the He has done and is doing, should we be surprised by the manner and depth of the teaching that awaits us both within and without? Consider, sunrise and sunset. Something that happens all over the world everyday, and has done so for eons.

If we, as an aspect of *final participation*, re-ensoul the world of the senses with *being* and *consciousness*, might we not then begin to see that when the Sun sets, when the *shape <u>representing</u>* (in its speaking-teaching) the Highest of the Mystery, recedes from our sight, at that moment the stars, one by one and then in groups, slowly emerge, slowly appear in the dark and by their order of appearing and by the shapes and forms they thereby render, they can be seen as singing praises to this Highest. He sets, and they rise and sing.

Then the night ends, the regular night-singing has passed, and as the Sun begins to once more return to shed Its light and warmth and life on humankind, the stars recede, and kneeling down, in groups and then one by one, they give way to that which they honor above all else. Yet, this is not all.

For the shape of time and space, of stars and suns and the world of humankind, is also *teaching*. We are there too, and what are we, we human beings, that the Highest and all the Angels look down upon us - surround us and gift us with such Love we hardly appreciate it. Not just that but more, for we are not only looked down upon from Above, but we are also carried through cosmic space by the Earth - Father Sky and Mother Earth - as the world's oldest peoples and cultures well know.

The dark moist earth is the Mother, from which all that grows and nourishes flows. The waters that give life, the very air we need to breath. There in the center of all, looked down upon by Father Sky, upheld and nourished in the Womb of Mother Earth, sits the human being, the upright shape with the hands and the creative and curious mind. That is the real question of final participation: *Who are we?*

****

recent news concerning Redshift
Sept. 12, 2008

Port Angeles, Wa. This week, dozens of leading astronomers, researchers and other scientists from around the globe met for a Cosmology conference.[1] The conference provided eight panels composed of experts in every facet of cosmology including the reality of expansion, quasars, dark matter, dark energy, black holes, and the true nature of the microwave radiation from space. One astronomer made his presentation live from Germany using video-link technology.

Organizer Tom Van Flandern said: This was a thrilling success. We heard and discussed three new mechanisms explaining redshift and a new equation modifying our understanding of gravity. If any of the Redshift proposals passes experimental tests that would mean we do not have an expanding Universe; that the Big Bang theory would be without its strongest foundation.

Physicist John Hartnett from the University of Western Australia said it is amusing that our conference occurred just as they fire up the Hadron Collider in Europe. Most of our presenters showed the deep problems with the Big Bang while a 40 billion dollar project starts up to trying to find an elusive particle to keep the Big Bang story from collapsing.

> *Redshift in the light from galaxies led to the belief that the universe is expanding, and this belief has persisted for 80 years. But modern observational evidence, especially from NASA European Space Agency space telescopes and satellites, has clouded the picture and raised many doubts.*

In 2004, an open letter was published in New Scientist magazine, and has since been signed by over 500 endorsers. It begins: The big bang today relies on a growing number of hypothetical entities, things that we have never observed-- inflation, dark matter and dark energy are the most prominent examples. Without them, there would be a fatal contradiction between the observations made by astronomers and the predictions of the big bang theory. In no other field of physics would this continual recourse to new hypothetical objects be accepted as a way of bridging the gap between theory and observation. It would, at the least, raise serious questions about the validity of the underlying theory. (<http://cosmologystatement.org>*)*

<u>*From the many lines of evidence presented at the conference, It now appears that those concerns were justified. Presenters also outlined the principles that a good cosmology should be based on. Chief among them is that it should not require a series of miracles to remain viable.*</u>
[emphasis added, ed.]

Letters on Magic (I. Through XII.)

S

A cogent article in the New York Times – SUNDAY REVIEW
Even Physicists Don't Understand Quantum Mechanics
Worse, they don't seem to want to understand it. BySean Carroll. Dr. Carroll is a physicist. The link is repeated at the end of these Letters.

t

<http://ipwebdev.com/hermit/lawspiritanarchy.html>
Something profound is happening in the World, yet remains unremarked in the common narrative of modern media institutions. To see this we need to remember how magical the world is, as we saw it once upon a time, when we were children.

n

Let us be children again, and remember … together.

e

Yesterday was Easter Sunday, and twice during the day I saw a fat rabbit, dining in the yard's fresh April rain's grass. She seemed pregnant, or perhaps recently so. She was not a baby rabbit by any measure. Like the daily wonder of sunrise and sunset, a wild animal gracing the yard is magical, … always magical.

In the 1960's the world was hit broadside with a cultural revolution that was itself magical, from the LSD, to the remarkable world-wide explosion of rock 'n roll, to the New Age of yoga masters, wizards, Tibetan and Zen Masters, Sufi dancers, and not the least strange, such as Osho (aka Bhagwan Shree Rajneesh), Rev. Moon, and, L. Ron Hubbard.

Christ – as Lord of the Dance – was everywhere, although few Christian religions recognized Him. Hermetic Science (the magic of the ancient Egyptians) is unfolding odd gifts, and making shamans and seers, all manner of psychic talent – within the individual biography. It is that – the individual biography – which is the core locus of Love, … what we call history, news, current events, wars, and all other kinds of folly is secondary, and merely context for the needs of the individual biography … a great and magical aspect of human existence on a personal level.

The Mother is back as well, for a time having been eclipsed in the public consciousness by the three male-dominated monotheisms, that participated in the birth of Western Civilization. As that Civilization dies into a new becoming, the previously unimaginable magical nature of reality will appear … everywhere. The trans-rational, i.e. the bridge between the rational and irrational, will appear inside human beings as a natural gift. People instinctively know that the ancients were far wiser than are we. We still only guess at how the Age of Megaliths, from Easter Island, to Central America, to Egypt, and to Stonehenge, happened: yes, via the oldest science: Magic.

That coming bak rides in on the Return of the Moon wisdoms, more commonly known as actual Magic. What is happening is nothing less than the very change in consciousness the New Age anticipated, albeit more dramatic, the Mother not afraid to make us face Justice, as well as the Love from Her Son.

All weather is delivered by Her, and Her adoring minions, the elemental kingdoms of Nature, the fire-folk, the water-folk, the air-folk, and, the earth-folk.

Knowledge of magic varies according to geographical and cultural eras. In the true West, the Americans, it is more apt to use the term "shaman" to denote a devotee of magic-knowing. Yogis and masters in the East, and magicians and initiates in the cultural Center work as well. Each place has a reality in which all their greatest Myths turn out to be true. Follow your local oldest earth religions, and that will renew the Way for the modern era.

Magic is the science of learning to find the right relationship to the Elemental Kingdoms, which ultimately needs to be a love affair. From a certain point of view, every individual biography is its own shamanistic path. If we are surviving life, we are surviving because of something in us that will not give up or give in. Survivors master their world, even in the darkest times.

In Her Scheme of Life, we are all shamans in training, for our essential personal intelligence is also Our Way. That individual Way is personal, and each day is a labyrinth of choices, not always navigated satisfactorily.

Each is to have their own talents. This person hears ghosts. That person makes sense doing astrology. Another brings herbal wisdom alive in their kitchen. A fourth studies the arcane, and finds wonder in the hermetic ideas of the electrical (fire/will) and magnetic (water/feeling) fluids.

Consider the storms, floods, earthquakes, wars, famine, … the Four Horseman work for Her, and Death includes that which we must see as Her Arts, as She has the whole world in His Hands.

Essentially cataclysmic events happen, some die, and She catches them as in the Pieta. The survivors, the shamans in training, have choices. Do I help just myself, or do I join with and help others? These storms are part of the divine world order, and we need to connect with that.

http://www.thecollectiveimagination.com/the-great-unsettling-the-3rd-millennium/ "the Great Unsettling & the 3rd Millennium"

http://ipwebdev.com/hermit/moon~%21~earth.html "Medicine Woman is Here"

_"Americans among the Lost: notes from inner space, the true Final Frontier"
http://ipwebdev.com/hermit/finalfrontier.html

If the most ancient magical science, Hermetics, uses the words electrical and magnetic "fluids", what is it about that aspect of physical reality that makes such a "metaphor" work? Perhaps modern science is clueless about just what lives in the so-called four fundamental forces of nature:

"In physics , the **fundamental interactions**, also known as **fundamental forces**, are the interactions that do not appear to be reducible to more basic interactions. There are four fundamental interactions known to exist: the gravitational and electromagnetic interactions, which produce significant long-range forces whose effects can be seen directly in everyday life, and the strong and weak interactions , which produce forces at minuscule, subatomic distances and govern nuclear interactions. Some scientists[1][2][3] hypothesize that a fifth force might exist, but the hypotheses remain speculative."

https://en.wikipedia.org/wiki/Fundamental_interaction
As these Letters about Magic continue, the mysterious/magical relationship between these "four" interactions, and the four classical elements: fire, air, water, earth, will be investigated, as well as the "fifth", known in certain circles as the "akasha" or the Source of Manifestation.

I will also reference works from my personal library. The main mistakes of classical physics, and even quantum mechanics, will be covered, although a cursory preview looks like this:

There is nothing existing that is not rooted in the wills of invisible to the senses Beings.

Letters About Magic
II.

where we left the work, in Letter #1 …

"If the most ancient magical science, Hermetics, uses the words electrical and magnetic "fluids", what is it about that aspect of physical reality that makes such a "metaphor" work? Perhaps modern science is clueless about just what lives in the so-called four fundamental forces of nature:

"In physics , the **fundamental interactions**, also known as **fundamental forces**, are the interactions that do not appear to be reducible to more basic interactions. There are four fundamental interactions known to exist: the gravitational and electromagnetic interactions, which produce significant long-range forces whose effects can be seen directly in everyday life, and the strong and weak interactions , which produce forces at minuscule, subatomic distances and govern nuclear interactions. Some scientists[1][2][3] hypothesize that a fifth force might exist, but the hypotheses remain speculative."

https://en.wikipedia.org/wiki/Fundamental_interaction

"As these Letters about Magic continue, the mysterious/magical relationship between these "four" interactions, and the four classical elements: fire, air, water, earth, will be investigated, as well as the "fifth", known in certain circles as the "akasha" or the Source of Manifestation.

"I will also reference works from my personal library. The main mistakes of classical physics, and even quantum mechanics, will be covered, although a cursory preview looks like this:

"There is nothing existing that is not rooted in the wills of invisible to the senses Beings."

Which leads us where?
"*the traditional kabbalistic worlds of Emanation, Creation, Formation & Existence*", or as Rudolf Steiner has it: "*Saturn, Sun, Moon, and, finally, the surface world of Nature, all inhabited at their core and in every particle by divinity in its immanent maternal aspect. Thus the Father God is One, the Mother God is Many.*" For essential details:
http://ipwebdev.com/hermit/Clarke5.html

Notice the Four aspect. repeated even in religious teachings. In the deeps of ancient religious ideas, there are four, and in the deeps of physics there are four as well.

The physicist imagines a big-bang, while Genesis says: Let there be Light. Emanation. The biologist imagines life emerging from the lifeless, which they call Evolution, and the ancients: Creation, Formation, and Existence.

One imagination leaves no room for invisible to the senses Beings, the other Imagination knows and meets these Folk directly. No theory necessary. To get to know the Beings behind/within Nature, involves a love affair, for the fundamental relationship is I&Thou.

Consider that for the last 500 years the Copernican Revolution took a path (for most) of taking Nature apart, and from the parts imagining the whole is made. The problem is that we experience the whole directly. Along side that historical Fall into Matter, no reality which is not us – not a human being – is, by modern scientific theory, allowed to have an interior life. A rather arrogant presumption, rooted in the arrogant fancy that modern materialistic science comes even close to "explaining" the human reality – the experiences through which we suffer.

If we look at Nature as having the same interior existence as do we, then everything changes.

Can this be proved? Sure. Here, we come at such proof via the Hermetic Sciences, aka Magic. Existence is. How does Existence work?

Consider getting up in the morning. We all have some aspect of the Labyrinth of the (Groundhog) Day to bear. Alarm clocks, coffee and carbs, routine, or not. We are not – in our essence – the same ~!~spirit/style~!~ … we are individuals having our own biography.

Where comes the power to start the Day? The ancient Egyptians had ideas like "primal fire", to describe the Will through which we move through time, seeing the element of fire/will inside everything, not just in us. These – the classical Elements – have meanings buried and lost, for those, who are critical of these ideas, have never actually understood that they refer to aspects of existence we directly experience.

Fire/Will; Water/Feeling; Air/Intellect; and Earth/Consciousness. Nor do we know these as "pieces". We and our experience are an indivisible whole. Not parts. Whole.

Part of the Fall into Matter ended in an Era of Existence in which our human consciousness more and more experienced itself as separate. I am over here, behind the typing of these words, and you are over there, reading with care or not. This "evolution" of consciousness is the real (non-material) evolution. "I am not my brain – the map is not the territory."
http://ipwebdev.com/hermit/brain.html

At the center of the confusion, is a long term habit of unnatural materialistic-only science, which took apart "things" (easier to do if you don't consider the "feelings" of the objects of experimentation and dissection). The quest was for the smallest entities, thus the four "interactions": gravitation; electromagnetic; strong; and, weak.

The virtue of those studies is that mathematics was necessary to find an exact and precise way to describe what is observed. The folly/danger is to imagine that these are separate from each other. They are always together, until we break them into pieces (Cern), by applying forces not observable in Nature. We imagine such forces forging what happens in the Sun, but that is theory and speculation.

Put down what you are reading this with, and get up and move around a bit. We know gravity in its wholeness state, as it grips us as a totality, and much of our behaviors are built around knowing the consequences of messing around with the gravity field authored by … What? Easily a whole that is greater than the sum of the parts.

At present, there is a kind of war going on between modern physics and certain aspects of philosophy. Physics wants to pretend "qualia" (qualities) don't have the same level of concrete existence as the quantitative … i.e. "things" we can count and measure. The taste of a ripe fruit, the thrill of a first kiss, and pain of birth – if it can't be measured, it doesn't exist – to physics.

To us? The qualitative is whole meaning of life. The ancient Egyptians knew that the qualitative was the essence of everything, and in the qualitative nature of the doctrine of the elements they hid their greatest secrets. Fire/Will; Water/Feelings; Air/Intellect; Earth/Consciousness.

Study those qualities in yourself, and miracles arise.

From my essay: "Medicine Woman is Here" which concerns the active presence of the Mother (Herself, also more than a part) http://ipwebdev.com/hermit/moon~%21~earth.html " … in the "light" of Rudolf Steiner's remarks regarding the future return of the Moon (Magic) back into the Earth, **and** in the light of the Emerald Tablet: *"The above from the below, and the below from the above – the work of the miracle of the One. And things have been from this primal substance through a single act. How wonderful is this work! It is the main (principle) of the world and is its maintainer. Its father is the sun and its mother the moon; …"*

Letters about Magic
III.

We are going to approach this relationship between the Four classical Elements, and the Four Interactions known to modern physics, from both directions. Here – in this Letter – we expand our qualitative ideas about the Elements. The main sources, besides our own observations, will be: Ernst Lehrs' book "Man or Matter – introduction to a spiritual understanding of Nature on the basis of Goethe's method of training observation and thought" https://www.amazon.com/Man-Matter-Ernst-Lehrs/dp/1482768364/ref=tmm_pap_swatch_0?_encoding=UTF8&qid=1556537143&sr=8-1 … and Franz Bardon's "Initiation into Hermetics – a course of instruction in magic theory and practice"https://www.amazon.com/Initiation-into-Hermetics-Franz-Bardon-dp-1885928122/dp/1885928122/ref=mt_paperback?_encoding=UTF8&me=&qid=1556537282

Lehrs, in the Chapter XI: "Matter as Part of Nature's Alphabet", points out that the elements involve eight qualitative ideas, for example: Water and Earth share the same quality: cold. Fire and Air share the same quality warm. Water and Air share the same quality moist, while Earth and Fire share the same quality: dry. Keep in mind that these are not separate aspects of Nature's Alphabet, but relationships making a single whole.

The physicist, for his imagination of the Four Interactions, has to smash stuff together in a Hadron super-collider, making the debris of these high energy collisions into his fantasy that first come the parts, then the whole. Matter is killed/broken leaving behind a corpse, and its pieces thought to be that out of which it was made.

Consider this, paraphrased from Rudolf Hauschka's "The Nature of Substance – spirit and matter" https://www.amazon.com/Nature-Substance-Spirit-Matter/dp/1855841223/ref=tmm_pap_swatch_0?_encoding=UTF8&qid=1556538254&sr=8-1 :

When we take apart water, through forceful physical interventions (electrical or chemical), we get hydrogen and oxygen. To Hauschka's way of seeing/thinking these two are the corpse of water, i.e. what is left after we kill the water. In addition, when we kill the water via these violent means, we also liberate heat and light.

Physics misreads the phenomena, not realizing that heat and light are additional corpse parts, but in their function/nature are aspects of spirit. In George Adams' "Universal Forces in Mechanics" https://www.amazon.com/gp/product/0854403256/ref=as_li_qf_sp_asin_il_tlie=UTF8&camp=1789&creative=9325&creativeASIN=0854403256&linkCode=as2&tag=bsra-roundrobin-20

(out of print, try the Steiner Library) Adams writes: "In all mechanical systems, be they at rest, be they in motion, elastic forces are involved … with every displacement of elastic balance, however small, shades of warmth arise …. [leading to] … revelation of the dynamic interplay of space and counter-space elastic resistant forces of matter have to do with something ethereal." (Adams, pp. 2, "Universal Forces In Mechanics").

We all have a direct experience of this when we take a wire hanger and bend it back and forth until it breaks. The broken ends will be warm, and there will be changes in the color of the metal as well. This color and this warmth are the arts of the materialization powers of Faeries. Beings. Rudolf Steiner called these Beings, collectively and abstractly, ethereal formative forces.

Bardon's work is very organized, and consists of instructive exercises. In the beginning section Theory, we are first introduced to a symbolic picture (not available in this venue). This is followed with explanatory materials, included remarkable discussions on The Principles of Fire (will); Water (feeling); Air (intellect); and, Earth (consciousness). All of which Principles we can self-observe in action in our own souls, in the course of the Practices. Keep in mind that these Practices and Principles are part of the fundamental organism of the Creation. There is, essentially, neither white or black magic. The deed belongs to the doer. The magical Laws (Steiner's Third Force?) exist because of the Divine.

For Steiner students, please keep in mind that from his knowledge we get this kind of statement (I paraphrase): The physical body is not the matter. The physical body is the Laws that govern the matter.

Emanation (Saturn-warmth will), Creation (Sun-light feeling), Formations (Moon-order intellect) & Existence (Earth-the What-Is consciousness). All that-is shares the same fundamental nature, where due to the Mother / Father Principle, everything is One. No parts.

These rules are universal. In the Indian doctrine (as explained by Bardon), there is the idea of the succession of the tattwas:
akasha – principle of the ether
tejas – principle of the fire
waju – principle of the air
apas – principle of the water
prithivi – principle of the earth

Bardon writes: "In accordance with the Indian doctrine, it has been said that the four somehow grosser tattwas have been descended from the fifth tattwa, the akasha-principle. Consequently akasha is the cause ultimate and to be regarded as the fifth power, the so called quintessence."

Missing Picture of the Magician: The First Tarot Card – Interpretation of the Symbolism:

Below you will find the mineral, vegetable and animal kingdoms expressed in a symbolic manner.

The female on the left side and the male on the right side are the plus (positive) and the minus (negative) in every human being.

In their middle is seen a hermaphrodite, a creature personifying the male and female combined in one as the sign of concinnity between the male and female principle.

The electrical and magnetical fluids are shown in red and blue colors, electrical fluid being red, magnetical fluid blue.

The head region of the female is electrical, therefore red, the region of the genitals is magnetical, consequently blue. As for the male, it happens to be in inverted order.

Above the hermaphrodite there is a globe as a sign of the earth sphere, above which the magician is illustrated with the four elements.

Above the male, there are the active elements, that of the fire in red and the air element in blue color. Above the female there are the passive elements, the water element in green and the element of the earth in yellow color. The middle along the magician up to the globe is dark purple, representing the sign of the akasha principle

Above the magician's head, with an invisible ribbon for a crown, there is a gold-edged silvery white lotus flower as a sign of the divinity. In the inside there is the ruby red philosophers' stone symbolizing the quintessence of the whole hermetic science. On the right side in the background there is the sun, yellow like gold and on the left side we see the moon, silvery-white, expressing plus and minus in the macro- and microcosm, the electrical and magnetical fluids.

Above the lotus flower, Creation has been symbolized by a ball, in the interior of which are represented the procreative positive and negative forces which stand for the creating act of the universe.

The eternal, the infinite, the boundless, and the uncreated have been expressed symbolically by the word AUM and the dark purple to black color.

Letters about Magic

IV

Books. If you don't have them, you won't learn their many secrets. Let us consider fairies.

https://www.amazon.com/Fairy-Worlds-Workers-Natural-Fairyland/dp/1621480259/ref=sr_1_fkmrnull_2?keywords=Marjorie+Spock+fairies&qid=1556719266&s=gateway&sr=8-2-fkmrnull

The world of occupied space, full of things to some, is actually the results of the work of elemental Beings. Above we have Marjorie Spock's Fairy Worlds and Workers: A Natural History of Fairyland. Helps to have good maps, given that part of the struggle, to learn to do&understand magic, runs against what has been instilled by us, from unnatural science: There is Only Matter. There is No Spirit.

It is within the hearts of human beings to re-ensoul the world of things, and start to treat all matter as involving real invisible beings, who will give us greater secrets than we can imagine, if we just … well that's the trick, isn't it. How do you treat the table at which you sit, and the machine on which you see these words, and perhaps type? Blessed are They who do not See, and Yet Believe.

Get this book: "the Slow Regard of Silent Things" https://www.amazon.com/Regard-Silent-Things-Kingkiller-Chronicle/dp/0756411327/ref=tmm_pap_swatch_0?_encoding=UTF8&qid=1556719988&sr=8-1

It is not possible to describe, although the link to Faerie goes like this: Auri lives beneath a great and ancient magic school … she seems lost, but her heart sees objects and places in all manner of imaginative and inventive Ways … and to point out that the character [Auri] in the above is a wonderful feature of two of the best/modern fantasy/magical journeys in recent years. "The Name of the Wind" and "The Wise Man Fears", by Patrick Rothfuss https://www.amazon.com/Patrick-Rothfuss/e/B001DAHXZQ/ref=pd_sim_14_bl_2/145-0041142-3236902?_encoding=UTF8&pd_rd_i=0756404746&pd_rd_r=4a4eb6eb-6c1b-11e9-8627-41445435c50e&pd_rd_w=j7jvL&pd_rd_wg=o62hj&pf_rd_p=90485860-83e9-4fd9-b838-b28a9b7fda30&pf_rd_r=YZX2KWFQ47C5A4TP1NQ0&refRID=YZX2KWFQ47C5A4TP1NQ0

About which, Ursula K. LeGuin, award-winning author of Earthsea remarked "It is a rare and great pleasure to find a fantasist writing…with true music in the words."

All magic libraries need to have LeGuin's "The Dispossessed – an ambiguous utopia". For Steiner fans she imagines into existence a world where the anarchy of personal liberty Steiner urged, has come to the ground of real human natures. At the same time, her discussions of whether or not a physics of sequential events needs to be joined by a physics of the simultaneous, are wonderfully inspiring for those understanding how we actually live in the prison/opportunity of the Now.
https://www.amazon.com/Dispossessed-Ursula-K-Guin/dp/B00HTJMH2E/ref=sr_1_5?crid=2OKIG8MKC4NTY&keywords=the+dispossessed+ursula+k+leguin&qid=1556721387&s=gateway&sprefix=the+disposs%2Caps%2C151&sr=8-5

In support of the questions of "physics", there is this journey into the nature of music and the physics of light: "The Memory of Whiteness – a scientific romance", by Kim Stanley Robinson

As all good things come in threes, there is this: "The Roads of Heaven", by Melissa Scott, where it is imagined that if a ship had a keel, made according to the rules of Alchemy, this tinctured keel could be made to vibrate (via a harmonium) in such a way that gravity wells repelled the ship. The stronger the "music" in the keel, the more de-materialized are both ship

and passengers. Once at the level – four/fifths of Heaven – the Roads are like complex images similar to Tarot symbols. A navigator of the ships has to see into the non-material in order to find roads leading to other worlds.
https://www.amazon.com/roads-heaven-Melissa-Scott/dp/B00005XTAM/ref=sr_1_fkmr0_1?keywords=The+Roads+of+Heaven%E2%80%9D%2C+by+Melissa+Scott.&qid=1556721938&s=gateway&sr=8-1-fkmr0

Speaking of Tarot, every magical library should have this book, attributed to Saint Germain: "Practical Astrology". A personal book-fairy – that sat on my shoulders whenever I wandered/wondered into serious used book stores, during my 14 years in the mystery school that was the San Francisco/Berkeley cultural landscape, – advised excitedly that I purchase this book. This is the only astrology book that combines into a single system: Tarot, Astrology, and, Numerology.
https://www.amazon.com/Practical-Astrology-Horoscopes-Language-Comprehended/dp/0265240409/ref=sr_1_fkmr1_1?keywords=Practical+Astrology+St.+Germain&qid=1556722894&s=gateway&sr=8-1-fkmr1

Keep in mind that we are studying the ancient Egyptian Hermetic Sciences, and this is their book about the starry heavens and the reading of their signs. The world is – at its fundamental nature – quite accurately described in terms of certain principles of order. Here is Saint Germain's book on Palmistry, another fun read, especially important for any magician who desires an easy way to learn about people. Who doesn't like their palm read?
https://www.amazon.com/Study-Palmistry-Professional-Purposes-Advanced/dp/1162563362/ref=tmm_pap_swatch_0?_encoding=UTF8&qid=1556723183&sr=8-1-fkmr0

And, certainly/finally last, but not least, Catherine MacCoun's remarkable book, which I sometimes call: "a Gospel of the Soul", wherein she combines Christian and Tibetan Alchemy into a single whole: "On Becoming an Alchemist – a guide for the modern magician"
https://www.amazon.com/Becoming-Alchemist-Guide-Modern-Magician/dp/1590306872/ref=sr_1_1?crid=3R6C2H9LSU7P3&keywords=on+becoming+an+alchemist&qid=1673814890&sprefix=On+becoming+an+%2Caps%2C107&sr=8-1

p.s.
Then, for the adventuresome, lengthy challenges, or books I have read many times: All the "Dune" books by Frank Herbert (there are six). Herbert was an instinctive Goethean scientist of social life. He saw the living in religions, societies, mystic practices, and more.
https://en.wikipedia.org/wiki/Dune_(novel)

The three volume, 2700 page, "Baroque Cycle", by Neal Stephenson. An adventure yarn, a history of modern money, a contemplation of the most important issues of science, the word

amazing does not begin to grasp the scope and the beauty.
https://en.wikipedia.org/wiki/The_Baroque_Cycle

Letters about Magic #5

Modern physics can be scary to a mind which believes there ought to be something "there", or at least – since I can't put my fist through a wall – the idea of there being no there there is a most curious mental affectation.

From Wikipedia:

"Each of the known fundamental interactions can be described mathematically as a *field* . The gravitational force is attributed to the curvature of spacetime , described by Einstein's general theory of relativity . The other three are discrete quantum fields , and their interactions are mediated by elementary particles described by the Standard Model[4] of particle physics ."

"In physics, a **field** is a physical quantity , represented by a number or tensor , that has a value for each point in space-time.

In order not to get too lost, lets weave a thread through this by attending to E. Lehrs distinction between matter which alert, and matter which is inert. Alert matter reacts to outside stimuli (the mosquito that won't let you sleep), while inert matter takes a good kick to get it to move (no, not the dog, or the cat, any stone will do, … for the moment. Please remember alert/inert are qualitative aspects of reality, not quantitative. No numbers need apply.

The picture below uses four colors: green, purple, orange, and, gold. The gold one is the famous "Higgs Boson" Google sez: "In 2012, scientists confirmed the detection of the long-sought **Higgs boson**, also known by its nickname the "**God particle**," at the Large Hadron Collider (LHC), the most powerful **particle** accelerator on the planet. This **particle** helps give mass to all elementary **particles** that have mass, such as electrons and protons."

A fun read to help the imagination not get too fixed in its habits. Has nothing to do with this essay, except to remind the read to take breaks on occasion.

https://www.amazon.com/Snow-Crash-Neal-Stephenson/dp/0553380958/ref=sr_1_1?crid=2UV8CROIQ06NC&keywords=snow+crash+by+neal+stephenson+paperback&qid=1673815710&sprefix=snow+crash+by+neal+stephensoni+paper+back%2Caps%2C77&sr=8-1
The names are so cool, … who knew physicists has such a neat sense of humor. The Purples (Quarks) are named: up, charm, top, down, strange, bottom. The Greens (Leptons) are more boring: electron, muon, tau, electron neutrino, muon neutrino, tau neutrino. The Oranges (Gauge or Vector Bosons) gluon, photon, z-boson. The one Gold (scalar bosons): Higgs boson.

We might just notice bits of symmetry as well: There are two sets of six each (Quarks and Leptons), and bosons divided into two kinds (Vector or Scalar), while the Higgs biggest claim to fame is that some still disagree that it was found, but perhaps all the more mysterious for being coy, and secret.

Keep in mind here, that if we do this carefully we can peel away the dramatic mathematical fuzz, and see that these physicists were trying to "describe" something. What they saw is real. Which is made all the more occult, when we realize the role that "consciousness" is said to play in quantum theory.

We are trying to get beyond the assumptions of what modern physics research means, and to take a look ourselves at the phenomena, without prejudice. For example particle detectors have evolved, becoming bubble detectors, then wire chambers, spark chambers, after which we have drift chambers and silicon detectors. What is the object of all these means of "detection"?

Wikipedia: "A hadron collider is a very large particle accelerator built to test the predictions of various theories in particle physics , high-energy physics or nuclear physics by colliding hadrons . A hadron collider uses underground tunnels to accelerate, store, and collide two particle beams ".

"In particle physics , a **hadron** is a composite particle made of two or more quarks held together by the strong force in a similar way as molecules are held together by the electromagnetic force . Most of the mass of ordinary matter comes from two hadrons, the proton and the neutron "
Let us skip a beat here, and add a theme: " …, for physics has entered a realm of a type of magic, dealing with the sub-sensible." from the last paragraphs of Georg Unger's "On Nuclear Energy", where he, Unger, also quotes Steiner this way: " … and we must carefully distinguish in our thoughts the difference between sub-sensible appearances and the sub-natural". There is a second essay with the above – "The Nature of Sub-sensible Forces", that can be read on-line here: https://wn.rsarchive.org/RelAuthors/UngerGeorge/OccultAtom/OccAtm_index.html

Google sez: "A hydrogen atom is about 99.9999999999996% empty space. Put another way, if a hydrogen atom were the size of the earth, the proton at its center would be about 200 meters (600 feet) across."

There a five models of the atom: John Dalton's atomic model: [1803] Dalton´s Billiard Ball (Solid Sphere) Model; [1904] J.J. Thomson's model: Plum Pudding model; [1911] Ernest Rutherford's model: Nuclear model; [1913] Niels Bohr's model: Planetary model; and, [1926] Erwin Schrödinger's model: Electron Cloud Model/Quantum Model.

Did something happen in 1926? Quantum Theories and Mechanics happened. All in all, we might suspect that the minds of physicists feel of the edge of a kind of flat earth type idea. Not real, but all the more dangerous because of the sense it seems to make.

More needs to be illuminated, but too much at one time asks too much of the reader, so let me pause this discourse on modern physics, and the elemental kingdom of nature, with this little tale:

Years ago when I was wondering/wandering in the Mystery School of the San Francisco/Berkeley culture, I came upon a little booklet, entitled: "On the Absence of Disorder in Nature". I lost the booklet, remembered the author's name wrong, but providence led to his latest book-sized version about ten years ago: "God Does Not Play Dice", by David Shiang https://www.amazon.com/God-Does-Not-Play-Dice/dp/0980237300/ref=tmm_pap_swatch_0?_encoding=UTF8&qid=1557063687&sr=1-1

"I, in any case, am convinced He does not play dice with the universe." It was addressed by Einstein to Max Born (one of the fathers of Quantum Mechanics) in a letter that he wrote to Born in 1926. The "Old one" and "He" Einstein refers to is God." Google

Essentially Shiang debunks quantum probability theories. An MIT engineer takes a look at his brother theorists, and finds there a complete failure of empirical thinking.

To be continued …

Letter about Magic #6

In the last letter it was pointed out that the "modeling" of the nature of the "atom", stopped evolving in 1926, with the: "Erwin Schrödinger's model: Electron Cloud Model/Quantum Model". In Georg Unger's "The Nature of Sub-Sensible Forces", he described a change in the approach of physics toward the smallest entities. Up to and through the end of the 19th and the beginning of the 20th centuries, physics was trying to find out what was "there", and that question morphed into "can we prove a theoretical (not 'there' yet) entity exists. The mind of the physicist imagines possible entities, based on the ideas of quantum-style thinking, and creates a device to see if what they fancy can be proven.

Let me say this again, because it is crucial to understand this. The physicist was no longer looking at the stuff, in order to "know" its secrets, but he/she is looking to blow particles up in a super collider, where photons are "smashed" together at near light speeds, producing in the observing "chamber" (which was also evolving) momentary traces (short half-life) of various kinds of "objects", or more accurately the debris of an event that is not clearly observable until we (not nature) create the event being observed.

We assume the Sun and the Stars work that way, but that is "theory", not empirical observation of the "inside" of these celestial objects. [For strange details, this: "the Misconception of Cosmic Space as Appears in the Ideas of Modern Astronomy" http://ipwebdev.com/hermit/space.html

"The total operating budget of the LHC runs to about $1 billion per year. The Large Hadron Collider was first turned on in August of 2008, then stopped for repairs in September until November 2009. Taking all of those costs into consideration, the total cost of finding the Higgs boson ran about $13.25 billion." Google

In the Fall season of 2017, the comedy show "The Big Bang Theory" did a story about how depressed the scientist characters were, because they had to admit that Cern was a failure and physics had not advanced in the last 50 years. Lots of theories, but no proofs. This theme was repeated in the first show of 2018. Keep in mind that these "seemingly impossible" to prove theories were derived from human thinking, and not empirical nature. Physics had run into a wall, which Rudolf Steiner had characterized as a problem with our concepts of the "atom".

The beginning of this difficulty for the physicist arose when they ran into an odd phenomena, where the instruments the "observer" was using could not "measure" positions of a smallest "entities" at the same time as their velocity. The instruments' "looking features" touch the phenomena and disturb it by this contact. An electron microscope is like a Star Trek Klingon disruptor-weapon, pointed at stuff.

This physical limit of our instruments was then seen as a problem with "nature", and not with us. We could not determine what we wished to determine, and this was not accepted as evidence of our limits, but rather evidence of matter's own indeterminate nature. Out of this assumption, that nature is indeterminate, probabilistic theories were generated/created in the minds of scientists.

Erwin Schrodinger's cat in a box analogy was born, where the state of the object is indeterminate until we open the box (by seeking to measure a tiny entity's position and/or velocity). We touch it, and the effect of this takes a probability and brings it into concrete manifestation. Physics basically acquires/invents its own religion about Nature (aka, looking for the God Particle – the particle that imparts mass to the object of investigation).

Georg Unger makes this analogy: stuff is not made up of parts, but like "safety glass" fractures along stress lines, as designed. As Designed. At the same time this thinking was developing in physics, Franz Bardon published, in the 1950's, his remarkable three volume teachings on the Hermetic Science of the ancient Egyptians. A science of how to work consciously with "the light", and the four elements, out of which everything created proceeds to manifestation.

We, human beings, are basically a potential (to ourselves) science experiment. Among the most serious Bardon students, Steiner is the next in line to be studied. This happened in my own biography, by "accident". First, five years of spiritual studies that soon led to Bardon practices/exercises, at the level of being able to "breathe in the fire element". Only then met Steiner through his books. A Moon (and Saturn via shamanistic studies) wisdom foundation, followed by the meeting of the New Sun Mysteries.

In Letter #5, I wrote: "Years ago when I was wondering/wandering in the Mystery School of the San Francisco/Berkeley culture, I came upon a little booklet, entitled: "On the Absence of Disorder in Nature". I lost the booklet, remembered the author's name wrong, but providence led to his latest book-sized version about ten years ago: "God Does Not Play Dice", by David Shiang https://www.amazon.com/God-Does-Not-Play-Dice/dp/0980237300/ref=tmm_pap_swatch_0?_encoding=UTF8&qid=1557063687&sr=1-1 "

Shiang begins with a discussion of the ideas of probability and potential, in the simplest way: coin flipping. We flip a nickel 1000 times, and it comes up heads 512 times and tails 488 times. If we repeat the experiment several times, perhaps the average gap will narrow, but still there is always the potential for an indefinite result – at least in our minds.

That physicists self-created jedi-mind-trick – a world of probability – remains a mental ghost (not in the real world) … is what Shiang points out. Whatever the number we invent, the scientific fact is our action will produce an actual empirical event. There will be a result even if we can't predict it. Just because our limit is the inability to predict, does mean Nature is not predictable. Our limit is only

Nature's limit, to the degree it lives in us. In the actual physical world, empirical results always happen. That these are preceded by a probabilistic state is our invention.

We (non-physicists) hear stories of what it all means, and many times a TV show, or other resource, talks about split screen experiments. Later in these shows, references are made to the obscure mathematics quantum theory produces, alleging it proves their point of view. Except for the anomalous situations, which are also in the popular culture, such as two entities/particles are separated (after being united), and if we touch one, the other one also reacts. Einstein called this "spooky action at a distance".

The question is not the experimental result, but rather the quality of thought which interprets the meaning of the results.

There is an important book to own: Catching the Light: the Entwined History of Light and Mind, by Arthur Zajonc, physicist and a former leader in the Anthroposophical Society in America. https://www.amazon.com/Catching-Light-Entwined-History-Mind/dp/0195095758/ref=tmm_pap_swatch_0?_encoding=UTF8&qid=1557153579&sr=1-1

We might grasp our differences here, from Zajonc's work, as involving the question of the Karma of Platonists and Aristotelians. For example, I studied magic (also theology and law) practices, ultimately to become a pagan Christian, as it were. The index to the above book briefly mentions Egypt, but neither magic, or elemental beings, or David Shiang's book. There is more than one way of seeing, but in terms of historical perspective, informed with the inspirations of Rudolf Steiner's indications, this book is excellent.

Overall, historically, natural science – starting about 500 years ago – began taking things apart, things that were assumed to lack consciousnesses or will (except Leibniz's monads). In the beginning spirit was assumed as necessary to what we are as human beings, expressed by our animation, ... that is we are alert-matter, not inert-matter. https://en.wikipedia.org/wiki/Monadology

"I cannot define the real problem, therefore I suspect there's no real problem, but I'm not sure there's no real problem."

"The American physicist Richard Feynman said this about the notorious puzzles and paradoxes of quantum mechanics, the theory physicists use to describe the tiniest objects in the Universe. But he might as well have been talking about the equally knotty problem of consciousness." By Philip Ball, 16 February 2017, http://www.bbc.com/earth/story/20170215-the-strange-link-between-the-human-mind-and-quantum-physics

So, physics runs into a limit of our ability as scientists to penetrate matter's secrets, about the same time the science of consciousness becomes less and less sure what consciousness is, all the while assuming an absence of spirit, given that we believe (science as religion) we can explain it all as a condition of matter. [See my: "I am not my brain – the map is not the territory" http://ipwebdev.com/hermit/brain.html]

Physicists at Cern, not realizing matter could have will and consciousness (as they do), shreds/devours/miss-imagines the real entities, such that the elemental kingdoms have ability to provide all the needed consciousness, by which nature is empirically determined. Just because We cannot Yet know this, does not mean there is a reality to probability physics. Cern is an altar on which the elemental kingdom is sacrificed, by the unconscious minions of Ahriman and Lucifer. None of the theories has been proved, although …

The claim is made that there are experimental results, which can mathematically be seen as proving aspects of the "theory" (tale/story/tragic delusion). So the math becomes (possibly) significant. To crack this nut, we have Godel's Incompleteness Theorems:

"Gödel's incompleteness theorems are two theorems of mathematical logic that demonstrate the inherent limitations of every formal axiomatic system capable of modelling basic arithmetic. These results, published by Kurt Gödel in 1931, are important both in mathematical logic and in the philosophy of mathematics. The theorems are widely, but not universally, interpreted as showing that Hilbert's program to find a complete and consistent set of axioms for all mathematics is impossible." Wikipedia: https://en.wikipedia.org/wiki/G%C3%B6del%27s_incompleteness_theorems This comes down to: You can't use math to prove anything, because all maths require unprovable assumptions – i.e. it is a system, defined into/with limits (yes, … limits again). Limits in the study of matter, of consciousness, and of mathematics.

For our purposes, we might think this: When a scientist proclaims, that his version of experimental probability theory is proven mathematically, we have the classic causal paradox: of a man lifting himself up by his own bootstraps.

Can Cern become a consciously chosen altar, where scientists meditate, study Goethean Science, and practice magic? Do we care? Magic is best known and understood by our own – personal/individual – experimental explorations. These are next … but first a mystery message from our Sponsor: Rudolf Steiner: "Think on it: how the point becomes a sphere and yet remains itself. Hast thou understood how the infinite sphere may be only a point, and then come again, for then the Infinite will shine forth for thee in the finite."

Letter about Magic #7

Given the nature of "number", which is very mysterious in a way, let us look again at the actor: Ourselves. Do we wish to do magic? What would that mean?

The deeper connections of the Four Elements (fire, earth, air, and, water), the four types of particles (Leptons, Quarks, Vector bosons, and Scalar bosons, and, the four interactions (gravity, electromagnetism, and the strong and weak nuclear forces) need to be illuminated through self-observation.

The Universe made us in its own imagine, the Hermetic Idea being that we are the microcosm, which is an exact analogue of the Macrocosm. Part of which means that the Elementals know the most about the nature of matter, playing the role of the last trial/passage on the Way to Manifestation. At the same time, this elemental "activity" is closer in our own "makeup", than it is in the allegedly outside world of things. That is true, but not simple in practice.

Our sense of dis-connectedness is an illusion – of sorts, which some may in the future seek to maintain. That is the final choice we get to make: individuality or community, or perhaps individuality&community – if we understand this basic Egyptian credo:

" … in the "light" of Rudolf Steiner's remarks regarding the future return of the Moon back into the Earth, **and** in the light of the Emerald Tablet: *"The above from the below, and the below from the above – the work of the miracle of the One. And things have been from this primal substance through a single act. How wonderful is this work! It is the main (principle) of the world and is its maintainer. Its father is the sun and its mother the moon; … "*
[Taken from my essay about the Return of the Mother: "Medicine Woman is Here" http://ipwebdev.com/hermit/moon~%21~earth.html   ]
Imagine you could see the future (a lot Steiner readers believe they can – a personal tragedy, a dear friend of mine calls: being doomed from this knowing) … anyway, imagine you could (and you would – in so imagining – join a few billion people that like science fiction), and what you imagined was the human race splitting into two races, one more "good/beautiful/heavenly" in form, because of its (moral superiority), the other "dark/ugly/earthly" in form, because of its "immorality".

If you carried this imagination into the spirit world you would come upon this: the bodhisattva vow.

Wikipedia says this (https://en.wikipedia.org/wiki/Bodhisattva_vow "The Bodhisattva vow's the vow taken by Mahayana Buddhists to liberate all sentient beings ." Oddly, according to my oral-given understanding/transmission, a major aspect of the vow [not generally mentioned] is the sacrifice of leaving the wheel of life (achieve the state of Nirvana). Even tho' enlightened (able to not again reincarnate) the Vow involves the sacrifice of going to that state-of-being until all can "liberated" from the need for corporeal existence.

So, here we are in a world with folk who want to hang around until everyone can get it, and maybe we forget to ask the question: Which race (of the light and dark races hinted at by Steiner) would Bodhisattvas enter? The ones already going up, or the ones falling down?

Just asking.

In an earlier letter I pointed out this: Fire-Will; Water-Feeling; Air-Intellect; and, Earth-Consciousness. In Bardon the exercises are designed to teach us – in practice – a deeper direct experience of these primal elements of all that is & has been created, yet. What I found most wonderful, in my Bardon studies, was that he hid important stuff in plain sight. This is a trope in magic fiction, but to find an actual magic-guru, whose mind was so subtle, in order to get it, some playful attentiveness is needed.

There are three books: Initiation into Hermetics; The Practice of Magical Evocation; and, The True Key to the Quaballah. They contain many ideas about how to do such stuff as make a talisman, and invest it with powers akin to Fire. How to create a beautiful circle to stand in for the evocation of otherwise invisible beings, into the ... well, read the books if you must. The Quaballah book is fascinating, and has some remarkable exercises, relating the powers of the Word, via letters/sounds/colors/and feelings.

The most important stuff, in each case, is right in the beginning. The first set of exercises concerns: on a Mental level = thought-control, discipline of thoughts, subordination of thoughts; on a Psychic level: introspection or self knowledge, and the creation of the black and white mirrors of the soul; and, for the Physical level: the Mystery of Breathing, The Magic of Water, and the conscious reception of food.

The background understanding is that thought is everywhere, and we are not isolated, such that for breathe, water, and, food, there is a practice in which our self-chosen thoughts can impregnate the matter which surrounds us. All theses practices then can be fit into all lives, because they are the stuff of daily life. What happens is we learn to see the sacred in the mundane, and take our routine and redefine it as ritual.

Then, depending upon our magical ambitions, we can learn all manner of typical magic powers stuff, although progress depends upon mastering the ability to do some work everyday. Let me repeat: everyday practice is crucial, even if it just a moment of prayer on going to sleep or on waking. Force-of-habit will take care of itself after a time. Life as a personally designed Rite, keeping in mind, if inner judgments of failure were to try to dominate, its all manure for the field of Bodhi. Don't seize the Day, seize the moment, one moment at a time.

For another example of an in plain sight secret, ... in The Practice of Magical Evocation, after spending many pages describing how elaborate we could make our temple and our circle, he writes: "The magician will always find that the magic circle is, in every respect, the highest symbol in his hand." Without directly saying, that these teachings of the summoning or communing with spirits requires – only – that we sit still, making – when seeking contact with beings – circles of our thumb and first finger, while practicing our exercises.

Everyone already leads a magic life. We are all shamans in the making, because our basic intellectual activity is about survival. Each person has different circumstances, in which to survive, not only physically, but more crucially in our Age, that our personality/style/spirit-individuality survive.

Shamanism also has a geographical aspect. The Earth is differentiated – spiritually/astrally/ethereally – and this means that a local region has import. We would do well to consider our own rooms as a locus-unique. We might, but ought not to, perform the Catholic Mass in a Hebrew Temple. The more we learn about magic, the more we need to respect what we can't yet "see".

Now this "seeing" is kind of a trick. There are many systems, or points of view. Some more ancient than others. Bardon modernized (since he did it in the 20th Century) the ancient Egyptian Hermetic Science, but other literature is deeply connected to the Age in which was authored. The crucial matter is to recognize the evolution of consciousness – our inward nature has/is changing considerably. Owen Barfield needs to be read here, e.g. Speaker's Meaning mentioned previously.

For example, a lot of literature, with an Eastern heritage, refers to "mind" and "ego" in a way that only worked for the stage of the evolution of consciousness dominant at the time those ideas were generated. I wrote a long essay on this: "West and East, or Wendt's critique of Osho's critique of Rudolf Steiner"

http://ipwebdev.com/hermit/WestandEast.html

For the magician, the central question (as for all of us) is: What am I as a human being? In Hermetic Science we study that question from the standpoint of the four elements, by a study of our own will (fire), our own feeling (water), our own mind (air), and the combination of those three in our consciousness (earth). Keep in mind that these are never separate, although magic exercises can make it possible to attend to various "parts", by magnifying our inner/soul/self perceptions through Bardon practice.

When we know fire in our Self, we know fire in the universe.

For some fun, as we end this letter, let us consider gnomes, they being close at hand as it were. Blessed are those who have not seen, and yet believe.

The process of manifestation isn't really in parts, but we can name an unfolding in different stages. Wherever matter is involved, we have to do with a process whose final stage is gnomish. Something becomes fixed, having found its rightful place.

Modern human beings have a trait now being called: porous mind. Our mind is not separate from spirit, but swims in spirit as it were. Thoughts are spirit. Real thinking/cognition is the creation of spirit form. All the same we are surrounded by other-presences, invisible and quiet. Not speechless, quiet. To meet/hear in your porous mind the thoughts of gnomes, find that mess of clutter in your living space and clean it. Carefully. Thoughtfully. Is this object, now less dusty and unkempt, in its right place. Thinking as listening. Thought/ideas/pictures and even feelings will be there, the more we keep our inner chatter silent. We hold the object, we care about it, and wonder – as shown: "in Slow Regard of Silent Things", a book suggested in Letter #4.

The gnomes will bring/being insights surprising. They are, by the way, a bit fussy. What I mean is the taste of the insight might not be to our liking. Gnomes doesn't think like us, but at the same time know a great deal. Lose an object in your house? Loudly call out to the gnomes for some help in finding it. They will know where it is.

Remember the bits above about matter which is alert, and matter which is inert? Consciousness is everywhere, and the elemental beings are the leading edge of what we experience through the senses. Once you start to trust that, your porous mind will make everyday a way of learning something new.

You don't see color without the salamanders (fire spirits). You don't hear sounds without the sylphs. The medium for perception is not through space empty of being. The cool beauty of water/undines is seen whenever you wash your hands or take a shower. And, the gnomes, busy and a bit grumpy for our failures to keep the place orderly, within reasonably aesthetic impulses.

Do you apologize when you hit an object against another object, that produces a tone you know means substance was harmed (dropped and broke a glass)? Will the physicists at Cern ever be grateful for the sacrifices of the little people on the altar of their atheist/agnosticism? Knowledge, of mutual intercourse with Elementals, was common in the times of the Goddess religions, for the little people ruled over the magics of garden, hearth, water-well, and a not too leaky roof. Hex signs were not superstitions. For details, check out any good books on Wicca.

Are Leptons and Quarks the corpse of elemental beings?

Next letter will give it a try ….

Letter about Magic #8

A particle accelerator is "an apparatus for accelerating subatomic particles to high velocities by means of electric or electromagnetic fields. The accelerated particles are generally made to collide with other particles, either as a research technique or for the generation of high-energy X-rays and gamma rays. " Google

"The aim of the LHC's detectors is to allow physicists to test the predictions of different theories of particle physics , including measuring the properties of the Higgs boson[9] and searching for the large family of new particles predicted by supersymmetric theories ,[10] as well as other unsolved questions of physics " Wikipedia

These practices are the result of mental activity. Nature didn't do this. We do it. Is our mental activity in need of some accelerated thoughts, crashing into each other, until we … what?

I'm trying to shift the scale here. Big machine, lots of money, sort of a toy for folks who … at the least believe they are doing no harm. Sure is a lot of stuff they don't know, although they also act as if they are on the right track, and asking the right questions. https://en.wikipedia.org/wiki/List_of_unsolved_problems_in_physics#High-energy_physics/particle_physics

Without a doubt the basic misconception in physics is that only the human being has an interior consciousness and free will, maybe – lot of uncertainty about that in some circles of brain science. http://ipwebdev.com/hermit/brain.html

Certainly they (the "they" that tries to act as if they can explain the finer points of existence) don't have room in their "theories" for spirit. The above document of "questions" is huge, and when I did a "find" search for the word "spirit", it was not there. Same with "mind", "thinking", "meditation", and, "prayer".

Really, … follow the link and gaze lightly over the list. At the least it is a story in a language-mysterious. Sort of like when the Catholic Church didn't want the Bible to be in any other language than Latin. Keep the membership from discovering that the whole field of Biblical meaning was a war zone of intrigue. Once regular folk could read the Gospels for themselves the whole situation started to change – history called it "the Reformation".

The level of disagreements in science is huge, and not always hidden. Rupert Sheldrake does a good send up of the whole mess, on a TED talk that some had tried to censor. "The Science Delusion" [Watch it!] https://www.youtube.com/watch?v=JKHUaNAxsTg

Are there Gospels of Science? Should there be? Well, if we admit spirit into the conversation, what happens … what changes?

Everything. A gospel of physics: "Man or Matter", by Ernst Lehrs; a gospel of organic chemistry: "The Nature of Substance", by Rudolf Hauschka; a gospel of "The Plant" (two volumes): Gerbert Grohmann; a gospel of water: "Sensitive Chaos", by Theodore Schwenk; a gospel of "Man and Mammals": towards a biology of form", Wolfgang Schad; a gospel of the soul: "On Becoming an Alchemist – a guide for the modern magician", by Catherine MacCoun; a gospel of the imagination: "Poetic Diction", by Owen Barfield; for starters.

Please note the repeated phrase: "a gospel", for there are many, not just these. As to Rudolf Steiner, a dangerous mind because of being so all encompassing. Didn't run into a situation for which he didn't have an answer. A lot of his students, are not very good at that – using Steiner to answer their questions, instead of their own minds.

All the same, without his inspiration, I could not have written my "gospel of theory": "The Art of God: an actual theory of Everything." My basic idea was to take the religious/spiritual question, and frame it as a theory, to compete with the neo-darwinian theory of evolution, and big bang cosmology, through The Art of God's superior explanatory power. Does a theory of God better explain the mysteries of human existence?

A friend of mine wrote a review, and a bit more at the same time: http://ipwebdev.com/hermit/artofgodreview.html
Another friend, a different review, … of my take on Anthroposophy, a la American: http://ipwebdev.com/hermit/JWendt-review-article.pdf
Commercial over … let us return to the Slow Regard of Silent Things, and wonder about that "nature" of which they are made. Elementals, or the imaginary wet dreams of materialists, with their leptons, quarks, bosons, and …. and what? Is there a there there? Let us revisit, a bit more deeply then, David Shiang's: God Does Not Play Dice.

(This is not a perfect work by the way, for Shiang has his own confusion in play, still being a bit of a materialist, and by re-enlivening the vanity of fixed determinism. That, however, is a whole other story, which a reader of the book can themselves take with a grain of salt.)

In Chapter Five he quotes in detail the essential trains of thought which led to the fantasy world of quantum delusions. While we approach these thoughts, let us keep in mind the efforts behind them – the lives and thoughts of many have offered what they could. These incursions into the deep structure of "things" are not to be thrown away. The language and ideas are real, and it would be helpful if we could imagine that the pieces of the substances, we destroy in a particle accelerator, might very well contain the most crucial of Nature's open in plain sight magical secrets.

The threshold between the material and non-material worlds is breached by these experiments, which morally weak thinking resulted in the atomic bomb. In the first nano-seconds of such an event, some rules are shredded, and entities not otherwise belonging to this world enter ours. However, the laws of the world of matter, require that an entity from the non-material realms become clothed in matter, once forced across this threshold. We call the related phenomena: flying saucers, and when folk otherwise not awake enough to fully encounter such beings we get: alien abductions. Spiritual experiences are given materialistic coloration by our minds, having been misdirected for generations by a matter only physics.

In the formation of authenticate crop circles, the elemental community (gnomes), ask of the "carbon" beings, that they swoon, while the aesthetics of the visible form are devised by guiding angels. Carbon, being necessary for structure, weeps out of the green wholeness, and falling through the well of gravity that is the Mother's Love, become those crystals found among the stalks that bend but not break – a very female gesture, yet separation leaves tears. Like the teaching of the speech of clouds, hidden in the inspiration of the movie Arrival, the "crop" circles are meant to be taken into the imagination and felt. A kind of class in the education of the human mind for a magical future, whose excesses will ultimately lead to the infamous War of All Against All, when everyone's a witch/wizard/shaman.

"Everything is determined … by forces over which we have no control. It is determined for the insect as well as for a star. Human beings, vegetables, or comic dust – we all dance to a mysterious tune, intoned in the distance by an invisible piper" Albert Einstein, Saturday Evening Post, 1929

"A common measure can now be applied to all forms of organization. Any loss of organization is equitably measured by the chance against its recovery by an accidental coincidence. The chance is absurd regarded as a contingency, but it is precise as a measure. The practical measure of the random element which can increase in the universe but never decreases is called entropy" Sir Arthur Eddington: The Nature of the Physical World.

" … the scientific world view contains the highly speculative, anti-factual belief that the "possible" could be the "actual"" D. Shiang.

It has been said – by materialists – that Nature prefers disorder over order. Eddington speaks above of the "random element", at the same time using the words: accidental coincidence; chance, and contingency. Shiang is arguing that whatever and however Nature does it, there ends up being an actual empirical event. No "chance" is involved.

Of course, we here are better informed, for even in just considering that the "Universe" is a co-participant in our lives, we have overcome the random, for which better proof is our own biography. We are story tellers, sailing seas uncharted, being beyond the edge of the world.

Letters on Magic #11

[Link to all the earlier Letters on Magic: http://www.thecollectiveimagination.com/2019/05/20/letters-about-magic/]

In a certain sense we are all shamans in making. If we survive, it is we who survived, and remarkable skills are thus acquired. For details: "Americans … among the Lost: notes from inner space – the true Final Frontier." http://ipwebdev.com/hermit/finalfrontier.html

The hardest lesson, for a shaman in maturity, is to accept the fact that if something exists, it has been approved from the highest and deepest spiritual communities. Bardon writes: "there is nothing unclean in the whole of the Creation."

My studies of Magic have led me to finding wonder in the hermetic ideas of the electrical (fire/will) and magnetic (water/feeling) fluids. Electromagnetism is one of the fundamental transformations in materialistic physics, so what did Bardon mean in using those words in the context of magic? A metaphor, of sorts?

Some Internet venues – on which these Letters on Magic are first published – are on Facebook (e.g. "Anthroposophy"; and, "Anthroposophy & Mechanical Occultism" = A&MO). These groups have a strong relationship to Rudolf Steiner's works. When it comes to our technological civilization, A&MO is taking a deep interest in these very questions: What is electricity? What is technology? Where are these aspects of existences going? Are these aspects of existences good for human beings, or very dangerous? What should be opposed? What should be encouraged?

Certain concepts/ideas discussed on A&MO have always bothered me. I have written these Letters about Magic in order to lay out the reasoning and experiences that lie at the root of my disquiet. At a basic level it comes down to this: the quality of the "how" of the thinking. "How" is quite different than "What", and much in Steiner communities is based of forgetting that fact. Reading Steiner gives us a concept/idea not rooted in experience. We need to increase the nature/disciplines of the How, drawing our cognitions not from words on a page, but directly from our own experiences.

In preparation, we need to add a couple of other Ideas, from Tomberg's "Meditations on the Tarot: a journey into Christian Hermeticism", in his letter on the Arcanum #11 Force. There he discusses the differences between Bios & Zoe, aka the terrestrial fires-electrical (Bios), and the transcendent fires-electrical (Zoe). Keeping in mind that Elemental Fire is also known as: the Will.

Bios is about the force=lawfulness/order of fire/will at the material level. Ernst Lehrs names this power: cohesion, … matter coheres … we have to kill it to find the parts. The father-powers of order giving are seen in the phenomena of electricity. No material universe without the power that holds matter in place. Taking stuff out of is "place" generally leads to trouble. We also need to better understand how "place" is maintained.

The force=amelioration is about fire/will, at the purely spiritual level. Amelioration: the act of making something better; improvement. Smooth over. Pacify. Succor. Hold dear. Accept. Receive.

The Tarot Symbolism is of a Woman seemingly holding open the Jaws of a Lion. Not by Her "command" is the animality gentled, but rather by the "the force of all forces, for it overcometh every subtle thing, and doth penetrate every solid substance." (Tabula Smaragdina).

Recall S. Clarke: *"the traditional kabbalistic worlds of Emanation, Creation, Formation & Existence"*, or as Rudolf Steiner has it: *"Saturn, Sun, Moon, and, finally, the surface world of Nature, all inhabited at their core and in every particle by divinity in its immanent maternal aspect. Thus the Father God is One, the Mother God is Many."* For essential details: http://ipwebdev.com/hermit/Clarke5.html
*"…all inhabited at their core and in every particle by **divinity in its immanent maternal aspect**." (emphasis added)*

Mom is Every-Where/When. Not in the sense of a collection of discrete objects, but "collectively" as in/via Wholeness. Her Consciousness penetrates All, and we gain some of the beauty here with this: She has the Whole World in His Hands. Christ is the unity of Mother&Father. Lawfulness&Holding Dear. Karma&Justice. Levity&Gravity. Stephen Clarke, in his "Close Encounters of the Fifth Kind"*** makes this conceptual array:

Table of Complements:
God the Mother God the Father
multifarious unitary
luminous darkness blinding light
questions answers
spontaneous playfulness fixity of purpose
fractal centripetal
below above
grief bliss
relaxation striving
immovable irresistible
forms life
mercy justice
chaos logos

[***Someone should see to having this published, for among many other aspects, there is deep work here regarding "flying saucers" and "alien" abductions. Also, Stephen's critique of the Anthroposophical Society: "Short Circuit", needs to be made available.]

Steiner, the esoteric Idealist (the best possible imaginary outcome is the one to pursue), was not perfect, although far too many treat his words as divine certainties. A folly he fostered by having points of view about everything spiritual.

In this regard, Andrew Linnell, in referring to a recent pdf file uploaded to the A&MO group, wrote this: "I feel this article from New View summarizes the best insights from Paul Emberson's voluminous works" I have no such faith in Emberson's work. For details, this link of my review – "A well intended* very flawed Book" – of his: "From Gondhishapur to Silicon Valley" http://ipwebdev.com/hermit/counter-silicon.html

From my own considerations of certain phenomena, these next links are must reads given that the Letters about Magic cannot even begin to cover every nuance:
"Electricity and the Spirit in Nature" http://ipwebdev.com/hermit/electricityandthespiritinnature.html

THERE IS NO "FREE" ENERGY: Space and "field" phenomena; Nature and sub-nature https://borderlandsciences.org/journal/vol/46/n05/Goethe_Space_Field_Phenomena.html

Why must reads? Read them and compare them to Emberson, and if not, don't pretend to being a scientist of the spiritual.
The title of the pdf file is: "Working with the Forces of Life". It contains many of the general defects I referred to in the above review. This new work also contains some very curious sidelights, which are good examples of an untrained imagination, coupled with too much antipathy toward the world which does not accord with Emberson's – or Steiner's – hopeful/dreams/idealism, planted in a garden of worry about the far-side future.

Emberson wrote: "In machine technology we are developing our own future physical bodies, because man will be "forged together" with his machines, to use Steiner's expression. What this means in a concrete sense, if we take only our present technology into consideration, is that, increasingly, artificial devices will be incorporated into our physical organism until our body has finally become a machine. It is not a question of being for or against developments of this kind: they have to come, Steiner said. The real question is whether they come in the right way or not. "

He also wrote this, referring to Life/Nature as she: "What we do not know is how she does it. In spite of all our scientific and technical prowess we are bound to admit that we have so far failed completely in our endeavors to discover what life is".

I assume the "we" he is referring to is materialistic science, for a spiritual science would know this theological poetry for truth, even at the level of physics: "In It (the Word) was Life, and the Life was the Light of the World."
One curiosity is where Emberson references in a positive way the wet dreams of Ray Kurzweil, of "The Singularity is Near" fame. http://ipwebdev.com/hermit/kurzweileffect.html The idea of artificial intelligence is by RK expected to end up with computers designing new computers, until "they" take over the world. My essay: "I am not my brain – the map is not the territory" http://ipwebdev.com/hermit/brain.html can be antidote to Kurzweil's confusion. The fusion of soul/mind with tech is more complex that folk realize, which is why the Platonist's experiences are a crucial help.

Some writings/statements of Steiner could be interpreted to mean that such a possibilities exist, yet even among the starkest probabilities, the world is not designed to become the dark&dry

nightmare/dreams of anthroposophists devoted to Steinerism, and unable or unwilling to think the situation through for themselves.

In order to grasp "electricity", with the mind, we have to go to the limits of the imagination and try to find and hold to the Idea, that electricity, in its essential nature, is a whole, not parts. We must try to see/intuit/understand that everywhere when there is "order" is due to the Father's sacrifice. Elemental Fire is a Being-Divine, and it (godly will) is everywhere, and – note – every when.

Steiner has described electricity as fallen light. In fact, there are several ethereal aspects of Reality given this characterization as "fallen". All that is "fallen" in the Creation takes this characteristic from what? There is, in the Creation, only one place to "fall", and this is into material existence. Christ's incarnation is a "fall" into materiality, which as we have been working out, the nearest spiritual aspect of Reality is the Elemental Kingdoms, aka Faerie.

Let me add some Steiner for the die-hards who are yet unable to know the moral nature of "Elemental Fire".
"…electricity in Nature is not merely a current, but that electricity in Nature is, at the same time, a moral element." … "… when we transform an atom into an electron, we do not transform it into a moral, but into an immoral entity." Lecture by Steiner, on Jan. 28, 1923

Electricity in Nature is not the same as the "electricity" grasped by the mind in the form of an electron attached to an atom. The former is moral by nature, while the latter is an ahrimanic abstraction, totally in denial of the Father and the Son, i.e. something born out of the spirit of the anti-Christ, via an untempered by the heart intellect.

Our technological future will leave a corpse. This is not news. Everything living in matter, abandons at some point the material. A lot of anthroposophists spend time worrying over milk that has not only not yet been spilled, but not yet created. Folks need to live now, not the imagined future of universal ahrimanic possession. Now is the only time we can do anything about the future. Will we tell worrisome stories, or find a way to illuminate why Steiner asked us to trust the future?

The world works in a certain Way …. we need to think in wholes, Reality is not parts.
A basic knowledge of modern human existence has to be founded on the recognition that the world is designed around the needs of the spirits&souls of individuals. Love cares more about us having the biographical experiences we need/want, than the "this to shall pass" of fashions in science, religion, art, education, politics, economics and so forth.

We are loved by Folk acting from Eternity. Long enough to love each one of us – who are doomed to materialism – with personal art and care. "The Art of God: an actual theory of Everything" http://ipwebdev.com/hermit/artofgod.html
Another curiosity, which I remarked upon in my Emberson review, and which is mentioned in the latest report, is that folk in Europe are seeking to know the How of the Strader machine, which mechanical occultism Steiner characterized as a gift possessed by Americans, or folk of the soul-West, via the streams of talents-genetic, flowing through our material-genetic ancestors. Work in Europe – the soul-Center – won't succeed for the simple reason that a Strader machine is put in motion by a magical

gesture, which requires knowing a lot more about the beings of Faerie. To do that you have to go down, into chaos and the spontaneous playfulness of the luminous darkness. Not up toward the idealistic as modeled by Steiner.

Emberson writes: "In order to become the master-craftsman of the living the human being has to develop a moral, etheric technology based on the forces given to the Earth by Christ through the Mystery of Golgotha

. These are the Grail forces

. If we think deeply enough about these things, we soon realize how vitally important it is for humanity to develop that moral technology before electronics, nanotechnology and robotics sweep the board. But how do we go about developing it?"

… then later: "Could acoustic resonance itself become a source of motor power if etheric forces were somehow involved? If you had a million identical tuning-forks set on their resonance boxes and you struck one of them, might they not all sound in unison by resonance if the conditions were right, producing waves of acoustic energy far greater than the small amount of energy required to strike the first tuning-fork?"

Remember the Platonists? http://ipwebdev.com/hermit/Culmination.html

Everywhere Steiner, and his quote lovers, uses the word forces, they are using an ahrimanic abstraction that is disconnected in the thought-ethereal-world from the actual beings involved. They deserved to be named and honored. If we (inspired by Steiner) want to find ways to help the future unfold in positive ways means that the Aristotelians need to listen to their brothers and sisters who are devoted to She, to the Mother.

To know the elemental spirits of existence is not a head-trip – for magic is simultaneously science&art&religion, but done in the mood of a heart filled with child-like curiosity, while on a romantic journey to wander among wonders, unafraid of caves, and moonless nights.

Ultimately, it is a question of starting to teach children to respect a world/universe/planetary system that is everywhere alive and self-conscious. Defeat scientific materialism on its own level by studying the Goethean scientists, and the pagan shaman/wizards.

Letters about Magic #12 {of twelve}

[Link to all the earlier Letters on Magic: http://www.thecollectiveimagination.com/2019/05/20/letters-about-magic/]

Last sentence of Letters about Magic #11: "Ultimately, it is a question of starting to teach children to respect a world/universe/planetary system that is everywhere alive and conscious. Defeat scientific materialism on its own level by studying the Goethean scientists, and the Platonist pagan shaman/wizards."

The Divine Mystery multitasks on levels beyond our capacity to imagine. A case in point is taking place in the river systems in the heartland of America. First there is what I have been calling: The Great Unsettling & the 3rd Millennium, which is the signature art of karmically/harmonically displacing folks from their stuck-habits of life-routine, through the Four Horseman, who work for the Mother when She is using Her Broom to clean the floors of the alchemical kitchen of Existence, especially the dark places left in our wake – the moral children playing with elemental fires. Keep in mind that angels help children to fall down, go boom, wake up, and notice the flowers.
http://www.thecollectiveimagination.com/the-great-unsettling-the-3rd-millennium/
Then there is Her Way of agriculture, which is to use great floods to distribute nutrients to the elemental kingdoms for their work with the future agricultural vitality of the American heartland. We've tried to dam Her water-ways, and harmed the land with poisons. Upending agribusiness is important, as an aspect of the metamorphosis of Western Civilization – a dying making possible a new becoming.

Human beings need to leave the cities and become farmers once again. Agri-Culture needs a reboot. One that is hands on, given that there is a divinity in the human being, which is on its personal Path to self-expression. Truly nutritious food is labor intensive, and a lot of people would like the life next to the earth, and the ancient rhythms built into all our systems

To do this redistribution/reawakening of humanity in a sane way, would seem to require political arts&crafts. Some of these are already in play, what with the anti-corruption work fostered by Jennifer Lawrence and Josh Silver of Represent US. https://mashable.com/video/jennifer-lawrence-political-system-corruption/
Meanwhile, Mother&Son released the Kraken (a legendary sea monster) of a Trickster/Trump into the stew of American political life. America's founders had it right, in the original Declaration of Independence:

"Prudence, indeed, will dictate that Governments long established should not be changed for light and transient causes; and accordingly all experience has shown, that human beings are more disposed to suffer, while evils are sufferable, than to right themselves by abolishing the forms to which they are accustomed. But when a long train of abuses and usurpations, pursuing invariably the same Object evinces a design to reduce them under absolute Despotism, it is their right, it is their duty, to throw off such Government, and to provide new Guards for their future security. —Such has been the patient sufferance of the American People; and such is now the necessity which constrains them to alter their former Systems of Government." http://ipwebdev.com/hermit/seconddeclaration.html
Next a picture of the thrice-bordered sphere, and the usefulness of teaching the own picture-thinking imagination to see changes over time, and review them. How does modern technology get here?

The life sphere of our world has three borders. An upper border where if you go too high, you can't breath. We have to take the earth with us, to go beyond the mountain tops, into the airless space. We also cannot go into the earth, without again having to take atmosphere and other life sphere resources with us.

The third border is within us, where hidden gates to the world invisible wait.

One way to see this is that humanity has an instinct to liberate itself from the Natural world. A modern city is the beginning of such a liberation. City light banishes from sight the starry heavens, and people not maintaining the prior ancient relationships (forgetting, and not truly knowing their own story – which is not about being an accidental animal) end up sleeping, drugging our Way across that landscape made of concrete, wearing shoes, breathing pollution, eating unwholesome foods.

The soil needs our attention.

A city needs what we have come to call: infrastructure. I am white-privileged. I live in a community where there are almost no minorities, the medium income is probably very middle class (no rich folk here, but still), little crime, the houses have indoor plumbing (we have four fire places, four TVs hooked up to cable. Our house is made of wood, as is a lot of the furniture. The wood was once in the forest I get to watch every day from my study.

Cities tame nature, control the flows of water, and eat electricity so densely that most of us on our block have generators, for when the power goes out. We have smart phones that are like Aladdin's magical lamp. Not like Haiti, or Syria are the lives of the American middle-class. No wonder folk want to come here, for the movies on the smart phone shows how we live.

Have you ever wondered why – when a sub-station directing "electricity" fails – all the lights in the affected region go out together?

There are a lot of people, these days, who see a world full of woe and danger, of deprivation and abuse, with governments and businesses basically insane. The technological tail seems to be wagging the grounded earth-nature of humanity, what with people starring at smart phones. Everywhere are the imaginations / fancies of bad things coming from machines. History teaches that those who hunger for power and wealth will weaponize anything, including sending children and women into village squares with C-4 strapped to their bodies.

Early on, when I began to seek for a living understanding of the world, I learned to see that given the liquid nature of the flows of wealth and currency, there would naturally be places where wealth coagulated. As well, the Americas are a very strange places, and the U.S. of A. more so all by itself.

The Genius of History cultivated the conditions that led to the U.S. Constitution, which was a seed formed from decades of mostly European political thought. Americans are becoming a People of Peoples (Steiner said peoples and cultures go here to die). A person comes here, and by the third generation much of the where they were from has disappeared. A melting-pot mosaic built from peoples hearts.

What is most special about the Constitution, is that the "people" emancipated themselves from a sovereign aristocracy, so that the individual citizen was to be seen then as the sovereign: "We the people … " begins this act. As the Kraken further helps weaken the two political parties, we can – at best – content ourselves with understanding that the metamorphosis of Western Civilization will involve a lot of chaos, and into that functional disorder, something new can be (and is being) born.

How extreme that transformation will be – if we read the handwriting on the wall of the Weather, and pay attention to our prophets – these changes will be very violent. If folks only knew the real relationship between Weather and our feeling life of soul, the minds eye would better be able to see what's coming, with some sanity. http://www.thecollectiveimagination.com/prophecy/

Chaos is an opening into the unknown future, with potential yet to be created.

If we are astute in our reading of history, it should be clear that change over time always involves a lot of drama. Wars and such. Many wish this was otherwise, but nothing about life suggests it is fair or perfect, forcing on the individual the necessity to author choices. All over the world, so seemingly filled with conflict, death, disease, people see "evil". But, is what is going on actually evil? Would the Cosmic Christ and the Holy Mother tolerate that? Are They so passive and/or uninvolved?

Our technological system requires moving around the world a lot of mineral wealth. When the basic systems of finance and governance begin to fail, that will put big obstacles in the ability to sustain high development on the current scale which technological advances require.

When the soul doesn't like something, the natural tendency is to find fault. If you see fault everywhere, you need to make an adjustment to "How" you thinking. See my "pragmatic moral psychology", for some help waking up to the own thinking, all based upon the Gospels:

http://ipwebdev.com/hermit/stgfr5.html

Our reasons are the same
But there's no-one we can blame
For there's nowhere we need go
And the only truth we know comes so easily

Moody Blues: The Actor. https://www.youtube.com/watch?v=sFHUJeTHznk
Experience is Mystery. Who do you want yourself to be? I used to think, given all the various spiritual development systems, that there was something I was not, and which I ought to become. The world posits many different kind of "attainments", such as: enlightenment, initiation, shamanism, and the teachers of such "paths" do a pretty good job of making folks feel a bit not enough.

During my lifetime (which began when this physical body, astral body, and ethereal body – in its 31st year – was given to another – me, by a remarkable young man. http://ipwebdev.com/hermit/Joey.html } … anyway, once I was in, and Joey was out, I started having spiritual experiences, although I did not understand this in the beginning. I've had many, some of which are as shattering as what happened to Paul on the Road to Damascus.

It is as if one's soul is a flute, which usually we play, often not as well as we might, but still the soul/flute can be "played" by Other-Presences. Eventually is was clear that these folk (the Cosmic Christ and the Holy Mother) had no need for me to be anything other than myself. The ambitiousness to be uber-spiritual was a driver from our own hungers, not from the Divine Mystery.

Except … in our age the Divine Mystery is "distributed". As the actor in our own biography, we are the artists of our choices. We are the microcosm. As above, so below.

This does not mean to not strive. We are also the part of god that is curious, playful, and on occasion a bit lost in space – out of it. When we get intoxicated, the goddess within is intoxicated. When we become obsessed, it is the god&goddess that is us, which is obsessed.

Freedom is only real if it is possible to screw things up gloriously.

and this too shall pass
~!~!~!~!~!~!~!~!~!~!~!~!~!~!~!~Q?~

The Mystery of Quantum Mechanics:

Time, as we tend to think of it, does not exist. Our picture is of us moving through time, from past to future, but the reality is only Now; and, we – our self-consciousness – which itself is never truly "at rest" (we die when we stop breathing and feeling), can reset & reboot our sense of our relationship to this condition of constant change, and grace these movements with a better name: the Eternal Now*. No one escapes this, and this present moment (seize the moment, not just the day) is always dying into a new becoming. The past is only in memory, and the future only in day dreams: "Strange Fire – a wizard's compendium of Ideas in the Light of Eros" http://ipwebdev.com/hermit/sfideos-eros.html
*[https://www.youtube.com/watch?v=H0wVwC6KwKE Moody Blues: "Forever Now".]
In Ursula K. LeGuin's remarkable novel on freedom, "the Dispossessed", she posits the need for a unification of our present sequential physics with a physics of the simultaneous. The old isn't so much wrong, as incomplete.

Arthur C. Clarke: "Any sufficiently advanced technology is indistinguishable from magic.". Although I do not believe he expected Magic itself to be the advanced technology. Yet, the Gate to the Future is through the Past Remembered – a past of the demon haunted ancient Earth religions, the world of gods&goddesses and elemental spirits everywhere/when.

The Quantum Confusion begins with the idea that if we can't predict an empirical result, there exists a pre-condition and/or state of reality that is not yet there, but only in potential. We take a limit in our ability to know as a condition of Nature, which as suggested above is a view of reality with an essential aspect missing: i.e. that we are not the only qualitative condition of reality with an interior self-aware consciousness.

Once we confess to the unreality of space-time, and the illusory nature of the quantum world, and then seek to know Nature through an I and Thou relationship, miracles appear. Do we want a way to deal with nuclear waste, and other poisons with which we have been killing the Life Sphere (the Cosmic Christ) of our Holy Mother, the Planet on which we are nurtured through material-plane existence, in between resting states as pure spirit?

Time to bend the knee to that which Created All, and ask for some help. Just keep in mind that we are a part of that All; and, we are the right people, in the right place, at the right moment.

At the same time, the world of particle physics is not without meaning. Again, an adventure in knowledge seeking, only troubled by our not recognizing we are missing attending to the direct knowing of reality. The condition of modern consciousness, with us seemingly as spectators and on-lookers, … that is not reality. Everything is interconnected. Porous mind is Everywhere = the Collective Imagination.

Still, is the quantum world real? Yes, tragically. Physics went from an art and craft of investigation, to an act of thought and fanciful imagination, lacking a sacramental quality. This broken and incomplete view of reality exists in the world of thought, which is real. The question, however, is are these human-thought creations good and true.

The Mystery of Quantum Mechanics is a trial for humanity. A trial of what/which truth will we follow, as we experience that the changes we call events-in-time are only a part of the Whole. The future, however explicit are the visions of someone like Rudolf Steiner, does not exist. Yet. For anthroposophists, a little humility might be of use, given that Reality Itself is Magical and in the magical world nothing is impossible. Unsure? Our existence is the most obvious magical fact, starring us in the face, in a presently unknown world of invisible beings, waiting for the return of Their prodigal children.

Several months after writing this, I came to a deeper understanding of Electricity: https://thecollectiveimagination.com/2021/07/15/the-father-at-rest/

~!~!~!~!~!~!~!~!~!~

I am not my brain
- the map is not the territory -

We all know this about maps. You can have a very detailed map of your home town, or even pictures from Google Earth, and the experience of that map or those pictures is not what we experience when we walk through the actual town - the actual territory.

This ordinary common sense truth points to a major flaw in the **thinking** applied by brain-scientists to what they believe they come to know through their studies. Regardless of how intricate their maps, how three dimensional, how colored, how full of data and time-stamped, brain-studies only give us maps to the mind. The real territory of the mind is only available to us as an experience, directly in our own consciousness, and directly to what ordinary consciousness conceives of as our inmost "self".

The central problem this essay addresses is not with the detailed arts and the hard work of the brain-scientists, but with the fundamental presumed logical assertions, *born in a misdirected thinking/cognition*, that fails to give us real explanations to what all that research is believed to ultimately mean. We will not find the true human being in the idea that we are just an inadvertent consequence of a random process, that has accidentally created a meat-organ with consciousness, however intricate and complex.

No doubt this research can and will provide advances in human knowledge of the nervous system. In fact, recent capacities developed to enable people with missing limbs to use *thought* to drive the action of the limb is not just a wonderment, but perhaps a kind of proof, which may lead to the opposite conclusion than the one held by those who currently say we have no free will.

The basic Riddle remains: Can these views of the outside (the maps to the brain) … logically give us real knowledge of what lives in the "inside-territory" of a dancing child - that whole human being?

Our languages are littered with expressions about this relationship between self and mind and experience. All personal pronouns used in any sentence have no meaning if there is not an experienced self, which lives within the actual territory of consciousness, making the relevant judgments. The same with most of the "rules" of grammar. Were we to accept the asserted implications of some of the brain-scientists, we are going to have to throw away great portions of thousands of years of language development.

The brain-scientist does not even have a way to "see" consciousness or thoughts or mental pictures or imaginative pictures or feelings or any of the thousands upon thousands of aspects of the actual rich and wise inner territory we all daily experience. The brain-scientists only sees surfaces, or "outsides", which he "maps", while only ordinary consciousness itself sees the "inside" (the territory). And, these reference to an inside and an outside hardly touches the reality of experience, which generally is known as a whole - inside and outside implicitly intimately linked in the total field of consciousness.

Yet, many of the brain-scientists are trying to tell us that consciousness - the territory - is rooted in the physical brain, that there is no self, and that there is no free will. Why?

Sadly, to answer the "why" question, we can't trust the brain-studies which brain-scientist likes to use to support his conclusions. Then arises an additional question: why can't we trust that work? The answer to these questions is not so simple, but nonetheless all the more crucial for being a bit complicated.

Everyone alive today is born into a culture and a language. Each individual culture is complicated. The religions are all different, and the historical paths through which that particular language arose are also complex.

Scientists like to act as if they are creating universal knowledge. A valuable effort if they were disciplined enough, but the historical facts of the development of modern science reveals that at far too many crucial steps it progressed by eliminating from its considerations aspects of existence that could not, in general, be counted or otherwise measured. Science in its youth (it can still mature, should its priests so choose), took things apart, and liked to count and measure these many parts, finding in mathematical relationships some logical surety that would otherwise seem lacking, if, instead of only quantities, this useful discipline tried to also be scientific about qualities.

For example, gravity, as a number relationship between masses is fine, but when we try to be scientific about what it "feels" like to fall from a great height, we don't know what to do. Weightlessness, sky diving, bungee jumping - to have knowledge about that experience, we have to have that experience. Keep in "mind" that the effect of many qualitative experiences is to change us. In the debate between

Nature and Nurture hides a very special question. The human being becomes something out of those complex and rich life experiences of their individual biography that can never be measured, counted or turned into a number.

The whole history of modern science since the 1500's is about analysis and counting and measuring (and similar eliminations of the qualities of experience), such that by the early 20th Century Sir Arthur Eddington was to say: "We are on a path of knowing more and more about less and less." The details (quantities) grow exponentially, while the understanding of the whole (qualities) becomes lost in the avalanche noise of more and more theories, requiring greater and more costly experimental apparatuses. This has gone so far as to produce a claim that the physicists studying at the super-collider in Cern recently discovered the theoretically imagined "god particle". Materialistic science, having banished God from its considerations (no qualities), now wants to borrow that name/word to describe some extremely tiny "thing", which will illuminate all of existence in some fanciful way.

This confusion (quantities without qualities) then (having arisen over centuries) becomes embedded in the meanings of the very language we use, such that when a modern brain-scientist is born, and then educated, the language paradigm by which he is initiated into his discipline already bears within it decades and more of numerous unproven assumptions and logical errors of thought. These then have come to live in the very meaning of many individual words.

Take for example, the words: subjective and objective. The brain-scientist strives for objectivity, and shies away from his own mind, because of its assumed subjectivity. Unaware perhaps that about 200 years ago those two words meant the exact opposite of how we use them today.

Of course, few in science like to hear such points of view, which is why in recent years a debate has broken out between leading scientists and philosophers, where these scientists want to put forward the idea that they no longer need philosophy at all. A lot of the basics of this problem were exposed in the 1950's by Thomas Kuhn's little book: ***The Structure of Scientific Revolutions***. Kuhn wrote this book, when as a beginning scientist in physics, he decided to look to the history of the themes about which he wanted to do his Ph.D. He then discovered that the histories of science he had been taught were false. The reality is that science travels a kind of zig zag path, encountering dead ends and false conclusions, before finding a way to move forward again. The problem was that the history of science he had been taught was written as if the path was straight, and there were no mistakes that later needed being corrected.

We still get taught today this made-up straight line history, which is done as if to suggest that the scientific method always leads to surety of fact. We are taught of scientific theories as if they were inevitable, and no other conclusions were possible. But that has never happened in the history of science, ever. The result is a kind of system of religious-like "beliefs", such that if a "leading scientist" says it, the general public is likely to believe it is true. Sadly, there are a lot of mistakes still out there, haunting the world-view many wish us to believe.

Some of these false "paradigms" involve the brain-sciences, and many of these false paradigms have become hidden in the words we use everyday. As I suggested above, the problem is complex, and more examples will be given as we proceed.

~~~~~~~~

Brain-studies require (and exist in) a general contextual background, and it is important to recognize that this background can not really be framed in the way many believe. Take, for example, two main theories commonly assumed to be completely true (in the popular mind): Darwinian evolution and Big Bang cosmology. In the case of each of these, a philosophically trained (logically rigorous) mind finds many difficulties. Self-conscious *thinking* and *thought* illuminates important unanswered questions.

A significant essay on this problem, as regarding Darwinian evolution (such as survival of the fittest), can be found here: ***Dogma and Doubt***, by Ronald Brady. In this essay Brady explains precisely why Darwinian evolutionary theory fails as a workable/testable scientific theory, due to its lack of philosophical/logical rigor. The main issue has to do with the idea of speciation, which evolutionary theory attributes to natural selection. Somehow in the darkness of a past we can never directly empirically observe, an incredible variety of species came into existence, one species being formed out of the previous. The amoeba becomes the tadpole becomes the lizard becomes the rat becomes the monkey becomes the man.

Almost every necessary transitional species is missing from the geological record. The gaps are huge, and our failure to note this problem carefully and fully is a serious weakness for the theory. What Brady shows is that, as presently formulated, the idea of natural selection can't be tested. If it can't be tested, it can't be falsified; and, if it can't be falsified then it is useless as a theory from a philosophy of science point of view.

The geographical record is supposed to consist of several very long periods of evolutionary stasis - what is there at the beginning of a particular period, such as the Cambrian, is what is there at the end. In this same version of the theory, the gap between one long period and another long period is much smaller in time, and filled with tiny micro-organisms not nearly as complicated as those in the longer periods of stasis. In order to "explain" this, the "theory" asserts that extinction events took place, completely eliminating almost all of the previous flora and fauna. The name given to this is: *punctuated equilibrium*. A better name would be metamorphosis, and the reader of this can find that discussion in my 2010 book: ***The Art of God***: *an actual theory of Everything*. A fully awake thinking learns that the whole of the geographic record is an ordered sequence of successive instances of metamorphosis, as a consequence of the activity over eons by the living Being of the Earth.

And, in spite of this failure, the theory has become so universally treated as factual, that it has became a dogma that can't be questioned, and which is used everywhere in biology to explain all kinds of phenomena, without anyone ever looking behind the curtain and seeing that the wizard has no clothes. Anyone wanting to refute what is said here in this essay, must become familiar in all its details with Brady's work, so as to realize precisely what the rules of authentic philosophic inquiry require, in order to produce, at the least, a workable/testable theory.

Science is full of such assumptions, which start out as theories, only to become unquestioned religious-like dogmas, and from there enter into our common understanding of the world as if they were scientific fact, when they are not by any means able to stand before the disciplines regarding knowledge and truth, that is the responsibility of philosophy (a responsibility many academic philosophers do not fulfill).

Big Bang cosmology, as a theory, is of a whole other order than Darwinian evolution. In biology, the material is much more accessible. Prior ages have left fossils and bones, and the geographic record (the strata) can be touched and taken to a laboratory to be tested. The starry world is very far away, and the actual physical phenomena, which constitutes the evidence, is only light vibrations of various frequencies (from infra red to ultra violet), including all kinds of oddities such as "cosmic rays". We capture their effects via such inventions as photographic-like instruments and large antenna arrays, but unlike biological artifacts we can't go into the field and pick up star-stuff, and take it to the laboratory in order to empirical confirm our many hypotheses.

Even the idea of the nature of "space" itself needs to be reviewed, which I have done previously in my essay: ***The Misconception of Cosmic Space As Appears In the Ideas of Modern Astronomy*** - *and as contained in the understandably limited thinking embodied in the conceptions of the nature of parallax and redshift.* The current theory has probably less than 1% empirical facts as aspects of its truthfulness. Most of it is made-up ideas, as various scientists tried to guess at what happened, in ways whose main virtue was that they denied a religious creation explanation. The reality of the starry world is that "space" itself at cosmic distances is no longer three-dimension, but two dimensional. The sphere at infinity becomes a plane, in accord with the rules of projective geometry. Rudolf Steiner: "*Think on it: how the point becomes a sphere and yet remains itself. Hast thou understood how the infinite sphere may be only a point, and then come again, for then the Infinite will shine forth for thee in the finite.*"

Presently the Big Bang theory is under a lot of stress even among astrophysicists, who are still uncertain as to the implications of quantum experiments, super-collider data, string theory, and that holy grail of physics: "a theory of everything", which is hoped to explain the relationship of gravity, electro-magnetism, and other forces seemingly involved in the organism of the smallest particles. Even that theory requires us to believe that everything is made up of parts, something that we don't actually observe in Nature. Recent explanatory "inventions" such as dark matter and dark energy, may, like the mutation/monster idea used at one time to explain speciation in evolutionary theory, make up for the anomalous aspects of the evidence, but anyone who uses the internet to get into the specifics will find many arguments hidden away in various journals and other places where scientists and philosophers disagree out of sight of such main stream fairy tales as in the recent TV series Cosmos series, staring Neil DeGrasse Tyson. Here is a statement on some of the cosmological problems:

Redshift in the light from galaxies led to the belief that the universe is expanding, and this belief has persisted for 80 years. But modern observational evidence, especially from NASA European Space Agency space telescopes and satellites, has clouded the picture and raised many doubts. In 2004, an open letter was published in New Scientist magazine, and has since been signed by over 500 endorsers. It begins: "The big bang today relies on a growing number of hypothetical entities, things that we have never observed-- inflation, dark matter and dark energy are the most prominent examples. Without them, there would be a fatal contradiction between the observations made by astronomers and the predictions of the big bang theory. In no other field of physics would this continual recourse to new hypothetical objects be accepted as a way of bridging the gap between theory and observation. It would, at the least, raise serious questions about the validity of the underlying theory." [the original source page for this is no longer available: (http://cosmologystatement.org)]

A point worth remembering: The reason Darwinian evolution and the Big Bang are both called "theories" is because we don't have the capacity to go into even the near evolutionary past, and certainly not the deep past of the cosmos, and actually see, hear and measure what happened. We lack the ability to be empirical about our past - we can't go there. Seeing is believing is the cliche, and in this case we never see this past at all. The minds of scientists imagine this past into existence, and then sell us their most popular tales as if they were facts.

So we take the small bits of aspects of our present, and then weave stories about the past we cannot test, and top that off by forgetting the huge number of assumptions involved in making up these stories. Check out this for part of the underlying issues: **_Uniformitarnianism_**. You could not find a bigger assumption about the universe and nature than this one, which assumes all known facts today, about what are called constants, remain unchanged into the most extreme past and conditions of space and time. Gravity is assumed to be constant throughout all time, etc. Any serious observation of Nature reveals the opposite: Everything changes, nothing is fixed, which observation doesn't even deal with the fact that we cannot go into the past and empirically prove that these constants in fact are constant, or that the radiation used in carbon dating existed in this same unknowable past. These supposed constant forever constants and radiation dating ideas cannot be empirically proved. They are just assumed to be true.

One honest way to describe this situation is to remember that for about 400 years physics has been too busy taking things apart, eventually in some cases just by smashing them together to see what happens, meanwhile leaving aside from consideration anything that can't be counted or measured. The development of physics preceded the development of biology, which itself eventually led to brain-studies. Both fields are littered with unprovable assumptions. By the time the basic riddles, about consciousness and the nature of mind, got sufficient scientific attention, and given that only that which could be counted and measured was allowed any scientific meaning, students of consciousness, in order to act as if they were being scientific, had to perform experiments that produced quantifiable data.

Here is an article about a physicist who actually pays attention to philosophy: **_Physicist George Ellis Knocks Physicists for Knocking Philosophy, Falsification, Free Will_**

Yet, of all the objects possible for scientific study, what realm of life could be more filled with qualitative phenomena than consciousness. Philosophers even coined a term for these phenomena, calling them: qualia.

From Wikipedia

Qualia is a term used in philosophy to refer to individual instances of subjective, conscious experience. The term derives from the Latin adverb quālis, meaning "what sort" or "what kind". Examples of qualia are the pain of a headache, the taste of wine, or the perceived redness of an evening sky.

Daniel Dennett (b. 1942), American philosopher and cognitive scientist, writes that qualia is "an unfamiliar term for something that could not be more familiar to each of us: the ways things seem to us."

Erwin Schrödinger (1887–1961), the famous physicist, had this counter-materialist take: The sensation of color cannot be accounted for by the physicist's objective picture of light-waves. Could the physiologist account for it, if he had fuller knowledge than he has of the processes in the retina and the nervous processes set up by them in the optical nerve bundles and in the brain? I do not think so.

The importance of qualia in philosophy of mind comes largely from the fact that it is seen as posing a fundamental problem for materialist explanations of the mind-body problem. Much of the debate over their importance hinges on the definition of the term that is used, as various philosophers emphasize or deny the existence of certain features of qualia. As such, the nature and existence of qualia are controversial.

The problem is that the Nature we have been studying doesn't come in pieces, but in wholes and systems. The logical problems can be kind of silly, once they are pointed out. So, for example, a physicist might describe a tree as made up of very small objects which we cannot see. Meanwhile, over in biology, evolution is described as a completely random and accidental process which evolved eyes for the purpose of survival, but oh, by the way, no need for this survival goal to include seeing atoms. To the imaginary hand behind natural selection, the seeing of cosmic rays, or protons is not much use. This leads to a really interesting question from a philosophical point of view, that doesn't have an answer (yet). We need to see the tree, so we see the tree, and the tree is very much there whether or not we say it is made up of very small, invisible to the senses, parts. For some details, read my essay on parts and wholes and analysis and synthesis in the thinking about Nature, see: **<u>Electricity and the Spirit in Nature</u>**.

~~~~~~~~~

A big part of the problem regarding the brain has to do with the experience we name by the word: consciousness. For all that the brain-students study, they have not even gotten close to explaining what consciousness is, or how the matter of which the brain is made produces it. In point of fact, this basic un-answered question is so crucial, that it is mostly resolved by ignoring it. The central mystery/riddle has been replaced with the assumption that the brain miraculously produces consciousness, thoughts, and all other mental phenomena, of which there is a considerable variety. But as yet there is no model for how this wonder is accomplished, and certainly no testable theory for its daily miracle.

Just as with the dogma regarding speciation, that is the central problem in evolutionary biology, the brain-student lives with an unproven dogma that consciousness is produced by the material organ we call the brain. The brain experiments are many, but have a common problem because present day scientific disciplines requires simple kinds of quantifiable studies. So the brain-scientist flashes some pictures at people's eyes, seems to watch what happens in the brain with some kind of instrument, and then asserts certain logical conclusions must follow.

The sad fact is that the brain scientist is not watching what happens <u>in</u> the brain at all. He has no clue what is happening there. The very best data the instruments provide is that the brain is doing something in certain previously mapped regions. What it is doing is entirely a made up theoretical construct, for which no test has yet to be devised. It is just assumed that the brain produces/contains consciousness in the way all of us recognize ourselves as being conscious. But that "consciousness" is not seen at all.

We know we can interrupt consciousness. We can put the mind to sleep. We can poke an electrode into a region of the brain and stimulate a memory. We can study people where the links between the hemispheres are severed. We can study people where all kinds of brain injuries limit their speech or the other sense. We just can't directly observe the central acts of consciousness themselves. Everything is inferred. And, all inferences are based on the assumption that the brain must produce this "consciousness", which is an "object" that no instrument sees, ever.

Except for one. *There is one instrument which sees consciousness directly.* Our own mind. But the brain-student does not study his own presumed subjective conscious experience. The one tool he has for conscious awareness of consciousness itself is ignored. Instead the brain-scientist uses instruments which notice electrical and chemical activity in brain cells in various regions, and *with his own mind* he forges what he believes are logical links about what that means. Then he has a press conference and announces there is no free will, and his studies have proved it.

Even the fields of psychology and psychiatry tend to involve the study of the conscious minds of others, from the outside. Questions are asked. Polls are taken. Dialogue arises. The student of the psyche, who tries to heal injuries to that psyche, does so by asking questions; and, if he is any good at that discipline, the main thing the healer does is get the subject to become more awake inwardly to his own life of mind. Instead of telling the subject what to think, the healer of the psyche tries to induce that subject to think more clearly about their issues themselves. This kind of healing of the emotional complexities of the mind makes no logical sense at all unless the individual being helped is free to make changes in his own psychology. Otherwise verbally based healing arts are meaningless. If

there is no free will, and consciousness is the product of a large ball of meat, then all that therapy is not only pointless, it never should succeed.

The brain-scientist can't do that. He can't fix the psyche. Perhaps he can fix some dysfunction in the matter of the cells - the neurons - but appealing to the self-consciousness of the individual with the problematic psyche is not in his repertoire.

Now there is a kind of study, which deals with consciousness in a very exact way, but at the same time somewhat indirectly. This is the science of philology - or the study of the changes in the meaning of words over time. Just about everyone that is not confused by the brain-studies knows that language is a central element in the act of thinking. We do an inner wording which we label: discursive thinking. We talk to ourselves in our own mind - we ruminate, we obsess, we worry. And, thinking is one of the main actions that takes place in consciousness. Not only that, but by thinking in words, we also engage (or become aware of) concepts and what we call: Ideas. Our languages would not have these words: concepts and ideas, if there was not some degree of inwardly experienced reality that observed such mental phenomena. At the same time, we need to never forget that a brain-scan does not see either concepts or ideas. Only the "I" of the own mind perceives such ephemeral phenomena.

For example, even in brain-studies the scientist has to obtain the participation of the individual whose brain he wants to watch with his scientific instruments. The brain-scientist still has to use language to explain the meaning of the study to the object of his study, and then stimulates that persons mind. After which he then asks that person to use language to report what they observed themselves, in their own consciousness. So while the brain-scientist is making his studies, that process is entirely dependent on what the object of the study inwardly observes, how that subject choose to act or cooperate, and both aspects of the experiment are dependent on language - on the meaning of words - in order to have any relevant discussion. And, as philologists know well, "meaning" is a much more problematic matter than we ordinarily realize.

These facts are generally left out of the brain-scientists considerations. He assumes that he can divine the meaning of his experiments solely from an inferred relationship between what his instruments see as various kinds of light and warmth and chemical activity in the brain, and the imaginary "consciousness" whose actions he believes he is thereby observing. This is not logically or philosophically sound.

Meanwhile, the acquisition of language itself, in the growing and developing child also remains a mystery. Lots of theories, but no means yet to perform experiments that actually "see" this crucial development in human nature. Why can't we see it? Because it has this odd quality which is that consciousness is invisible to any outside observer. We can see (experience) our own, but any thoughts we have about the consciousness of another human being can only be inferred - they are not empirical or otherwise observed. That fact alone has not been given enough attention by the brain-scientists, which is a crucial lack from the point of view of the natural rules underlying any philosophically pragmatic and logical approach to knowledge.

~~~~~~~~

Let us, for a moment, recapitulate our situation, perhaps adding a few helpful nuances.

Four to five hundred years ago, natural science was born, originally called: natural philosophy. Philosophy already had existed for thousands of years, but with the advent of a change of "consciousness" in human nature in general, something arrived which a few thinkers and writers on this question called: the onlooker separation. The best source for this is the works of the thinker and philologist Owen Barfield (a member of the Inklings, with C.S. Lewis, J.R.R. Tolkein and Charles Williams).

Barfield observes the changes in the meaning of thousands and thousands of words - in many languages - over time, and then reasons these changes as revealing an underlying change in human nature at the level of what we call consciousness. This is called: the evolution of consciousness. While we generally recognize a physical evolution, we are yet not fully awake to an evolution at the level of consciousness, the very central problem/riddle for the brain-scientist. Barfield has written a number of well-recognized, thoughtful, and challenging books. For example, Barfield's book, ***Worlds Apart***, placed in imaginary conversation various disciplines of thought, such as: a lawyer with philological interests; a young man employed at a rocket research station; a professor of physical science; a retired school master; a biologist engaged in research work; a linguistic philosopher; and, a psychiatrist, which led T. S. Eliot to describe it as: "*An excursion into seas of thought which are very far from ordinary routes of intellectual shipping*". The title, Worlds Apart, gives an apt description of the struggle for members of these disciplines to find ways to even be in the same conceptual universe, much less find common solutions to crucial modern questions. It was Barfield's genius of spirit that enabled him to so accurately grasp this disconnect among separate intellectual disciplines, and then unveil the resulting confusion.

Before this change of consciousness, human beings felt themselves as participating in the world of Nature, not as separate from it. Barfield gives many many details here, so this really can't be questioned, unless we are willing to take up several years of study. The main effect for the brain-scientist is that this new knowledge, which Barfield and others produced during the 20th Century, is as yet mostly unknown to the brain-scientists. His university experiences trained him in his field of interest, but his "education" is not likely to have taught it the wider views living outside his field. Remember Eddington: "We are learning more and more about less and less".

Natural Philosophy, on its way to becoming natural science, begins (from an onlooker point of view) to take everything apart. Thus a changing evolving consciousness inaugurates the progressive effort to analyze down to the level of its smallest bits all sense objects (forms of matter), yet for a considerable time in the first couple of hundred years a religious or spiritual view remained. Our histories of science (remember Kuhn?) forget that Kepler was an astrologer, and Newton an alchemist. For a long time many early natural philosophers (scientists) were also believers in God. And, in the earliest days, the Church murdered natural philosophers if their views conflicted with Church dogma (Bruno was burned at the stake in 1600, and Galileo was forced to recant under the threat of torture and/or death).

A crucial juncture was reached around the years 1700 to 1730, when Newton and Leibniz argued about who invented the calculus, and what was the real nature of the smallest parts of matter. Newton was inclined to take the view that the smallest parts were inanimate (the "atom"), while Leibniz had the inclination to view these smallest parts ("monads") as having consciousness and will. For both the main difficulty was that matter, in the form of the human being (as well as animals), was *animated*. It got up, moved around and thought and spoke. An explanation for where that "animation" came from needed to be found.

In Ernst Lehrs' book ***Man or Matter***, (published in 1950), Lehrs points out that some forms of matter are "inert" (don't respond to being stimulated from the outside such as rocks) and other forms of matter are "alert" (react to being touched or stimulated).

While those questions appear to be settled for the main streams of science, especially modern physics and biology, the philosophical-logical problems remain.

For example, while current theories in Big Bang cosmology and Darwinian evolution conceive of that which is alive (alert) as having been built up of matter which was originally not alive (inert), we have no way to go back in time and empirically observe such processes. In fact, we can't find such a process anywhere in Nature today - a process whereby the living is derived from the lifeless. We only empirically observe, in presently manifesting Nature, processes whereby the living produces the lifeless.

For example, the growing and developing human being in the womb starts out alive (derived from living seed and egg), and only after a long time do the "bones" appear, which with age are more and more lifeless (stop growing and become very brittle), ultimately surviving death as ""inert" remains in burial sites. When we get wise enough, we will realize that the "living" earth has done the same thing (all rocks are extruded remains of a still living self-conscious organism existing on a planetary scale).

While some modern scientists strive to synthesize the living out of the non-living, they are doing that in a laboratory, and can nowhere point to where Nature does that as part of its normal processes. Evolutionary theory and empirical reality cannot be made to conform, which from a philosophical logical point of view, makes for a really serious problem for theory. If we are going to posit a creation process where inert matter produces alert matter, then we very much need to observe it, not just theorize (imagine) that everything had to happen that way, regardless of how many billions of years (we can't actually observe) were available.

Part of the problem, from the standpoint of the history of natural science since the 15th Century (as it arose from a change in human nature - consciousness - at that time), is that the process of analysis that arose, where physics spent a lot of time taking things apart, became more and more involved in the counting and numbering of "things", seemingly lacking consciousness themselves.

Mathematics became a powerful tool. As this tool became more dominant in the thinking of scientists (only what we can count has meaning), philosophy (with its inconvenient questions about "qualia") more and more took a back seat, as if it had nothing more to contribute. On the chessboard of science, the queen (mathematics) became more important than the king (philosophy), because the queen's powers were in a way more "sexy".

However, the rules of the game of rational inquiry require that the king - philosophy - is the essential piece, otherwise the game is lost if the king is made immobile - or checkmated. Remove philosophy from the board and science becomes religious - a system of dogmas and beliefs, rather than a system that is rational and logical. This is in fact the present state of natural science today. Everywhere dogmas, such as observed in Brady's article above, and most especially today in the completely unproven assumption that the material brain produces "consciousness", an invisible quality of human nature that scientific instruments cannot even detect, but which every human being knows directly and intimately.

Let us come at this once more, perhaps a bit more poetically. Art often "sees" the world in a way neither reason or faith can alone. I know I am somewhat repeating myself, but this basic picture is important to grasp from as many different points of view as possible.

The brain scientist swims in a sea of ideas, but doesn't notice them. He is born into this sea as he acquires language, goes to school, is raised and educated. The better his education (which is something different from mere training), the richer is his apprehension of the sea of ideas. Certainly he becomes familiar with specific kinds of individual concepts, and acquires some skill in their manipulation, something he needs in order to get his degree - the license which allows him to do research and earn a living at it. Specialized language, belonging to the discipline of brain-studies, is required in order to enter the temples wherein those arts of brain research on consciousness and thinking are celebrated.

The more trained and the less educated the individual brain-scientist is, the less rich is his ability to see the forest for the trees. He knows the neural landscape, but not the essence - the whole (for a wonderful "education" in how the part relates to the whole - to the _context_, go to **_The Nature Institute_**). The brain-scientist's discipline, by shunning an empirical self observation of his own consciousness, fails to notice the greater part. *"Imagination is more important than knowledge. For knowledge is limited to all we now know and understand, while imagination embraces the entire world, and all there ever will be to know and understand."* (Einstein)

Sure, ... we all know this greater part, for we have many names for it, such as "human nature" and "self understanding". But the brain-scientist, like many other scientists, is fascinated with trees (the brain cells) and comes to believe the whole - the forest - is just a complex collection of trees, without the whole being something very different in itself. Dogma and belief overwhelms reason, and the total modern paradigm built over the hundreds of years of the existence of natural science decrees in its queen-like power that all is matter, and there is no spirit. This vast sea of ideas (named by Plato, as one part of two realms: the material realm and the transcendent realm of forms.) is not noticed, for its patterns and currents (in the world of ideas) are ignored, while specialization focuses on the one object the brain-scientist assumes answers all questions: That the mind and the brain are one individual "thing" - a kind of living stuff, without any other feature. The fact that he directly himself observes the essential mystery (consciousness) in himself is forgotten. Why?

Fear.
In response, please allow me a brief rant (to be polemical):

Every human being knows they have dark places within. They know they lie and cheat and steal, and suffer and forget and experience loss and other terrors of life. But, the disciplines of the brain-scientists too has its holy grail, just as does the physicist with his worship of the "theory of everything". Take apart the brain-structures with enough care, they seem to believe, and all of human nature will then be explained. Some think to test for and find in the matter even the source of morality, which suggests - clearly - that one should also find there the source of immorality. Poppycock.

The disciplines of Natural Science are modern. They are no more than 500 years old, and many within that temple want to believe that all ancient peoples were stupid, did not know how to reason and just made stuff up to fill in the gaps. Only modern science can unveil the real "truth". More poppycock.

One of the ways we moderns are so much like our forebears is expressed in our hubris and our arrogance. Every Age believes it has arrived at Truth, which will be eternal for all time. What could be more arrogant than for the natural scientist to assert that he can tell us what actually happened billions of years ago, and billions of light years away in space and time. That faith in our own minds is hardly different at all from the same impulse we attribute to those who wrote the creation myths that everywhere survived from the deeps of time. We accused the ancients of inventing stuff, when (we assume) they could not explain what they experienced. Yet we do the same - when we don't know (can't empirically observe the past), we invent stuff, which we call "scientific theories", to fill in the gaps. Pray tell, what is the real difference between the great Myths of humanity and the grand Theories of modern natural science? If we read Barfield, he would explain these differences as arising from different kinds of consciousness, which have evolved parallel to all human development. The ancient Greek did not have a consciousness like ours, nor did the ancient Sumarian have a consciousness like the ancient Greek.

I am not my brain, whatever the brain-scientist with his dogmas and beliefs wants to assert. Everyday of life proves this to me, and I don't need some faceless group wearing white lab coats and torturing monkeys to tell me otherwise. They need to get some authentic "education", and rediscover what the ancient wise have always said: "oh man, know thyself".

The whole evolution of language, with all its open secrets, defies the assertion of some brain-scientists that there is no I - that self-consciousness is not real. The personal pronoun is everywhere, and even the brain-scientists could not get through a day without appearing essentially insane, if they didn't use: I, you, we, us, and so forth. It is totally hypocritical to assert there is no self, and yet go through life using the very aspects of language and grammar that have no meaning unless our perception of self is real. Human nature is not the stupid.

Such brain-scientists are like a new version of drug addicts, drunk on what they seem to conceive is some kind of special knowledge about human nature, when all they have done is lost sight of the vast integrated contexts in which all knowledge arises. Excessive knowledge of the details of parts consumes our wisdom/intelligence and makes us incapable of seeing anymore the whole.

What reality is there to quarks and muons and bits and pieces of stuff, that only appear in an experiment that smashes tiny bits of matter together at outrageous speeds - a process which Nature never uses. A flower does not need a super-collider to blossom.   And, the mind does not need neurons running fantasy quantum events in order to create poetry.

End rant.

The English language has the word "mind". At the time of Freud and his friends, when they were exploring the unconscious and other phenomena seeking to explain human behavior, ... - the Europeans, particular the Germans, used the words geistes (spirit) and seele (soul) to reference the "interior" life (consciousness territory) of human beings. Jung even posited that there was a collective or common aspect living in the unconscious - which had transcendent characteristics. In his book ***Freud and Man's Soul***, Bruno Bettelheim points out that when Freud's works were translated into English (in the 19th Century), even though English had both "spirit" and "soul" as words, those kinds of references in Freud were translated as "mind". We can call this a slight materialization of the idea of mind, one which moves away from any idea of spirit (transcendent form), and begins to more firmly root itself solely in matter.

As science developed further, during the 20th Century, the concept/term "mind" became even more materialized and was replaced, as it is today, with the concept/term "brain". As well, a kind of split arose in academia, whereby the physical scientist of the brain became less and less able to have a meaningful conversation with a psychologist, for the latter could not treat his patients unless he believed in the interior life and in the free will of the individual to grow and heal from emotional trauma. Arguments among some philosophers and brain-scientists have, at the same time, become more polarized.

For a delightful example of a passionate philosopher trying to deal with the various things scientists tells him must be true, some of which he fully believes (principally, that the brain produces consciousness), watch Professor John Searle : Consciousness as a Problem in Philosophy and Neurobiology - the lecture runs about 57 minutes: *https://www.youtube.com/watch?v=6nTQnvGxEXw*

In that lecture Searle refers to what he calls: dualism, and attributes to Descartes as being a prime exponent of this view of there being something other than matter, which might be called soul or spirit. Searle casually dismisses such a view, considering it obviously flawed and unreasonable. We could say that in the use of the word dualism in such a negative context, modern philosophers so inclined stepped fully into a materialistic explanation for "mind", i.e. that mind or consciousness had to clearly and obviously be product of the biology of the brain. This was to be the only conclusion possible.

All of this was connected to a tendency in biology to only see material causes for all aspects of the phenomena we call "life", eventually resulting in the present-day conception that the human being is only matter, and never spirit. In a way, what was known to the explorers of the unconscious as an interior aspect of human nature (the territory) became then over time something that was itself a kind of illusion produced by a material "brain" (the map).

The reader needs to realize that above is very superficial. Books could be written, and have, which go into great detail providing a solution to the problem of dualism. Their main present-day feature is that they are little known outside of small circles, where individuals are more open to spiritual truths and practices. In effect there has arisen a kind of counter-Copernican revolution, involving the Romantics and the Transcendentalists, and now Rudolf Steiner's Anthroposophy (c.f. **_Man or Matter_**, by Ernst Lehrs; **_History in English Words_**, Owen Barfield; **_Art and Human Consciousness_**, Gottfried Richter). Barfield even wrote a book about Anthroposophy, called: **_Romanticism Comes of Age_**.

Let us remind ourselves here: The brain-scientist does not see thoughts or consciousness. These are invisible to his instruments. Only the sometimes presumed illusory individual-self knows consciousness and thoughts directly. A very important point to recognize here is that the brain-scientist too has an interior life (a territory), and seeks to explain that territory by creating a complex map, which, whatever else it may do, remains only a kind of outer surface. The reality of a real territory - an "interior" - is trying to be denied. Again, why?

One way to answer that question is to see that there is a kind of war going on at the leading edges of science, between a fully materialistic conception of a human being, and a more humanistic/spiritual conception. Perhaps this war is between abstract thinkers, and intuitive feelers. The former are more disconnected, and the latter seek out connection. What the humanist might call "I and Thou", the abstract intellect sees only as "things" and "its".

A good example is the difference in their relationship with Nature, between aboriginal peoples and modern peoples influenced by natural science. Nature has no interior for the latter, while it has a transcendent interior for the former.

~~~~~~~~

The strange/funny aspect of all this is that the disconnected abstract thinker also has children and spouses, and co-worker relationships. Does he treat his family and colleagues as things and its? As if they were not persons, but only the product of a piece of meat called a brain, however complex? What kind of politics does a piece of meat have?

We have some interesting language phrases that are illuminating here. Someone might say: "I have a gut feeling", possibly meaning they trust their intuitive connected thoughts. While another might say: "Its only in my head", meaning they doubt the abstract disconnected thought.

To bring this into a more concrete situation here, let us describe and contemplate recent brain-scientist experiments that are alleged to prove there is no free will. The below in italics is from Wikipedia, and I have inserted a small comment inside [brackets]:

Neuroscience of free will refers to recent neuroscientific investigation of questions concerning free will. It is a topic of philosophy and science. One question is whether, and in what sense, rational agents exercise control over their actions or decisions. As it has become possible to study the living brain, researchers have begun to watch decision making processes at work. Findings could carry implications for moral responsibility in general. Moreover, some research shows that if findings seem to challenge people's belief in the idea of free will itself then this can affect their sense of agency (e.g. sense of control in their life). ...

... Relevant findings include the pioneering study by Benjamin Libet and its subsequent redesigns; these studies were able to detect activity related to a decision to move, and the activity appears to be occurring briefly before people become conscious of it. Other studies try to predict a human action several seconds early. Taken together, these various findings show that at least some actions - like moving a finger - are initiated unconsciousl ["unconsciously" is a curious term to use here], *at first, and enter consciousness afterward.*

In many senses the field remains highly controversial and there is no consensus among researchers about the significance of findings, their meaning, or what conclusions may be drawn. It has been suggested that consciousness mostly serves to cancel certain actions initiated by the unconscious, so its role in decision making is experimentally investigated. Some thinkers, like Daniel Dennett or Alfred Mele, say it is important to explain that "free will" means many different things; these thinkers state that certain versions of free will (e.g. dualistic) appear exceedingly unlikely, but other conceptions of "free will" that matter to people are compatible with the evidence from neuroscience.

"Unconsciously" above, as an observation, comes from the fact that scans detect neural activity before the individual in the experiment reports to the research scientist that they have made a choice of some kind of which they were "self-aware". The reasoning seems to be, that if the brain is active first in time, before the "individual"(?) reports a choice (second in time), that the brain (the matter by "itself") is the initiating cause and the seemingly self-aware individual is in one way or another out of the causal loop. On occasion, in some experiments, the measure of the "gap" in time is only milliseconds.

Keep in mind that we are not actually observing the highly complex mental (brain?) activity of someone driving a car in traffic, or making love. The brain-scientist has to make his experiments very simple, such as asking someone to move a finger. Hidden in plain sight in the experiment is the assumption that the only causal element is the brain in some way or another. Consciousness is assumed to be rooted in the material brain, and that view is hardly questioned any more at all, except in some odd corners of philosophical inquiry. Not only that, but whatever "individuality" turns out to be, that too is rooted in the brain.

Part of the offered explanation is that because there are billions and billions of neurons and pathways, this complexity itself somehow has to make for how consciousness works. Keep in "mind" that there is no evidence for this, it is just assumed to be true, and has resulted in borrowing all kinds of computer terminology to use as metaphors for "brain" activity. The brain stores memories like a hard drive. The mind runs sub-routines to carry out bodily activity. The wet-ware - the brain - has hard wired software provided by millions of years of evolution. In the near future, we will be able to upload our individual memories and consciousness to computer storage, and live in essentially immortal robotic bodies (the singularity).

When I first encountered this philosophical/religious/scientific question in the late 1980's and early 1990's, I read a lot of neuroscience and cognitive science. It was very clear in these readings that the mind/body dualism problem had been bascially set aside, although at that time, the '80's and '90's, scientists seemed to still notice that this conclusion that consciousness was rooted in the material brain was a working assumption. Since those decades, I no longer encounter any recognition of the assumption character of this conception   For details, see my essay ***The Idea of Mind***: *a Christian meditator considers the problem of consciousness.* That consciousness is rooted in the material brain has, as with Darwinian evolution and speciation, become a unchallenged dogma in these fields of inquiry.

The basic working assumption in modern experiments then is that if the scans of the brain showed activity before the individual reports it, the brain - the matter - is somehow itself "acting". Few other causal views are argued or considered. Forgotten, almost always, is the fact that the brain scan does not actually see either thought or choices or consciousness itself. That the brain is assumed to be the seat of these common human experiences is apparently no longer questioned.

To repeat, for this is important. Brain activity in certain already "mapped" regions is observed with a device. Then the individual reports that they made a choice. The actual choice, or what really inwardly happened within consciousness, when the brain activity was observed, is not seen. Not seen, but inferred; and, inferred in accord with the unproven, now dogmatic, assumption that consciousness is rooted in a physical material organ.

As this will naturally be asked, let me offer a very brief and different "explanation" for what the brain scientist sees:

First recall that if we move our mind's attention toward a hand, this additional attention will cause warmth to arise in that hand. Blood flow also can be increased by moving our attention's focus to a single part of the body. Now picture the possibility that "spirit", a transcendent feature of consciousness, moves free of the body ... hovers around it in a kind of way, but not in physical space. So when tasked (or stimulated) this "spirit/attention" uses the brain as an interface between its normal non-spacial realm and the physical realm, much like imagined in the film Avatar, when the consciousness of an individual is moved from their body to the manufactured body. As this "spirit/attention" is drawn toward the physical brain on the way to achieving the task which the research scientist asked the "I" (or spirit) of the experimental subject to do, the spirit/attention dips into the matter in the region of the brain previously mapped as habitually used for certain tasks. Also keep in "mind" the speeds at which this all happens. There is an important riddle hidden in that fact.

This "dipping in" is what the brain-scientist's instrument sees - the natural warming due to the movement of the attention, drawing the blood into that region. The subject was also asked to report to the research scientist when they accomplished the asked for task. This is actually a second task, and requires of the subject that they become active in the region of the brain associated with speech. There are then two tasks, one the action and the second the report.

Now in order to accomplish the first task, the inward (in the territory of consciousness) activity of the subject is an inner action of which they are not likely to be consciously aware. Why? Because the attention was not tasked with ***watching itself*** act out the first task. Only to ***do*** the first task - not to watch itself do the first task. In a few paragraphs we will take a brief look at those disciplines that deal with the task of self-watching, a rather peculiar inner activity, which is not normally done. Doing and watching-doing are two different acts. Anyway, it is the time gap between the doing and the reporting that is observed by the research scientist. The brain itself never "acted". Only the "I" or spirit acted, using the brain as an interface between its non-physical realm and the physical realm.

What is then not "seen", or understood, is that the unconscious aspects of this are just that: unconscious. That term only means that the cognitive-self does not notice what it does instinctively, because it is more focused on the doing, than on the watching-itself doing. This pretty well describes a great deal of the activities in which we engage, which Searle's lecture seeks to portray in this question: How does this consciousness act in the physical world? But the sea of ideas in which nearly everyone swims today, only conceives of the "animation" of the "alert" matter of the body as accomplished by the brain-organ of the physical body itself. There is no other "actor", as when Freud used the older terms for mind: soul and spirit.

Arguments at this level could go on forever, and most philosophers don't even know the relevant ideas described just above, which can be used as an alternative explanation. Thus, even many philosophers are trapped in the endlessly repeating argumentative nature of the discussions, as evidenced in the previous Wikipedia article, with its last comment repeated, here:

In many senses the field remains highly controversial and there is no consensus among researchers about the significance of findings, their meaning, or what conclusions may be drawn. It has been suggested that consciousness mostly serves to cancel certain actions initiated by the unconscious, so its role in decision making is experimentally investigated. Some thinkers, like Daniel Dennett or Alfred Mele, say it is important to explain that "free will" means many different things; these thinkers state that certain versions of free will (e.g. dualistic) appear exceedingly unlikely, but other conceptions of "free will" that matter to people are compatible with the evidence from neuroscience.

Perhaps something is missing. Perhaps we are confused precisely because we can't be other than confused (the snake of the raw intellect eats its own tail). Perhaps, in throwing out dualism (the mind/body distinction), we threw out the baby with the bathwater.

~~~~~~~~~

What is missing is a recognition of the real implications of the fact that to each actor in this play - whether scientist or philosopher or experimental subject - all have a direct experience of consciousness itself. The very complexity of the "object", the brain-scientist is unable to measure with his scans and instruments, is visible to every human being. What does not happen is an investigation of this territory, which is not an aspect of the very limited brain-map - actual consciousness is far more complicated than the structures of the brain. So, an old question resurfaces ... dualism is back, but perhaps a Way past its prior difficulties has been found.

Here we get to something rather remarkable, because the fact is that human beings have been studying their own consciousness for millennia. This embarrassment of riches, however, is a problem for the brain-scientist, because it defies the underlying assumption of mainstream science, in that these riches perceive not just matter, but what has to be called spirit as well.

Here are some names: Yoga, the Tao - or Way of Lau Tzu, Tibetan and Zen Buddhism, Kabbalah, Sufism, Gnosticism, Tarot, Alchemy, Rosicrucianism, Hermeticism, Hermetic Christianity, Romanticism, Transcendentalism, and Anthroposophy. Go to any serious New Age store, or any store or library with a wide selection of "spiritual" books, and its all there. Studies of human inner life - or "consciousness", with all manner of ways of understanding and practices in which the individual student can engage.

These do not all agree on the details. Some even claim to be non-theistic (i.e. no need for the idea of God). Yet, all posit a aspect of consciousness that is transcendent of matter. Why are these "sciences" of consciousness, that work with the actual territory and not the maps, ignored? This is a really good question.

Owen Barfield, in his book ***Speaker's Meaning*** suggests that the minds of modern Western educated scientists encounter, in their fields of interest, contemporary kinds of taboos. If scientists, working in evolutionary biology or big bang cosmology, are forced somehow to admit that there might be matter *and* spirit, then all those theories have to be rethought. The huge theoretical edifice of modern materialistic natural science gets a very big flat tire - several in fact. A scientist who offers a spiritual explanation will risk being shunned within his own community.

What is at stake here?

Basically, the truth. If science is no longer interested in the truth, then it has just become another religion competing with other religions. If it is the truth that scientists desire, then any competing theory, even one which posits spirit as real, has to be on the table. The discussion has to shift, and the cutting edge of that need to shift is in the brain-sciences, for here a kind of natural limit in the search for knowledge has been reached.

You cannot, without being a complete hypocrite, ignore the fact that consciousness is only visible to the individual (the map is not the territory), and that this territory has already been studied by individuals, successfully, for thousands upon thousands of years.

What is also funny/strange/odd is that the same limit was encountered by physics during the 20th Century, when it had to start to consider the possibility that "consciousness" participated in the shaping of quantum events. Scientific materialism has run into the limits of the possibilities it has created for the "explaining" of the world - and that limit is this still unanswered question: What actually is consciousness and how do we come to scientific knowledge of its real nature and actual influence.

Outer space is very far away. But inner space is not. Dare the brain-scientists go where none of them seem to have gone before? A territory well explored for hundreds of centuries? Aspects of the whole future of human existence may well depend on getting this one right

As someone who has empirically studied their own mind for four decades, I can assure you it is an adventure well worth taking. There are in fact, real maps to the territory, that can help the introspective investigator begin his journey. Here is just one example, Rudolf Steiner's book: ***The Philosophy of Spiritual Activity***, which has the sub-title: "*some results of introspection following the methods of natural science.*" This is a much better map to the territory, than that produced by brain-scientists, because it actually accepts the basic existential fact that consciousness is an open book to each individual that has the courage to take up the task, and observe empirically what stands within himself (again, the ancients: know thyself).

A few brief observations/conclusions, from my own investigations of the territory of the mind as inspired by Steiner's various "maps":

Thinking (spiritual activity) can observe its after effects in the consciousness (the soul), and thereby come to self-knowledge through empirical self-observation. Consciousness is a kind of mirror of thinking's spiritual nature. Not all thoughts arise by our own efforts of will, but this un-willed territory too can be observed by its effects, and was previously named the unconscious.

The self-conscious thinking (concept creation) can be studied and developed like any other willed activity. Skill can become Craft can become Art. Its main will-components are the *act of attention* and the *act of intention*. That is, toward what object of thought do I direct my thinking activity (the attention), and for what reason (moral or otherwise) do I engage in that act of thinking (the purpose or the intention). The content which the method of conscious intentional thinking produces will be observed to vary according to how and in what way I vary the attention and the intention.

Awake thinking has a variety of modes, or ways of operation. These include, but are not limited to: organic thinking, pure thinking, reflection, theorizing, figuration, comparative thinking, associative thinking, picture thinking, imaginative thinking, concrete thinking, abstract thinking, warm thinking, cold thinking, thinking-about, thinking-with, thinking-within and thinking-as. The mind is an instrument which we can learn to play, and many acts of thinking can be accomplished as a kind of harmonic cord of more than one mode simultaneously.

Aspects of this play of the instrument of the mind also have to take account of feelings, or moods that can go with or otherwise drive the modes of thinking. These include: sympathy, antipathy, pain, pleasure, anger, fear, love, joy, sadness etc. Moods can also be cultivated, not just reactive (spontaneous and undisciplined). Cultivated moods include such as awe and reverence. Moods and modes can be observed working in concert, sometimes like the resonant harmonies that arise in other objects, when some particular instrument produces the primary tone.

All of this means that the qualia, which many philosophers accept, but can't yet figure out how to approach scientifically, can be investigated empirically via the skills, crafts, and arts of self-aware thinking, which I call elsewhere: The Rising of the Sun in the Mind***, or **_Sacramental Thinking_**. "Sun" in this instance needs to be seen in the way Rudolf Steiner tried to describe our Sun. Our Sun is a kind of emptiness in physical space, a kind of hole as it were. It is a place that is not there in physical space at all. What is there is concentrated ethereal space - the kind of space at the cosmic periphery where light and life are created. What we see as the physical "Sun" is the boundary conditions where at the "edges" of the spherical hole in physical space, light and life creation forces abound, arising from concentrated ethereal space, which is of such a qualitative nature that cosmic spiritual Beings can find a home there.

[***For anyone wanting some a more personal and self-directed approach to these questions, I have created an app-like web page: _"The Rising of the Sun in the Mind"_.]

A curious fact to keep in mind about the Sun, well known to physics, is that the Sun-body itself is not as hot as the "space" surrounding the Sun. The Sun surface (described above as the boundary condition of the transition from the physical to the ethereal) is about 6,000 degrees F. Meanwhile the "space" surrounding the Sun is one to two million degrees F. The frying pan is considerably hotter than the fire. This is one of those huge anomalies physics ignores, because it is so inconvenient to its current theories about the physical Sun.

The Rising of the Sun in the Mind then is the creation/opening of a hole in the mind-space, where the peripheral or "edge-like" conditions allow light and life forces to arise before the inner eye of the self-consciousness. Tradition calls this inner eye the third-eye, but it is not a physical eye - it is a spiritual eye. At the same time, this inner eye is creative - it makes thought. It draws/invents thought out of the realm of timeless and spaceless conditions, through the state of pure ethereal space, into the "place" of physical space, ultimately descending into the words in discursive thinking, and then into speech. It is also not "dramatic", but you might say: just the opposite. It is subtle and delicate. It is where the still small voice can speak. Where angels offer their insights, in tune with the quiet slow-motion and soundless beating of butterfly wings.

It is: **_Living Thinking_**. It uses the brain stuff in order to interact with the physical world. But it is not itself physical. The true I is not the brain. It is pure spirit, like the wind as described by John in his Gospel: "_What's born of the flesh is flesh, and what's born of the breath is breath. Don't be amazed because I told you you have to be born again. The wind blows where it will and you hear the sound of it, but you don't know where it comes from or where it goes; it's the same with everyone born of the breath_". John 3: 6-8. The soundless sound. The lightless light. The spaceless space. The lifeless life, the deathless death, and the timeless time, or ... the Eternal Now, where it is always: In the Beginning
~~~

There is a great deal more that is reported in the mostly little known modern literature on the territory of consciousness, and its major components: thinking, feeling and willing. See my website **_Shapes in the Fire_** for details, as well as references to the works of others.

~~~~~~~~~

Some additional links:

A current article on Near Death Experiences in Salon

An article on why the math shows that thought cannot be encoded in a computer

~!~!~!~!~!~!~!~!~

Is the brain a computer? Is the mind the brain?

Cowboy Bebop
and the physics* of thought as moral art

[*The term physics is here meant to suggest a set of general rules and processes that in part can be labeled: the Way of a science of thought and thinking. That thought and thinking are also moral and artistic then too becomes part of a true "physics" of thought. This means that the three sciences, art, and religion cannot actually be separated, as they form in the soul an organic whole.]

*

Cowboy Bebop (1) was a Japanese anime television show that was also made into a movie. It was short lived(1998-99), and critically acclaimed. The main character was a bounty hunter working from Mars in the year 2071. Many sequences in this very original animation were accompanied by music often dominated by a jazz and blues background. From the beginning this anime was a fusion of American cultural influences and modern Japanese artistic sensibilities.

In a certain way this work of art carried both instinctive esoteric Christian and instinctive Zen components, which to elaborate might take a whole book, and therefore will not be attempted here. The Cowboy motif fits in with the fact that the Western is the main mythical archetype of the American Soul (2), and the use of jazz and blues rests the musical themes within the creative heart/roots of American music, fostered mostly out of the culture New Orleans.   In fact, many of the sequences or scenes in the show are basically spontaneous dance. Feet and limbs often move to the underlying jazz and blues bebop of the music.

The visual artistic style is very modern in a Japanese sense, as are the ideas which positive criticism has come to recognize, such as: philosophical concepts including existentialism, existential ennui, loneliness, and the past's influence (1), again). The main character's morality is very much of the Western cowboy type - the lone stranger doing good while entirely uncertain as to his own meaning in the great schemes of existence. The dialog is clever, philosophical and pointed, in the same fashion as the American film-noir movies that were common in the late 1930's and on into the early 1950's. (3)

These undercurrents within the American Soul influence the path of thought-creation in Americans. These undercurrents arise from the whole world in a way - each emigrating culture adding its distinct influence to the whole. In America is being born the People of Peoples. Cowboy Bebop is a good modern expression of certain undercurrents that have greatly influenced the American Soul, beginning with the Western in the 1920's, and then later in the 1950's when Zen was brought to our shores in California by Alan Watts (4). California then became a kind of stew pot of soul-themes, such that West and East met at that edge of the North American continent and had cultural intercourse.

If we want to look for evidence of this subterranean influence of cultures, we need go no further than the writings of the modern crime novelists: Robert Parker and Elmore Leonard. Their dialogue is crisp and spare, zen-like in wisdom. Their characters are the stranger-other - the Cowboy archetype who rescues damsels in distress and lays down his/her life to do the right thing.

That the heroes themselves are flawed, even criminal, really only points to the fact that in America the soul also can take a path near and through the Underworld - the ancient world of Faerie, and dark and dangerous impulses. America is the world's most earthly culture, and this density of fallen striving and suffering should not really surprise anyone paying attention to social phenomena in America.

Not all Paths of development wander among the stars and the clouds. The American Soul gave birth, with the aid of Christ and the Holy Mother, to <u>the Twelve Steps of Alcoholics Anonymous</u> in 1933, which is the most practical spiritual path for dealing with the threefold double complex, or the shadow in the soul. (5) Addictions and their kin are not the only issues human beings may solve in the company of others with similar flaws. The hungers for wealth and power can be addictions. So can be lying - how many of us know the individual whose every word is an exaggerated tale told to advance their image, and impress their acquaintances.

The point of the immediately above is to set a tone for what is to follow, for it will be useful and practical to understand from what well of wisdom do such writers as Parker and Leonard draw their art.

Let us examine this carefully …
Thought exists. Everyone knows this. Ordinary mind also is often naturally virtuous, and the below is what can be understood if one makes a study of ordinary mind, in a scientific and empirical fashion.

The brain scientist, never actually examining the intimacy of his own mind, does not understand the art of how to come to an empirical knowledge of thought. To know thought, through thinking, we must investigate the own mind. But this journey is rooted in the challenges of the moral. It requires the encountering of life-trials. There is no substitute for this is very personal investigation, which is often costly in terms of suffering.

We are dark <u>and</u> light, which fact makes any exploration of the basics of the life of the own thought dependent upon an excruciatingly moral self-honesty.

Not everyone needs to do this on purpose. The modern biography, particularly in America which is at the cutting edge of the evolution of consciousness, is itself a spiritual developmental Path. (6) The life-trials of the biography lead to a natural spiritual development. The main difficulty is an absence of the needed language to describe this fact of existence. Anthroposophy can provide to modern culture this language of the Consciousness Soul era if we tease apart the traditional reliance on the dead thoughts of Rudolf Steiner, entombed in books and in the tragic overuse of Steiner <u>said</u> (note the use of the <u>past</u> tense of that verb). Steiner is well worth quoting, but to rely on him as an authority is to violate his own stated wishes.
Anthroposophists must discover how to think for themselves, outside the past utterances of Rudolf Steiner.

That religious and moral metaphors might be practical could be denied by many seeking an operating manual of the mind. The truth is otherwise, however, for the journey begins here with the "washing of the feet". The higher elements of thinking cannot be consciously known other than by actions in the spirit-mind that are profoundly moral. To unveil the secrets of the will-in-thinking begins and ends with appreciating the nature of the "intention" (or purpose) from which the thinking is born - or, the Why of the How.

These moral/heart forces are the only way in which the cold and arid, almost lifeless, thinking of the intellect alone can be mastered. The intellect is brilliant, but not wise. Obviously we are a mixture of light and dark. But to better understand the light we have to also appreciate the dark.

Washing the feet means thinking must be put in the service of the Thou. Thought which is self-directed, and meant to only benefit ourselves, will lack the warm clarity and strength to find anything other than superficial meaning. The cold thinking of the intellect alone - without the guidance of the heart - leads only to the error of misunderstanding. For thinking to find the truth it must sacrifice personal consequences for those results which are meant to benefit others.

The striving for empathy already is washing the feet. It is very important to realize that the biography itself, especially in and among Americans, does this naturally. Here is Rudolf Steiner, from a lecture to the workmen, on 3 March 1923:

"The time will one day come when this American woodenman, which actually everyone is still - when he begins to speak. Then he will have something to say very similar to European Anthroposophy. One can say that we in Europe develop Anthroposophy in a spiritual way; the American develops it in a natural way."

This natural development happens because American social-cultural forces tears the individual away from its original language and cultural roots. We speak of a third generation American, for example. Our parents may come to America bringing with them their cultural past, but generation by generation this past dies away, and the "individual" emerges. This is true even of the so-called: Native Americans. Individuation will triumph, and tradition will fade away.

The same process of development also arises because the family and community matrix too is falling apart. Elsewhere in the world what Steiner called the group-soul tends to rule, and the individual bows to those social forces that define group behavior as against individual and independent of family and community life choices. Growing up in America takes away our cultural and language past, strips us of the normative rules governing families, and spits us out into the modern world forced to stand on our own. Natural here does not mean painless.

This is not an easy course of life, and once freed of the past of our ancestors the washing the feet trial is only the beginning. Ultimately we will travel all of the Seven Stages of the Passion of Christ: washing the feet; the scourging; the crowning with thorns; the carrying of the Cross; the crucifixion; the entombment; and finally, the resurrection. Each of these is an exact metaphorical archetype of the various arts of thinking in the fullness of soul and spirit, and their related trials in life.

Christ warned us: Matthew 10:34-40:

"Don.t think I came to cause peace across the land. I didn;t come to cause peace, I came to wield a sword, because I came to divide a man against his father and a daughter against her mother and a bride against her mother-in-law, and to make a man's servants his enemies. Whoever prefers father or mother over me is not worthy of me; and whoever prefers son or daughter over me is not worthy of me; and whoever does not take his cross and follow after me is not worthy of me. Whoever found his life will lose it, and the one who lost his life because of me will find it. Whoever receives you receives me, and whoever receives me, receives my Sender.?

Not only that, but these trials do not confine themselves to linear time - that is, they do not follow one after the other in sequence. In the same way a plant lives in an ecology, the life of soul and spirit - in the biography - lives in a psychological and mental ecology of social existence, in which various events (trials) arise and become the center of our lives. The social, with respect to the biography, provides both inertia and momentum. Life resists us, while at the same time certain impulses and actions propel us onward.

For example, to become a mother or a father places before the soul the trial of the washing of the feet in a quite natural fashion. Parenthood creates a necessity, and the "I" in responding to this necessity can begin to learn to put the other - the Thou - before self. In the same biography, family conflicts exist over life choices and meaning - do we do what our parents want us to do, or do we follow our own star - the unfolding of this trial of individuation in our family life will evoke scourging and crowning with thorns. Details will be described below.

These stages then do not always appear in sequence. Different life experiences draw them out, although over time, the general pattern produces a transformation of the artistic skill level of thinking, which starts as a natural skill, then (usually with maturation) becomes craft, and then finally wisdom or art. Maturation, by the way, is not a given. Many there are who never develop past late (early 20's) adolescence. When such a person becomes a political or corporate leader, disasters happen.

The mystery of thinking is then trained by the moral struggles in life - not just the successes but the failures as well. All experience can be turned to developmental nourishment when the "I" reflects on its actions. The intention behind thought determines the nature of the realm of the thought-world in which we travel. This intention is instinctive (natural) in the beginning, becoming more and more conscious over time. The path, which we in anthrposophical circles conceive of as a path of development, for the American (and others all over the world at this same leading edge of the Consciousness Soul) occures in the biography. We do not have to go to the Swiss Alps to engage it. We just live our life, for it is - through Divine Intention - the very best School possible.

Recently I was saying some related words to my girl friend, and she wanted me to take the time for a more careful and somewhat formal illumination of the nature of thought. What follows next is based in large part on her notes to that conversation, which mostly consisted of me making an attempt at an skeleton-like organized presentation, which on occasion was inspired by questions she asked me during this verbal intercourse. These notes give order to what follows next ... and flesh has been added to the observations of structure alone.

The plane or arena of matter is bound to space and time. You can't put your hand through matter. That's how we know its exists. Two cars crash into each other on a highway, and the violence is so powerful it crushes steel and human flesh, perhaps bringing death in its train of causes and effects.

We live in a physical body and act in a material world. We also act in the non-material world of thought and thinking. This non-material life survives death.
Above the plane of matter is the plane of soul, or consciousness. This "astral plane" (to use a more ancient form of expression) is bound to space, but not to time. It is also the plane of perishable or mutable spirit. We know this realm when we use picture thinking or the imagination. The imagination needs "space" in order to appear before our mind's eye. It is, we should note, not three-dimensional, but plane-like, or two dimensional. We can move around its surfaces and sometimes right through it, but it remains in essence an arena of organic (living) thought that longs to be investigated and known directly.
For now we see through a glass, darkly; but then face to face: now I know in part; but then shall I know even as also I am known.

In the final episode of Season One of the television show Joan of Arcadia, the God character there says: "You have to trust the world behind your eyes", and, "learn to see in the dark"
.

Our biographies do not take place, in general, when we are alone (although a prisoner and a monk or a nun, often live lives of virtual isolation). We live as members of a community. As we grow into the truthful possibilities of our thinking, we may often find ourselves needing to speak truth in circumstances where others do not like it. In order to avoid what this truth has to mean to them, they will deflect, or act angry or many other forms of finding a way to ignore what we have said or done (based on what <u>we</u> "thought", independent of the cultural or social norms).

This deflection can often take the form of attacking the truth-speaker, and this is experienced by the truth-speaker as a scourging - the own soul experiences a trial of emotional (astral) pain. Where someone confronts a gossip, for example, in a community that likes the false content of the gossip, the whole group may turn upon the person who challenges these lies. Everyone who seeks to speak or act on the true and the good experiences such trials, even though we yet have no vocabulary in our shared social existence that recognizes this fact.

On a wider social scale, we have today what is called "political correctness", which are ways of individual doing or speaking that large portions of the social body do not like. Modern social-media allows scourging of this kind to apply a huge unjustified condemnation of acts or words of specific individuals. This public shaming is the problem of the mote and the beam writ large, forgetting the admonition: he who is without sin, let him cast the first stone.

Matthew 7: 3-5: Judge not, that ye be not judged. For with what judgment ye judge, ye shall be judged; and with what measure ye mete, it shall be measured to you again. And why beholdest thou the mote that is in thy brother's eye, but considerest not the beam that is in thine own eye? Or how wilt thou say to thy brother, Let me pull out the mote out of thine eye; and, behold a beam is in thine own eye? Thou hypocrite, first cast out the beam out of thine own eye; and then shalt thou see clearly to cast out the mote out of thy brother's eye.

Everywhere that we see social conflict, we see those naturally occurring trials that for some individuals are best described in the metaphors of the Seven Stages of the Passion of Christ. When the I-am is authoring what it can of the Christ-Impulse, this produces social conflict - social strife and heat. Not peace, but a sword.

The mental plane, or sphere of pure thought (or spirit), is spaceless and timeless. We are an active creator in this sphere, and through a thorough study of this capacity to create thought there comes to be one of the best Ways we can learn to understand thought's properties and nature - however, only if we are so inclined. It is not necessary for everyone to do this, and in fact the understanding of such facts is the point of any science of thought or thinking. The scientist of thought makes the journey and then shares that understanding with others.

Rudolf Steiner writes in the first sentence of the First Leading Thought: "Anthroposophy is a path [Way] of knowledge [cognition] from the spiritual in man [the human being] to the Spiritual in the Universe."

Human beings create thought, but we are not usually conscious of this creative activity. When we create thought we are active ourselves as a spaceless and timeless spirit in the realm of the uncreated and formless. As thought then descends from this formless state, it takes on form, ultimately descending into the words that comprise our languages. To be intuitive, in the sense of Zen for example, is to always be awake in the creative act that results in the flow of thoughts. That's why it is difficult to get "Zen", because its locus is outside the realm of "naming", so the Zen masters speak of "no-mind" or "no-name". (7)

Thought is also living. In the arena of the "astral", where the imagination resides, organic thought as spirit is clearly perishable and mutable, for unless we maintain the mental picture with our conscious intention and attention it fades away. That Goethe came to perceive the Ur-plant shows that he eventually entered the realm of the timeless and spaceless and met a Being, through the gate of recreating, in the imagination, the changes in matter-based form over time. The arena of space and time bound matter; and the arena of imaginative space or astral space; and, the arena of timeless and spaceless thought, - all interpenetrate at their boundary conditions.

The thought-world, or the ethereal world, has an upper and lower boundary condition. At the upper boundary we experience the garments of non-material Beings in the form of Ideas, after the indications of Plato. Steiner, in A Theory of Knowledge Implicit in Goethe's World Conception describes an Idea as a "complex of concepts".

As social beings we sometimes find ourselves in conflict with others over the Ideas of the Good and the True. Here too we can be attacked, for our expression of this mental/spiritual world disturbs those who do not agree with it, or otherwise need a justification for ignoring our expressions or deeds. These attacks represent a crowning with thorns. Our head is where we develop thought toward its higher qualities, and the socially induced crown of of thorns is meant to penetrate the idea-matrix we have offered, and through pain banish our ability to express ourselves here.

The Beings of the super-sensible spiritual worlds wear (or appear) as Ideas so that we can approach them without having to experience the full impression/power of their real nature. At the upper boundary of the ethereal or thought-world (8), they "step down" their nature as an act of loving kindness. This is also the "meeting ground" between the 9th Hierarchy, the realm of the Angels, and the 10th Hierarchy, the realm of human beings. Christ, as an aspect of His Second Coming, appears in the ethereal in the "form" of an Angel.

Like our personal guardian Angel He is now available to "speak" to us in the realm of discursive thinking - our inner wording - the same way our Angel is able to speak to us there. Steiner called this speaking inner thinking: Inspiration. But first we must learn to silence our inner discourse - to become poor in spirit, or what in the cultural East might be called: empty consciousness, or no-mind. Our original experience of this Angelic contact is via the still small voice of the conscience. With practice (especially praying out loud and in private) we can learn to "hear" other inner voices besides our own.

At the lower boundary of the ethereal or thought-world, we experience the living aspect of this thought-world as a train of thoughts, in the form of discursive thinking (inner wording). The speed of the primal or original thinking is infinite, and that takes place in the realm of the uncreated and formless. In this realm everything is simultaneous - in the Now, in the Eternal. This is the gate to the Akashic Record. Everything that happens, happens Now. "All things happened through Him and not one thing that happened happened without Him."

When we bring a thought out of this realm, through the space bound astral world of picture thinking, or imagination, into the realm of concrete words, we also bring it out of the realm of the simultaneous into the realm of linear time - that is, out of the realm of timelessness and spacelessness, through pure space (the imagination), and then into sequential time.

In life, when we do this, it is best called: carrying the Cross. The weight of the true and the good, as it is born in naturally developing thinking, to become realized in speaking and doing, - this moral weight is a burden. At the same time we are not alone. Matthew 11: 28-30: Come unto me, all ye that labour and are heavy laden, and I will give you rest. Take my yoke upon, and learn of me; for I am meek and lowly in heart: and ye shall find rest unto your souls. For my yoke is easy, and my burden is light.

In our ordinary thinking we experience all of this. We just don't notice it, because our thinking usually has as its object some important (or playful) aspect of our day to day existence. Thinking serves our existence, as does thought. It is just that we do not attend to it, or know yet how to practice our intention in full consciousness.
That's why Steiner wanted us to "turn around" in our consciousness (soul life) and wake up through the path or Way of an empirical and scientific study of our own minds, following the map he created through The Philosophy of Spiritual Activity, whose subtitle was: "some results of introspection following the methods of natural science", and whose last sentence of the original preface said: "One must be able to confront an idea and experience it, otherwise one will fall into its bondage."

Here is what Steiner said about "cognition", from the preface to Truth and Knowledge, his doctoral dissertation:

"The object of knowledge is not to repeat in conceptual form something which already exists, but rather to create a completely new sphere, which when combined with the world given to our senses constitutes complete reality. Thus man's highest activity, his spiritual creativeness, is an organic part of the universal world-process. The world-process should not be considered a complete, enclosed totality without this activity. Man is not a passive onlooker in relation to evolution, merely repeating in mental pictures cosmic events taking place without his participation; he is the active co-creator of the world-process, and cognition is the most perfect link in the organism of the universe."

We have today the concrete terms or words: consciousness and self-consciousness. Two or three hundred years ago in Europe, they would have used the words soul and spirit to mean the same experience. In between our Now and this most recent past, as those terms - soul and spirit - were translated into the English language, the term/word for soul and spirit became "mind". This materialization of our concepts of our inner life has intensified so that now people no longer use the term mind, but instead use the word "brain", believing that there is only matter, and never spirit. (9)

The truth is that the "brain" is a material organ by which the spirit is able, with the aid of the soul - or astral body - in a mediating fashion, to integrate itself into a physical body, much the same way consciousness is moved around in the movie Avatar. The "idea" that there is only matter, but no spirit, so common today is due to the existence in the "mind" of beliefs. A "belief" is an idea that has placed the self-consciousness of our "I" (or spirit) into "bondage".

Steiner called such belief-like ideas aspects of the Ahrimanic Deception, which I name (for artistic/aesthetic reasons) the Ahrimanic Enchantment.

Errors in the act of thinking produces illusory thoughts, which realm of illusions Tomberg has called: "the Realm of the False Holy Spirit". This is that portion of the ethereal or thought-world ruled by the legions of Lucifer. It is at the boundary of the ethereal and astral planes of existence. According to Tomberg, to get through this realm one needs to be accompanied by the Holy Mother.

In this experience in life we begin to come to know the crucifixion. We die inwardly in order to travel higher into the thought-world consciously, yet in this death we are "caught" by the Holy Mother, just as is depicted in Michaelangelo's The Pieta. The thinking "I" gives up its "self" for the other - for the Thou, thus experiencing a kind of death in the astral.

Steiner has said there are more illusions in the spiritual world than there are in the material world.

This is looking at the process of thinking from below upward. When we view this process in the fashion it creatively happens, we travel it from above downward - from, as pointed out before, the realm of the uncreated and formless, through the space bound world of imaginations (and mental pictures) into the space and time bound realm of discursive thinking in the forms of words (language).

Belief is different from true Faith, the latter being an act of trust in the Divine, not an "idea" of the Divine. When we encounter fundamentalism, of either the religious or the scientific kind, we are meeting a rigidly held belief, which possesses (or holds in bondage) the mind of the speaker.

MacCoun, in her book On Becoming an Alchemist, writes: that the belief in absolute facts is ahrimanic (she doesn't actually use that name, but it is obvious she means to refer to a Being), and the belief in absolute truths is luciferic (again the same caution).

If people treat the works of Rudolf Steiner as an absolute authority on anything, they are falling into a relationship of bondage with those ideas. In a way this is a kind of self-generated entombment. This is different from social entombment, where the expressions of the good and the true are experienced by the "I" in the soul as an inability to effect the outer world. However hard we try to manifest the good and the true in the social world, it is rejected or otherwise not heard. We feel we are alone and powerless. Like someone buried alive (entombed, but living), we fight and struggle against the social world's refusal to hear us.

There is a way out of the Tomb. Our empathy must be so rich, that we realize that the other - the Thou - does not need to be like us. The Thou is entitled to Its own version of the true and the good, and we must then sacrifice that version which is ours, and learn, as Steiner pointed out in The Inner Aspects of the Social Question: to hear the Christ Impulse in the other's thinking. For our own biography we need the true and the good in order to act the Consciousness Soul, but at the same time part of the true and the good is that the other - the Thou - is not seen, if Judged.

Thinking as Perception:

This is not a commentary on the nature of sense perception, but only on the characteristics of thinking as perception - as "seeing". (10)
In a crisis situation thinking is aided by the adrenaline to focus and concentrate. We can ourselves learn to focus and concentrate without this chemical (astral) support. Through either process we can wake up in the realm of the uncreated and the formless. We will then "see" with the thinking. To consciously experience this, and to also act in the world on the basis of this seeing is the experience of the resurrection at the level of our inner life. The social world often compels our "seeing".

The Zen master "sees" the situation of his student. The mother, when thinking selflessly, sees what to do in a moment of crisis with her child. The soldier, or first responder, sees with their thinking what the right action is. An athlete calls this: being in the zone.

The "mind" in this condition, which is generally completely spontaneous, is free - no longer in bondage to its old thoughts and mental habits.

This, when sustained while in contact with the world of pure spirit, Steiner called: Intuition. In our ordinary life we call it likewise: intuition, without the capital letter. We are united with the Idea in either case, although Steiner's Intuition means a fully aware experience of the Divine Being, free of our own body - or sense free (body free) thinking. In the more ordinary types of consciousness, where our self-consciousness is seeing/perceiving, we have taken to having our ordinary language talk about a "bright" idea, or in a cartoon we have someone with a light-bulb going off over their head. The concentrated action in thinking "lights" up the mind.

"More light!" said Goethe on his death bed.

In spontaneous action we have what MacCoun describes as "see, do". Perceiving and acting are united. Because our attention is focused on the needed action, we don"t notice the inner activity of seeing/perceiving because we are too committed to the outer world action to notice the inner world lighting up. In the East, if this state of pure intuitive experience is constant, it is called: enlightenment. I had the following personal experience one day. I was in my kitchen with a friend, and also with my youngest daughter, who was about 3 and one half years old at that time. My daughter was skipping around the room, tripped over her own feet, and fell forward with her chin striking the corner of the clothes dryer which was also in that room.

I immediately picked her up, and sat her on the dryer, looking at her carefully to see her condition. She had not yet started to cry, something one ordinarily expects to happen very soon. I next immediately recalled that there was a bottle of Arnica in a nearby cabinet. I quickly took the bottle out, unstoppered it and placed some on a finger tip, which I then placed under her nose for her to smell. I next took another bit on a finger tip, and rubbed up between her eyebrows over the astral/ethereal doorway to the pineal gland. Only after these actions did I look at her chin, notice there was no open wound, and applied the Arnica there.

I had never before thought about any of these actions, other than the last one. All the same, I saw/I did. She did not cry at all, and was soon very calm, and sat in my lap for a while before returning to play.

My visiting friend, who was also a curative eurythmist, said to my daughter: Your father is very wise." Perhaps. What I did know was how to think - how to be empty or poor in spirit. I didn't need a content of knowledge already existing, stored somewhere in memory - I only needed to know how to think. I do not mean here to denigrate experience and memory, but only to point to the capacities of the purely intuitive mind.

I trusted the world behind my eyes, and saw in the dark.

This Pure Thinking is pure in three ways: It is pure in the sense that the <u>attention</u> of our I is oriented fully away from sense experience (we don't actually have to leave the body to do this). It is also pure in a consciously <u>intended</u> moral sense - that is our thinking is fully other-directed. We have no egoistic stake in the outcome of the thinking activity, for we do it for others not for ourselves. The third way such thinking is pure is that it is only of concepts and ideas - that is the object of thought is the thought-world itself.

Rudolf Steiner described this kind of inner moral activity in The Philosophy of Spiritual Activity, as moral imagination, moral intuition, and moral technique. This activity can be applied both in the outer world of our social environment, and in the world of contemplative thought alone. To apply it contemplatively, or while in a state of reverie or meditation, means to turn around and enter into the thought-world on purpose - as a place in itself.

The deeper (higher) we go, the more consciously we become able to wake up in the realm of the uncreated and formless, where moral thought arises out of our own creative activity. When we live the true and the good from out of this realm of experience, then we are truly free - no bondage to the idea. We've become a spirit-thought-creator, and then we are seen. Again, as pointed out by Steiner in Truth and Knowledge:

"Man is not a passive onlooker in relation to evolution, merely repeating in mental pictures cosmic events taking place without his participation; he is the active co-creator of the world-process, and cognition is the most perfect link in the organism of the universe."

Ordinary consciousness, as it faces the social-trials of the biography, is the naturally arising expression of the Seven Stages of the Passion of Christ. This then is the science or "physics" of the life of thought as religious or moral art.

For the American Soul, we now have cowboys and cowgirls, as women more and more claim their rightful places society. Again, following the mythical archetype of the Western as regards the American Soul, and remembering that this Soul is the leading edge of changes in consciousness occurring on a world-wide scale, those who "think" their way to the true and the good, or live in what Steiner called the Consciousness Soul, burn with a kind of fire for the true and the good that involves them becoming Christ-like in their biographical environments, however small and intimate.

As such fore-runners they then are destined to live the Seven Stages of the Passion of Christ in their individual biographical niche. This can be true even if someone is in a prison, or works in a large Corporation, or is homeless.

In this biographical niche they will run into, and become involved with, those individuals serving other impulses. Our Age then is an epic social conflagration brought about by the naturally occurring differences among individuals, which is bringing in its train that Age of Earth Existence the Hopi Prophets called: the Day of Purification. As a first act in this true New Age, Western Civilization is failing.
Those serving other impulses are not necessarily wrong. Each biographical Path is perfect, and overseen by the most profound Love (see note 6, again). Each follows their own drummer - their own music. In my Father's House are many mansions.

Is the brain a computer? Is the mind the brain? Can a computer be moral or create art? (11)

a brief summation

The above was mostly parts ... now it is our task to string the parts into a whole, and as a whole we will then arrive deeper into the realm of the true and the good ... of the "physics" of thought and thinking ...

Original thought is created by human beings, in the realm of the uncreated and unformed - a realm connected to the spaceless and timeless Now that is Eternity. From there it descends, through the realm of perishable and mutable spirit - the realm of the imagination and mental pictues, which arise in that mental/astral space bound existence we more easily experience. Then from there the descent is into the the inner wording of discursive thinking in the form of concrete language, and in that way finally, via speech (12), into the world of social space and linear time. Steiner's map of the mind: The Philosophy of Spiritual Activity, via its practices of moral imagination, moral intuition, and moral technique mirrors this process just described. Moral imagination takes place in the middle realm of the perishable and mutable spirit, through which activity we ask a question of ourselves, and in forming the moral intuition that is the answer to that question, we rise into the realm of timeless and spaceless cognitive creation. Then through moral technique we once more descend, from our previous assent, into the process of incarnating the true and the good into deeds, which can include speech.

Not all thoughts that we utter come from this organic and living sequence of ascent and descent. Some thoughts come from memory, such as where we store Steiner-<u>said</u>. We also speak out of habits of thought, which too live in the astral/ethereal matrix, often in the Realm of the False Holy Spirit. The liar is trapped in the illusions spun by his or her lies - a false idea we don't confront places us in bondage. Steiner called speech without true thought: <u>the empty phrase</u>.

The Creator, named Christ in our current perception of the Now, has made a world-encompassing social organism in which the human biography unfolds, in such a way that each individual receives the Love that belongs to them to receive (see note 6, again). As an aspect of this organism, there also exists a Path, which we have called The Seven Stages of the Passion of Christ. The Creator became human and then went through the gate of death, because He could not ask of us something He could not himself do - namely be human. Many people believe falsely that the Passion is something we did to Christ. It is not.

The Passion is the mirror image of something humans do to themselves as a result of the Fall into Matter. Christ follows us in living out this Passion. It is our Passion for material existence that He imitates.

The social organism is so perfectly endowed, that what Christ experienced in the Seven Stages - during the Turning Point of Time as Steiner phrased it, we can now experience as well. This is possible because the social world reacts to us, and in reacting plays the same role as did the Romans and the Hebrews, in the moments when the Creator God became human. The profound Now of the Turning Point of Time reverberates through All Time - all Nows. The Seven Stages are also the ultimate process of metamorphosis.

What Goethe observed as the various renunciations in the Plant, can also be seen in such a way that in that the totality of all the single renunciations also reflect the Seven Stages of the Passion. The Ur-plant, first as seed, washes the feet of material existence, burying itself into Matter, engaging in its own Fall. This Fall goes ever more deeper into matter, and the life of the Ur-Plant, on a planetary scale, experiences the resistance of matter to its generative powers as scourging, crowning with thorns, carrying the cross, crucifixion, entombment and then resurrrection in the masterful creation of the new seed. This life is yet without consciousness or self-consciousness. It is pure life-process, without even instinct.

The animal kingdom and the human kingdom too suffer the Fall into materiality - and in overcoming the density of matter in order to express their true spirit, they too go through this Passion. And the human kingdom, in forgetting its own true nature, adds to the suffering of the life (plant) process, and the instinctive consciousness pain of the animal kingdom - by our efforts to manipulate what we do not understand (the fundamental "sin" or error we commit by our efforts to genetically modify organisms - including ourselves). Not appreciating matter, we also harm spirit, including the spirit of life itself ("In it - the Word - was Life and the Life was the Light of the world").

The Light of the Sun does the same thing (see note 11, again). In photosythensis It dies into Matter to become food (energy) for the human being (take and eat for this is my body), only to return/become the inner sun-light of thought and the mind. The deeds and sufferings of light also mirror the Seven Stages of the Passion.   Everything is part and parcel of everything else. Those people who vex us, and scourge us and help us be socially entombed - that's just us wearing a different face in a different aspect of the Eternal Now (13). Our biographical Time is not their biographical Time, which is one of the reasons Christ encourages us not to Judge, for it is ourselves we judge. The other - the Thou - is us wearing a different face and experiencing a different time-oriented biography. We only appear to share the same Time.

When asked what is the most important commandment, Christ spoke this way: Love the Lord your God with all your heart and with all your spirit and with all your mind. This is the first and greatest commandment. And the second is like it: Love your neighbor as yourself. All the Law and the Prophets hang on these two commandments.

God is everything, everything is god (14). We are all Cowboy Bebops - stranger others - dancing and singing throughout all Eternity; and, seeking the true and the good is just one Chapter of many in our own eternal dying and becoming.

Notes
(1) http://en.wikipedia.org/wiki/Cowboy_Bebop
(2) Learning to Perceive the American Soul http://ipwebdev.com/hermit/learning.html
(3) See the movie Payback starring Mel Gibson, for an updated film-noir representation. http://en.wikipedia.org/wiki/Payback_(1999_film)
(4) http://en.wikipedia.org/wiki/Alan_Watts
(5) The Mystery of Evil in the Light of the Sermon on the Mount http://ipwebdev.com/hermit/mysteryofevil.html
(6) The Art of God: an actual theory of Everything: http://ipwebdev.com/hermit/artofgod.html
(7) see "Zen Anthroposophy": http://ipwebdev.com/hermit/ZenA.html
(8) The IDEA of the thoughtworld:
 http://ipwebdev.com/hermit/thoughtworld.html
(9) "The Idea of Mind: a Christian meditator considers the problem of consciousness": http://ipwebdev.com/hermit/tidom.html
(10) Carl Stegmann, in his book: "The Other America: the West in the Light of Spiritual Science" called this new thinking: clair-thinking:
 http://www.amazon.com/The-Other-America-Carl-Stegmann/dp/0945803281
(11) Electicity and the Spirit in Nature .. - a tale of certain considerations of the present state of science, in the light of a modern practical understanding of the nature of mind

- http://ipwebdev.com/hermit/electricityandthespiritinnature.html
(12) The Gift of the Word (a poem - meant to be read
aloud): http://ipwebdev.com/hermit/giftoftheword.html
(13) See the Beatles "I am the Walrus": http://www.youtube.com/watch?v=42luHhrsNhg
(14) also: All You Need is Love http://www.youtube.com/watch?v=ydfH7iuLR0I

~!~!~!~!~!~!~!~

Healing the Insanity of Psychiatric Medicines and Practices

for artistic perceptions see these videos: Define Better:
  http://tv.naturalnews.com/v.asp?v=D54DD96EF224FA5B562DABF91B666B8E

Side effects of Quiting Smoking:
http://www.huffingtonpost.com/2012/01/08/snl-chantix-parody-side-effects_n_1192612.html
Labelling Kids:

http://tv.naturalnews.com/v.asp?v=79F04FDDB029F7E5DF59E508D1281DE0

psych visit:
http://notyet30.wordpress.com/2011/01/06/psych-visit/

It is one thesis of this small paper that common sense thinking, applied to the question of the efficacy of modern anti-psychotics and similar medicines, will reveal that such drugs cannot generally be healthy for either the mental or physical health of the human being. They only seem to work, and then only if you define the goal of the application of such medicine in a quite limited, and anti-human, fashion (behavioral modification instead of healing). [For supportive details from a self described "dissident psychologist" go here.]

This is not to say no good at all comes from the lifetimes of effort put out by many professionals in these fields, but rather that the picture we have of this work is spun, just as politicians spin their versions of the truth. Spin is not the truth, and in this essay we are trying to come nearer to the social reality represented by our institutional mental health systems. They are mostly not about mental *health* (those problems of the mind are not being adequately researched or solved), but rather about power, wealth and social control.

It may help some possible confusion in the reader to distinguish the psychiatric profession, from the psychological profession. Most psychiatrists no longer participate in talk therapy (classical analysis on the couch), but by and large engage in the practice of diagnosis of mental illnesses according to the DSM* V (a system of labeling various symptoms into a name that can be recognized by the mental health system for purposes of insurance payments and other institutional processes). Following such a diagnosis the psychiatrist (being also an MD) prescribes medications designed to adjust the behavior of the patient. More will be said about this later.

*[***Diagnostic and Statistical Manual of Mental Disorders V***, for interesting details look it up on Wikipedia.]

Psychologists almost universally engage is some form of talk therapy, although often in connection to some kind of prescription medicine, and as well often using the same classification system as the DSM V.

The important point above concerns *the general method of thinking* involved in the practice of this discipline (psychiatry), for that is where the failure begins and ends. It is not so much the individual thinking, but rather the institutional thinking - the generalized paradigm which serves as the context and background to all the rest. Let *us* begin the examination of this method of thinking, by first looking at something with which most of us today are quite familiar: the movement toward organic food. Some history ...

In the 19th Century natural science reached a kind of pinnacle of sorts. Great advances in knowledge were seen everywhere, and technical devices of all kinds were being created in the hope of solving any number of humanity's pressing problems. The industrial revolution was a seeming success, and not a week went by without some scientist somewhere announcing another breakthrough, in either pure knowledge or in some practical art.

In agriculture the plant had been studied in the laboratory very carefully, and how it was composed of basic elements, such as carbon, hydrogen, oxygen and nitrogen (plus a few trace elements) was now assumed to be quite clear. Farms as a result started to become more and more modeled after factories, where what is now called mono-culture started to flourish. Machines planted the seeds, watered the plants and artificial fertilizers were added to the soil to make up for any missing elements such as are related to the plant's need for clay, silicon or calcium.

Large corporations grew into existence, many of them chemical factories creating pure and ofttimes synthetic substances that were applied at the farm or then later during procedures by which food was processed, manufactured and distributed to consumers via grocery stores. Needs of commerce became important and shelf life required new chemical methods of preservation. Foods were enhanced, adulterated, preserved, and supposedly purified. Flour was bleached. Sugar was too (keep in mind you wouldn't, yourself, directly drink bleach).

In many places, however, things were not coming out so well. Large farms using mono-culture and artificial fertilizers found themselves more and more attacked by insect life (nature, sensing something dead or dying or ill, sends its littlest workers to take it apart, and return it to the whole). This required the application of poisons to kill the insects, and also to kill any weeds (unwanted plants). The farm became essentially a chemical factory siting astride the land. Ordinary farmers couldn't compete, and the whole of agriculture, as a way of life, changed radically.

Eventually, people began to question whether this was sane. After some time organic farming (which is really only a return to the pre-industrial farm) became important, as ordinary common sense was applied by ordinary people to examine the assumptions of mono-culture and corporate industrial food processing and practices.

This is a brief, but I believe quite worthwhile picture. What is the nature of the thinking that produced this history of farming practices that ultimately have failed on such a huge scale to provide healthy food?

The first step was in natural science itself, which has followed primarily a method of analysis (taking things apart). For example, the plant was burned in the laboratory to produce ash. Then the ash was analyzed to see what were the basic elements of which it was made (the burning only eliminated the water from the harvested plant - although that is not precisely true, for the combustion process creates many products such as light and heat, but which come from where - the burning takes something less quantifiable away from the once living plant.). In any event, the modern scientist looks at plant biology on the farm as a process by which the plant was created by the DNA of the seed out of certain basic elements available in the soil.   Already, before DNA, if the soil was lacking something, these could be added later (fertilizers etc.).

This turning of the farm into a chemistry factory was before the need for ecological or holistic thinking was understood. Pure analysis needs to be followed by wise synthesis. After you take something apart, you have to know how to put it back together, in order to prove you actually learned something. The later discovered flaws of mono-culture have pretty much proved that the original thinking about plants and foods was in error.

To this analytical thinking was added the thinking involved in mass production. Machines were seen as useful replacements for physical labor and the farm became large and mechanized (leading to mono-culture or farms sowing and reaping only one plant, such as wheat or corn). The profit motive was added to the search for scientific facts, with the whole thing becoming a bit distorted because as agricultural colleges grew in size (and developed more research capacity), a great deal of the funding for research in these schools was provided by business (and sometimes government), neither of which had pure agendas and motives.

Ultimately, regulatory bodies such as the Food and Drug Administration became less the defenders of the public interest, and more the creatures of the lobbyists for big agricultural and chemical corporations.

Everyone today is more or less aware of these facts and tendencies.

As common sense was applied, it became clear that the earth in which plants were grown was itself alive with microorganisms and worms etc. The more chemical fertilizers and anti-weed and insect poisons were added to the farm, the more "dead" the soil became. A kind of vicious cycle arose, which required more and more chemicals on the farm, that has since resulted in more and more a denaturing of the food itself. We could try to look for laboratory evidence for this, but since it was the human population itself upon which the experiment (denatured and processed food) was conducted, we need only look at people to see the results.

Now it is not usual to relate to this certain other facts, but it is clear to a holistic thinking that modern diseases of the heart, and many cancers began to arise at the same time as changes in farming. In fact, the so-called obesity epidemic in America is clearly related as well. True experts in nutrition realize that the real reason so many people are fat is because there is no actual nutrition in the food you get at the grocery store. As a consequence the body keeps telling people to eat more, but the only thing in the food is empty calories which the body then stores (converts the excess of sugars into fats) if one has a certain body-type (an endomorph). Other body types burn all the calories, but need stimulants such as caffeine and cigarettes in order to function at work and in home.

What is worse is that many today in the medical field want to castigate the consumer, and leave aside or ignore the responsibility of the producer of the food, as well as the role of the government (or absence of a role, might be a better way to phrase it). Wealthy corporations and corrupt government officials get a free ride, but the fat person has to take the whole blame for his choices. Somehow we are to be able to overcome corporate and government power, and the influence of advertising, while at the same time raising the children and creating through our work all the wealth.

So to the flawed excess of analysis without synthesis, and the flawed excess of corporate greed, we must now add the flawed reasoning which wants to blame the consumer for buying products that should never have been sold to him in the first place.

Now why did we bother to look at this, in an article partly on problems with mental health medications. The reason should be clear to the reader with common sense: the same flawed thinking that debased the food supply has come alive in the realm of soul-healing, and is currently debasing the physical and mental health of millions.

Natural science remains locked in an excess of analysis, and an absence of wise synthesis. Corporate greed in the creation of pharmaceuticals has led to a need to force the sale through advertising of products after products whose side effects kill and injure. If these so-called medicines were truly healing, there would be no need to _sell_ them - they would sell themselves.

Government has become corrupted, as are many universities and hospitals where research is conducted. In the absence of holistic thinking, suffering is produced directly on many minds. Lets look at some examples.

The writer of this essay has 18 years experience in the trenches of the mental health field, including ten years as a mental health worker in a for-profit psychiatric hospital in Nashua, New Hampshire. I could tell a lot of stories, but I'll just tell one, after making a few basic observations.

First of all it was clear, to my observation and experience, that psychiatrists working at the hospital were basically poorly supervised experimenters. I seldom saw a diagnosis made at the beginning of an admission remain the same over the whole course of treatment (unless the patient had been in the system for years). It was routine to order one medication (or more) in the beginning, and then change that as treatment went forward. The goal, of course, was not to heal the patient, but to modify behavior. The diagnosis defined certain behavior as socially undesirable, and then the psychiatrist experimented using various medications until the desired behavioral result was reached.

During this process the subjective inner life of the patient was often not a factor, although many patients came seeking help with their inner states of being. Of course, such inner states often led to deviant social behaviors, such that people would come recommended by various agencies (social services, the police, the family etc.). The new patient would have a complaint, of sorts, but the social matrix surrounding this person would also have its own separate complaint.

The patient was worried about their state of mind, and the family or job was worried about their behavior. What we did was modify behavior, often by what was essentially a chemical restraint on some aspect of the patients subjective state of mind. We pressed down the personality with drugs in order to make them more easily fit into their social environment. Obviously there went with this process a number of side-effects (physical and mental collateral damage is probably a more accurate term), some of which were more or less permanent (such as tardive dyskinesia).

Now in appreciating what I write here about the psychiatrist as an experimenter, the reader should be clear that I am pointing out a great deal of ignorance and some degree of arrogance (just as was done to the farms we need for the food we eat). At the same time it is the institutional system of mental health that perpetuates these problems, because these flaws are well known and are everywhere criticized, although unsuccessfully   (Google: psychiatric polypharmacy; psychiatric and organic reductionism; ecology of mind; and anti-psychiatry, for example). Psychiatry is a "soft" science, not a "hard" science. It is more art than science, and a lot of people practicing it clearly don't have any talent.

Lets do the horror story now ....

The hospital where I worked had a Chief of Psychiatry (a different job than the business head of the facility). He was also paid outside money by various pharmaceutical companies to manage research projects. When a new experimental drug had to be tested, we were one place such tests were done. This process costs a lot of money (the drug company paid the full admission costs of all patients in the study as well as additional staff time needed to support the study, such as through frequent blood tests, physicals etc.).

The Chief of Psychiatry maintained "professional" relationships with the Nashua community, and was in fact already the "doctor" for a number of individuals with chronic mental health issues. All these individuals were provided living support through local social services agencies, as they couldn't work and often needed help just with basic living skills.

A new drug for schizophrenia was to be tested, and shortly thereafter a number of regular patients of the Chief of Psychiatry were admitted to the hospital to participate in the study. They were not in crisis, but were admitted solely for the study. Because the study was a double-blind study, some would get a placebo, instead of the experimental drug.

One patient, clearly receiving a placebo, began in a couple of weeks to show severe symptoms. He had been taken off the medication that helped him live (with aid) in the community, and brought into the hospital for the study. He was, in the jargon we used, decompensating.

He began to be awake for 50 hours at a time, and then crash for about 16 hours and then be awake again (I know this because I was the one who went carefully through his chart to develop these and other facts in order to confront the Chief of Psychiatry with the torture of this individual). He wasn't eating and existed mostly on coffee and cigarettes. His behavior was erratic, and his speech pressured (speedy and incoherent). He pestered staff and other patients constantly. Fortunately he was not violent, just a terrific nuisance to others, and of course miserable inside himself (for which his "madness" - as it were - offers him no understanding). We forget, or ignore, that the world seen from inside such a mind is not the same world we see at all.

Lets look at what happen here - the reality. People with known mental health issues were brought into the hospital to suit the convenience of the Chief of Psychiatry and the drug company, and used as guinea pigs. This is not only shameful, but it ought to scare us that such callous and indifferent impulses fill in the structural nature of the mental health system, such that no one objects on an institutional level. Of course, the professionals put a good face on all such activity, because as anyone knows, we can with our thinking justify anything.

Even today in the food industry, that system still lives in denial of what has been done (and is being done that is worse) to the food supply. The same attitude is rampant in the field of mental health. Natural science does not understand what it is doing. Commercial interests mine this field of confusion for profit making purposes. And, the human beings, the patients and their families (as well as society) are not being well served.

One really doesn't need to be an expert, but just use common sense; and, in fact recognize that the expert has his own agenda, which is often the preservation of his status and his income. The only way to stop the insanity of the mental health institutional system is for public opinion to marshal its common sense, and ask of their representatives in legislative bodies to use their common sense as well.

Human beings shouldn't be the subject of experiments by psychiatrists no longer interested in their subjective inner well being, but only in changing the behavior, all supported by a pharmaceutical industry which has proven it will lie and cheat in order to make money. There are alternatives as everyone who looks at this question knows.

To come at this from another direction ...

There is a field of science that is called (or was called) coal tar chemistry. Basically this field (and its related industries) took something that was already quite dead (petroleum in the ground) and killed it some more (took it apart on a massive scale). Those smelly gasoline making plants you drive by were at one time called "cracking plants" because what they do is heat the oil to very high temperatures, while keeping it under pressure (crack the petroleum coal tar into pieces that don't exist in nature) and then as the various vapors rise, they cool them and make gasoline, kerosene etc. (a kind of distillation process). From this same chemistry we have ingredients for plastics, cosmetics and even medicines. These are all synthetic, which among other things means nature didn't make them, man did (with all his selfish motives, and his ignorance and arrogance).

We are aware today of all those allergies that comes with the proliferation of these products throughout human society. Cigarettes are full of this stuff. It has a lot of uses, of which one is that it makes some people a lot of money. Lets make a synthesis, a common sense picture.

As science matures in knowledge, human impulses everywhere look for personal advantage. The industrial revolution includes a chemical or synthetic revolution where all kinds of substances are created that never before existed in nature. Human beings now swim in a sea of synthetic (artificial) chemistry, for which their bodies were never originally adapted. Nature made us, we made synthetics and synthetics are ruining our food, changing the climate and torturing mental patients.

Seen as a whole social process, we've essentially conducted a huge set of experiments on the human population of the world. That's right, we are the experimental subject of a lot of badly thought out theories, acting in collusion with profit making industries.

We played with the world in ignorance and arrogance and now must reap the consequences. Yes, a lot of the time we were trying to solve problems and meet genuine human needs. But at the same time we were not humble. We believed we could try anything and fix any mistake. We were childish, and as all of us learn growing up, when you are impulsive and childish, you screw up, and sometimes ruin the rest of your life. Humanity, as a group, has been doing the same thing on a very large scale for some time.

Here's the rule that is frequently violated: Just because you *can* do a thing, does not mean you *should* do a thing.

At the beginning of this small paper I made an off-hand remark regarding modern psychiatric medicine, which now needs some elaboration. I said: *"They only seem to work, and then only if you define the goal of the application of such medicine in a quite limited, and anti-human, fashion."*

I have watched all kinds of people receive all kinds of medications over my 18 years personal experience in the trenches of the field of mental health. By "trenches" I mean direct patient care (the psychiatrists see their patients briefly, sometimes not even daily). It is people like me who see them all day long and talk to them as one human being to another (instead of as treating doctor to insane patient).

What we call "mental patients" are individuals of great personal courage, who suffer inwardly in ways few of us can imagine. They live in an Age where they are not understood. They are often lucky to have caregivers (nurses and mental health workers) who treat them as human beings - with sympathy and compassion. The mental health *system* treats them as things and as numbers on summary sheets. If they are really lucky they sometimes get compassionate doctors, but these doctors are themselves caught up in the institutional system, which has a quite distinct life of its own.

\Years ago an acute observer of the business world (Peter Drucker) put forward something called "the Peter principle", which stated that: *in a hierarchy people naturally rise to level of their incompetence*.

A truism for sure, but certainly not always true. Sometimes people are competent, but the nature of that competence can often be solely for their own benefit. The present-day financial crisis in America is an example of that truism. Our mental health institutional systems, and their related pharmaceutical allies, are full of folks not very good at anything but serving their own interests. We really shouldn't expect them to produce something that helps mental patients - that's not the agenda under which they operate.

John Maynard Keynes wrote this about our economic system: *"Capitalism is the extraordinary belief that the nastiest of men, for the nastiest of reasons, will somehow work for the benefit of us all."* A similar statement can be said about the mental health system. But we (patients, and families of patients, and Society, and state and federal law-makers) fool ourselves if we expect the institutional mental health system to benefit those unique individuals we label "the mentally ill". The evidence showing this failure is overwhelming. Hopefully this paper will reveal that even common sense can know and understand this, and that we need to not be dependent upon so-called experts to realize something is badly wrong. Further, we need to realize that only we can fix it. The system won't fix itself.

Of course, we often think of certain people as violent and aggressive, and with good judgment want to exclude them from our communities. This need to exclude is a theme we'll come to at the end of this paper.

Lets add another approach to our consideration ...

Above we noted that the scientist in the laboratory sought to understand the plant through reducing it to ash. He did not study the living plant in its natural environment, but removed it to the laboratory and disassembled it.   The medical doctor in this same period of scientific development spent a lot of time taking apart the cadaver - the dead body. He did not concentrate on the living organism, but on the dead organism.

A similar kind of thinking has gone on in brain studies, where the physical apparatus is assumed (if we read the literature carefully) to be the basis for all mental activity. The scientist studied dead brains, and if he studied living brains, he often studied ones with problems - that is ill or dysfunctional brains (such as people with the split brain problem).

If we do a survey of psychological literature, we find different attitudes there as well. Some study optimum states of consciousness, others only diseased or deviant states of consciousness. Recall the Chief of Psychiatry, and his allies in the pharmaceutical industry - he tests his drugs on an already ill (socially deviant) population, who can't truly consent, because the real nature of their abuse by the system is not apparent to them. Like most people in the field, he and his allies consider their activity (the use and abuse of the unfortunate in the pursuit of limited goals, such as behavioral modification, knowledge and profit) to be normal - that is okay. Remember, the psychiatrist and the pharmaceutical company are not even trying to heal the patient, but only modify behavior.

In the background here is a very deep question, upon the rocks of which Western Civilization now founders. Natural Science has taken the course where it has rigorously decided that there is no spirit in the world - no spirit in Nature, no spirit in the human being.   All we are, to this materialistic outlook, is matter.

In large part this view comes from an unfortunate truth in the field of psychological studies: that the investigator never studies his own mind, but only that of others, and then only through processes which take apart (destroy or eliminate the living element), or which only look at a dysfunctional consciousness. From an ontological (or basic premise) point of view, natural science mostly uses death processes and disease processes to try to wrest, from the once living and healthy, its secrets. Were natural scientists to study their own minds objectively, the presence of the spirit would soon be quite apparent.

The application of a little common sense logic might suggest that the secrets of the living and the healthy will be found in the study of those elements of existence, where they arise - that is in the family and social environment. This is not easy, however. While certain thinkers in these fields have looked to the positive (Abraham Maslow etc.), the institutional *system* does not take such an approach.

There is a view held by some in the field of psychology that speaks of the "identified patient". This is the person who comes to a soul-healer (the psychologist) in order to resolve certain personal problems, and many mental health professionals realize that the so-called "identified patient" might be the most mentally healthy person in that family. At the least this person recognizes a problem, but the root of the problem may not be discovered in the individual, but only in the family-matrix.

A related theme ...

It took a while, but women finally understood that this same method of thinking had led doctors to think of birth as a disease process, and such views had to be opposed and eliminated (a struggle not yet over). In a similar way, we have to resist taking the so-called deviant out of Society in order to study them in isolation, but rather we need to keep the whole together, and recognize that they aren't so much deviant, as unique and highly individual. It is in fact Society that needs to be healed of the assumption that unusual mental states (and their related behaviors) are an "illness".

That is the true insanity - to take the living personality and treat it like the plant in the laboratory where we first destroy it before we can understand it. To repress the unusual personality through powerful and intrusive artificial (not living) chemical forces, simply to coerce changes in behavior, is not healing.

It is in fact the worst kind of tyranny - the tyranny of the majority (who declare themselves superior psychologically) over an essentially helpless minority (the different). It says more about us, as a Society, than it does about them. It reveals _our_ "us and them" assumptions, and _our_ moral weaknesses in shunning them and setting them outside our company, all the while pretending as if we were helping them, when the raw truth is that we are only helping ourselves.

It is Society that lacks the sanity of true charity, and an honest impulse to help (and or heal) the weak and troubled. Its far past time for us to grow into a greater maturity in our social relations with the different.

Lets come at this once more with a slightly different emphasis ...

Healing the Healer: the first steps in a sane future evolution of psychiatry and psychology -

When Freud's works were translated into English, from the German, the terms *geistes* and *seele* were translated as mind, and not as spirit and soul, which easily could have been done (c.f. Bruno Bettelheim's **Freud and man's soul**, A.A.Knopf, 1983). Thus continued and deepened the materialization of the underlying thinking of those who sought during the 19th century to treat problems of human inner life - of the psyche - the soul (which as everyone knows is the root term for the words *psych*ology and *psych*iatry).

Modern scientific thinking on the brain now seeks to explain all inner states of the human being today as consequences of material causes. Mind and brain are now seen as equivalent. The Fall, from a one time appreciation of the human spirit and soul dimensions of existence, is, within scientific thinking, nearly complete. At least at the level of assumptions.

"It is old hat to say that the brain is responsible for mental activity. Such a claim may annoy the likes of Jerry Falwell or the Ayatollah, but it is more or less the common assumption of educated people in the twentieth century. Ever since the scientific revolution, the guiding view of most scientists has been that knowledge about the brain, its cells and its chemistry will explain mental states. However, believing that the brain supports behavior is the easy part: explaining how is quite another." (**Mind Matters: How the Mind and Brain interact to Create Our Conscious Lives**, Michael S. Grazzanica Ph.D. pp 1, Houghton Baffling, Boston 1988). [emphasis added]

This process of materialization of our ideas of human inner states of being has now gone so far that some believe today that there is no "I", or "ego" or "self consciousness", and that this perception of *self* by the brain is nothing but a chemically manufactured illusion.

Into this minefield today come those who feel called to what remains of the profession of "soul healer". Even Grazzanica, in a recent dialog with the writer Tom Wolfe, when questioned on this very issue, was loath to admit such could be possible. This interview, broadcast on C-Span Books, shows Grazzanica rising from his chair and moving around so certain was he that the I or ego was real. All the same, he had to confess that some evidence more and more suggested otherwise.

To appreciate the depth of this problem for modern humanity, the reader is urged to try to speak or write of human interactions without using personal pronouns, for this is the ultimate implication of this train of thought: If there is no I then there is no you, nor he, or she. All is simply *it*.

This last was dramatically portrayed in the film *the Silence of the Lambs* when the serial killer commands the "it" to rub on the oil and for "it" to obey all commands. If it is an imagined serial killer madman that refuses to acknowledge in his victim the reality of an I, how equally insane then has become certain kinds of thinking in natural science that would, in the name of some kind of hyper-objectivity, declare as a complete illusion the idea of any human subjectivity at all.

In a very real sense, we can see that scientific thinking has run up against a wall of sorts. At the same time, a careful review of the research reveals that this wall only really exists in the conceptual frame of reference in which all this research is conducted. It is not the facts of experience that are flawed, but the thinking that makes the errors. It is the _paradigm_ itself that has reached the limit of its viability (c.f. Thomas Kuhn's **The Structure of Scientific Revolutions**).

Now the writer of this little essay is not unfamiliar with these fields of interest, but as previously noted was in his work life drawn into them, albeit not at the professional level of the doctors. I have 18 years in the trenches mental health, from lay therapy in California in the 1970's, to group-home work with adolescents in the 1980's to ten years in a for-profit psychiatric facility in New Hampshire in the 1990's. I've been a counselor, an orderly and a mental health worker. Nor am I uneducated, but I have degrees in pre-seminary (B.A.) and Law (J.D.) My avocation (now full time in retirement) is philosophy, and this at a level far beyond ordinary academic philosophy. With this aside set out, let us continue.

These limits of the paradigm of scientific materialism have been reached everywhere. The studies of consciousness and how that might arise from a material brain still are unable to explain how this happens or what consciousness is. There are theories, but nothing testable. In reality for this thinking, the sacrifice of the idea of self-consciousness is just a cheap and easy way to get rid of a very big problem.

Over in physics, the natural scientist has his own problem with consciousness, for his split-beam experiments prove in this field that the fundamental indeterminacy of states of matter does not become "real" until the observing subjective self-consciousness acts upon the experiment. The observer can't actually keep any longer his own subjectivity outside the work - the two remain interconnected.

This is true also with regard to a great deal of research being done on the brain. The researcher in these fields often has to ask the subjectivity (the "I") of his subject to engage in certain "mental" actions, in order for a brain scan to have something to look at. The subject is to look at pictures, try to access memory and so forth. The problem comes when the experiment is thought about afterward, and researcher tries to create his "model" or theory, and not include the facts that the subjectivity of the researcher and the researcher's subject, first had to make a social agreement before the "mental" act even arises.

The physicist knows he can't do this (refuse any longer to recognize the participation of his own consciousness and self-conscious choices) anymore, so perhaps it is time for those who do research on the mind to recognize the same fact.

In **Mind Matters**, Grazzanica, having already likened brain to a mechanism, then says paradoxically: "*A thought can change brain chemistry, just as a physical event in the brain can change a thought*". My question for Grazzanica is: what does he think causes the thought which changes the brain chemistry?

Clearly to the naive experience of any thinking subject, it is their own self-conscious activity that directs thought. In point of fact, there is no experiment and even no theory, without the thinking of the scientist.

Where this leads us then is to this:

Since the psychiatrist and the psychologist are human, and flawed (as we all are flawed), can it not be possible that hidden within modern theories of consciousness are assumptions that are no longer justified precisely because we have arrived at the above noted limits?

To make the question as stark as possible: Can a researcher or "healer" in the field of "mental" health, subject his patients to treatments he would not do to himself or to his own children? Have any doctors prescribing ECT, for example, actually had ECT?

The easy answer is that it seems necessary to engage in this kind of treatment in order to help the patient. But this is falsified by the fact that quite often the soul healer no longer believes he is healing a subjectivity or self-consciousness, but in fact is really only altering behavior. Certainly, in many circumstances, the subjective self-consciousness of the patient wants some kind of relief from inner torments, but simultaneously the social order surrounding the patient seeks and needs a change of behavior, which this same social order considers to be deviant, or outside the acceptable norm.

Further, since the soul healer no longer thinks of the subjectivity as real, but only the material brain, then all kinds of gross processes and adjustments become possible, because one is really only dealing with the alteration of a mechanical system. Biological to be sure, but (and this with a kind of unrecognized denial) essentially a thing, not a person.

The system of mental health seems to run itself these days, and the soul healer is just a cog in a unhealthy aspect of the social organism, whose purpose more and more requires of its participants that they not feel either sympathy or empathy with their patients.

Is it not one of the costs to the psyche of those who work in this field that they have to stop having normal human feeling, and basically dehumanize their patients on some level in order to subject them to such powerful forms of suppression of the individual spirit? Mental health professionals routinely subject their patients to chemical restraints on behavior, while at the same time never actually believing they are curing the patient of a treatable illness.

Remember, please, psychiatry has become almost entirely behavioral in its approaches. No longer is the subjective inner state of being of the patient relevant. All is driven by the need to define certain behaviors as undesirable (the DSM-V), and then to attempt to modify them without respect for the subjectivity of the patient. The subjectivity (how *they feel* about the treatment) of the patient is less and less a concern, and modification of unwanted behaviors the entire goal, for the individual spirit is here being sacrificed to the assumed needs of the social organism for order. Any individual unable to conform to social order is quickly defined (already in school, and sometimes even earlier in the family) as either criminally or mentally defective. (for a sociological perspective on this read: **Deviance and Medicalization: from Badness to Sickness**, Conrad and Schneider, Merrill Publishing Company, 1985)

Is there a way out?

Before trying to answer that question, lets take a look at the whole situating in its basic form.

Are the individuals crazy, or is Society crazy

First lets step back a bit and think about growing up in modern culture. What was it like to live in a family and go to school and then join the work force?

Some examples:

Suppose you didn't like to sit still in class. You were curious and perhaps gregarious. You wanted to touch things, and play with them and talk to the other kids, and do fun stuff. You were full of life and full of spirit.

But the adults around you had, even prior to your arrival, already "conformed" to the social norms, and so they expected you to "conform" too.

In the family, if you didn't behave you were probably physically and/or emotionally punished, although no one likes to admit how much this still goes on today.

When you survived your families rules and the school's rules, you went to work. At work you had a boss and he had his rules too. These also you need to survive, because in order to live you had to eat, in order to eat you had to have money to buy food, and in order to have money you had to work for a boss.

Unless you were criminal or crazy, that is deviant and non-conformist - that is irrepressible of spirit in one way or another and wouldn't follow normative social rules "just like everyone else".

Everywhere while growing up some "authority" (with a great deal of practical power over you) demanded you do what it wanted you to do, and not what you wanted to do.

We all go through this and it seems to make a lot of sense. Everyone more or less agrees this makes a lot of sense, and it is the normal or standard thing to do, so most everyone does it.

Shouldn't be a problem, right?

Except for a couple of things we tend not to connect to growing up and learning to conform to the social authority which has spent this enormous amount of effort to get us to be what it wants us to be and not to be what we want to be, such as:

STRESS and ILLNESS, both PHYSICAL and PSYCHOLOGICAL!!!!!!

Opps?!?!?

All that energy and spirit that gets pressed down during growing up, through the power exercised by the "authority" towards the social conformance urged upon us by society, moves into our psychological and physical organism and causes stress and illness.

So for all the good we believe we do by using our authority on children to get them to conform to social norms, maybe that's not such a good idea after all.

The spirited nature of the child has a kind of kinship with water and similar fluids (there are other kinships as well).   The one I have in mind here, however, is concerned with a well known physical law: the incompressibility of fluids. This is how your brake system on your car works. Because the brake fluid is incompressible, when you push your foot on the brake pedal, this fluid, trapped in the tubes of the brake system, pushes the brakes (whether disc or pad). Because of other laws of physics the force of the foot gets multiplied, either by changes in the diameter of the tubes or assisted by engine power (this makes no difference to the analogy).

What this means is that when we use authority, either in the family, and/or the school and/or the work place to repress the spirited nature of the individual, we **_stress_** the rest of the "system" of our being and nature, both physically and psychologically. [See the film **The Village**, by M. Night Shyamalan, for a fairy tale like metaphorical look at these kinds of social issues.]

Then later, when the stressed individual acts "mental", or "criminal", we treat this problem with those social systems, which are even **_more_** authoritative and not less. Even with physical illness we do the same - the medical profession uses its "authority" to get us to take drugs, and the drugs are a "physical authority" applied to our bodies and minds. Instead of offering more freedom from stress, we increase the stress (remember all those nasty "side effects"?).

Maybe we really need to think out the whole damn structure of our social culture better from top to bottom, and in the meantime we ought perhaps to stop whacking the "mentally" ill (overstressed spirited human beings) over the head with more authority to conform (whether the rules of a hospital or the physical rules of a drug).

From this point of view, its just might seem like *society* is more crazy than the individual; or, that the collective is more stupid than the one.

To return to the question of what might be done...

The point of this little paper is not to attack those called to the professions of soul healing. They are, in fact, caught in between. On the one hand there is the social order that wants something done about "them" - the deviants. On another hand is the massive presence of the paradigm of scientific materialism, which will not tolerate any mention of spirit or soul, but rather insists (with less and less evidence everyday) that all is matter, and all explanations of human existence must be based upon materialist or physical conceptions.

Some even create prophecies about the end of the human, and the supplanting of the human with the biomechanical. They imagine we will discover how to transplant the consciousness of the human being into the memory chips of a machine, thus giving us imperishable bodies and immortal consciousness.

At the other end are those - the "them" - the deviants. We still don't know how much behavior is derived from Nature and how much is derived from Nurture. What we do know, those of us lucky enough not to be caught up "in the system", is that we don't want someone messing with our inner life. This most personal sphere of autonomy - our own thoughts, feelings and impulses of will - this we will guard even to the point of violence if necessary.

We understand the American and French revolutions. We applaud the iconoclast, who manages their individuality without getting too deviant - we even often call them *artists*. We worry about tyranny, especially the tyranny of the majority. We even have gone so far today, that *conformance* itself is often seen as a character flaw. That is, until your <u>non</u>-conformance goes too far.

Today more and more the parents and friends of psychiatric patients find what is done to their kin to be unjust, even criminal. Since the patient is often unable to advocate for himself, others must take up the task.

Pressures then mount on the soul healer. If we step back from this, and look at it as a kind of an organic process in cultural development, we could ask whether or not the soul healer is in fact just that person who can do the most for all parties, given that the soul healer is already in the center of the storm. If the soul healer takes a stand, then all will be forced to pay attention.

the weight of scientific materialism

+

need for social order -> the soul healer <- the kin of the patients

+

the patients themselves

The soul healer is himself a spirit struggling to be scientific, a member of the social order, kin of some in need, and perhaps has even been a patient. All which surrounds the soul healer socially should help the soul healer, instead of demanding that the center conform to their one-sided point of view. If we find a way to heal the soul healer, we might well begin to heal the whole.

Some practical suggestions:

First, concerning scientific materialism: This approach, in that it seeks knowledge of consciousness, makes one glaring fundamental error.   It assumes nobody has studied consciousness before. The whole cultural history of mankind is full of such studies, all of which are practical and experimental and rational. Some seem to lean toward a vague mysticism, but this is only when see from the outside.   The more modern are eminently scientific.   A partial list: the Middle Way of Lua Tzu; Yoga; Tibetan and Zen Buddhism, Quabbalah; Gnosticism; Sufism; Alchemy;

Rosicrucianism; Transcendentalism; Christian Hermeticism; and, Anthroposophy (this last is the most modern and scientific).

The soul healer will find much to aid his ability to help scientific materialism overcome its own one-sidedness, by taking in hand his own path to *self* knowledge.

Second, concerning the social order: the soul healer needs to speak plainly to power, and recognize that while political power can want almost anything, a great deal it wants is not possible, and let us still have a free society. Go too far in eliminating deviance (something more and more hard to define), and all other freedoms will be eroded. The soul healer, being in the middle of these social forces, needs to have his views particularly respected, for only he sees and knows certain aspects of the whole. The social order needs to follow the guidance of the soul healer in how money is spent and on what.

Third, concerning the kin of the patients: more and more the kin must accept that they are often (but not always) the best caregivers. Their hearts are most open and committed, but such care must be cooperative in nature ... all four groups, who surround the soul healer in the center have to work together. In practical terms this means that families and communities in which special individuals have been born and raised, perhaps need to stop wanting to send these individuals away, and hide them in institutions.

Fourth, the patients themselves: they need to realize that the more they want to indulge in socially deviant behaviors, the more necessary they make it that they be isolated from the rest. No one, the conformist or the non-conformist, can force themselves on another individual human being. Actions will have consequences, and no one will have a perfect life.

What becomes essential, for all five parts of this organism directed at soul health, is mutual trust and cooperation. Each has a role. *All must sit at the same table*. Nothing can change overnight, but with patience and agreement the whole can make progress, one day at a time.

This following also needs to be said to the soul healer:

Immediately you define deviant behavior as symptomatic of a disease (mental or otherwise), you have locked in a box a whole other set of questions that need to be asked. Predominant among these questions are whether the social order itself is healthy. If the social order breeds deviance, then why do we blame the deviant? If all causes are material, why do we even have a debate about Nature and Nurture?

The main problem, from a philosophy of knowledge point of view, is that we live in a time where there is an excess of analysis, and hardly any synthesis. Remember: the scientific enterprise (at the present, this can change) is dominated by analytic thinking - thinking which takes apart what it observes in order to make it easier to analyze. The fewer variables, the easier to define the experiment.

Eddington called this, at the beginning of the 20th Century, knowing more and more about less and less. Detail multiplies far faster than wise synthesis.

So for example, physics, having confined itself to dealing only with what it could count (*quantities* to the exclusion of *qualities*), can only create a world view (the big bang) based upon number relationships - no other relationships having been investigated or understood. The soul healer, trapped in the scientific model which only counts and takes apart, can't any longer understand his patient whose subjective psyche is complex in the extreme, and completely inter-related and inter-dependent - not just inwardly, but more crucially socially.

For the soul healer there are almost too many variables, at least in the sense of what is acceptable science today. Thus, everything has become dependent on material chemistry (in its widest sense), while the reality the soul healer faces is obviously a mixture of material chemistry and emotional or social "chemistry". Perhaps we need an entirely new discipline: *social alchemy,* which would be concerned with how we transform the soul-lead of human weakness and darkness, into soul-gold for the benefit not just of the individual but the community as well.

Part of the problem is the pursuit by the soul healer of pure objectivity, following the lead (in a sense) of physics. By various kinds of rules (developed over time in the history of soul healing such as the problem of transference), the soul healer more and more abandoned his own subjectivity. Yet, and everyone in this field knows this, the best talk therapy work is often done in groups, and involves a great deal of perception on the part of the soul healer of "feelings".

Unperceived emotional chemistry has to be brought into the open. In order to do this, the best guide is actually the self-awareness of the soul healer's own feeling life. A therapist not seeing his own therapist on a regular basis is not upholding the necessary standard of self discipline. An explorer of the spiritual dimensions of human inner life, that is not studying with someone more experienced, will also fall into error. If the soul healer combines his work (that is he studies his own mind and the art of soul healing), will need to work not only with other soul healers, but with those whose spiritual practice is mature.

Those who want to move in this direction will find, obviously, a mine field. Therapists are human and subject to much temptation - sexual manipulation of the patient being an obvious case in point. The soul healer who pursues real self knowledge in an objective fashion, will discover that his best guide is his own moral attitude, a problem that is not at all simple.

Feelings are best perceived when we develop the ability to think with the heart. Thinking with the heart, however, is best done when our conscious motive is to realize the good. We will the good, and then think with the heart. Moreover, the gesture of what is the good begins in the head. We think first, what is the good, then we will the good and let the heart be what it was designed to be: an organ of perception.

Why does this work in the realm of soul healing?

Because what every human being wants is to be known and cared about non-judgmentally by other human beings. This is where the child begins its life, and where all the deep pain of growing up is lodged. At the same time this is a very frightening want. We want our truth to be known, and our social order discourages us from expressing our truth. The social order already in the family doesn't want the truth of who we are, but rather some kind of mask. Everyone there is already wearing masks, and this we imitate from childhood onward. The very first thing deep psychological art we learn is to put on a mask.

That is the fundamental nature of childhood and it leads easily to the correlative creation of an outer personality - it is a mask designed to navigate troubled emotional seas. We have how we behave, and then who we really are inside - known to our secret self. Conflict arises between the two modes of being - the mask and the reality. Everyone solves the conflict in unique ways. Some parts we mask, other parts we share.   The variations on the mixture are remarkable, and once we really appreciate the nature of individuality - the true spirit of the individual human being - we will discover that scientific materialism has been itself a mask hiding our fear of religious domination for a long long time.

The social order itself put on a mask. The whole advertising industry exists to manipulate this conflict for the benefit of commerce. The soul healer will find that in order to truly heal the individual, he must simultaneously help to heal the social.

And, all the keys to this vast work lie within his own humanity. We discover and heal the truth of ourselves, and we at the same time discover and heal the truth of the world. Fully half of what the soul healer can know is available to him only through a scientific and objective introspection. At present the soul healer only knows what is available through his senses. What lies interior, a vast landscape already explored by many others, remains potential. Unexplored, the rest of the world is incomplete. Once explored, no secret is prohibited.

What happens when we do this

Consider now two common problems: hearing voices and serious depression.

From the side of scientific materialism, these often reported phenomena are diagnosed as defects at the level of brain chemistry. The mind, as a mechanism, is seen to be producing such effects because those who are not seen as deviant supposedly do not experience them.   The sub-conscious thought of the soul healer is that since I do not experience voices or become paralyzed with depression, such phenomena must be a flaw in the brain chemistry itself. The logical conclusions then is that if I can change the brain chemistry with drugs or ECT, I have fixed the problem.

This is very reasonable, as long as we refuse to recognize the inherent contradictions and present day limits of scientific thought about consciousness.

Suppose, for example, we do something very dangerous (only at this time, and in this essay, as a *thought experiment*), and consider the possibility that the paranoid schizophrenics' report of hearing voices is in fact accurate. They are hearing voices that are real. Granted this is not a normal condition for a human being, but why do we assume that because it is abnormal, it is not true. The one fact does not automatically follow from the other.

Further, if we turn to the understanding of the historical (and recent) mind sciences (who dangerously don't accept that the mind is based in matter only), we will find all kinds of explanation for the voices. So as to not complicate things, let us just consider such a view as might arise in the West, and is modern and scientific: Anthroposophy.

If the voices are real, what, possibly, is the patient hearing?

To say invisible people is to mock the experience of the individual having the experience, but at the same time, this is precisely what we see when we notice a paranoid schizophrenic walking down the street, seemingly talking to the air - talking to someone that is apparently not there (we don't see anything).

Our culture defines this as insane and seeks to rid this individual of this experience. Yet, in Western mind sciences, two clear possibilities are recognized. One is that the schizophrenic is talking to the dead, or that they are engaged in a kind of spiritually abnormal dialog with the double or the shadow. These mind sciences would not say that the individual talking to invisible people is behaving in a spiritually healthy way, yet at the same time they would say that what the schizophrenic experiences is real, and not illusory (albeit warped by psychic imbalances).

This turns everything on its head, certainly. Yet, it also redefines the problem, and in a quite significant way. The problem at once ceases to be one of ridding the brain mechanism of a mechanical dysfunction, but of actual soul healing, for something is out of sorts in terms of the self-consciousness of the individual. The inwardness is out of balance, and what is out of balance can be restored to harmony.

Nor does this exclude physical therapies. Rudolf Steiner, the discoverer of Anthroposophy, gave a series of lectures to an audience of both pastors and doctors, which he called **Pastoral Medicine**. He talked at length and specifically about mental illness, putting forward the idea that many such individuals needed both medical care and pastoral care, simultaneously.

Just to give an example from personal experience. I was working on a woman's unit at a for-profit psychiatric facility where was admitted a nun. She was a member of an order that teaches children and she no doubt was exhibiting anomalous behaviors. What struck me as particularly tragic, was that while she was in the hospital, the inner ground of her spiritual life (daily prayer and Mass etc.) was ignored. If fact, I was the only one who would talk to her about her spiritual life, and it was clear how much she hungered just to have someone listen to that aspect of her soul.

Of course, the reader may now say this is ridiculous, but the reader no doubt has not practiced meditation and other inner disciplines for years. Had they engaged in such practices, the schizophrenics' experiences then take on an entirely different meaning. Hearing voices and seeing things that supposedly aren't there is a common stage of spiritual development well know to those on a meditative path. When mind becomes sufficiently inwardly silent, it also becomes receptive to that which is otherwise too subtle to be experienced by ordinary consciousness.

Our self-conscious subjectivity is actually more real than matter, and when it wakes up to itself sufficiently, it discovers another world along side the one we normally experience through the senses.

It would go too far here to give meditation instruction, but at the least lets revisit some of what science thinks is knows. For example, it is common in an experiment, where the brain is being watched with a CT scan, to observe a certain sequence: the subjectivity is asked to perform a certain mental function (solve a puzzle, for example), and then at some point there appears to the scan a great deal of activity in some part of the brain, after which the subjectivity reports the solution. These observations are seen as demonstrating not only that the brain solved the puzzle (after all the observed electrical activity occurred in time prior to the report of the solving of the puzzle), but also what part of the brain was involved.

The problem here isn't the observations being made by the investigating scientist, but rather with the interpretation of their meaning. Remember above that we pointed out the tendency in brain studies to leave aside the social agreement between the investigating subjectivity and the subjectivity of the one whose brain is being studied. The physicist knows he has to reinsert this into his appreciation of what happened in his split-beam experiment, so lets do the same here.

Causally the first thing that has happened is the social agreement by which the self-consciousness of the scientist asked the self-consciousness of the research subject to engage is certain activity (solve the puzzle in this case). Without that request, nothing happens.

Just as with the indeterminacy problem for the physicist, there is no brain activity to observe without the social agreement asking the subjectivity of the one whose brain is being studied to engage in self-conscious mental activity. The next thing observed is the electrical discharges in the brain. Prior to this, however, the subject has inwardly acted (which the subject certainly experiences, and the scientist if he is honest about his own introspective knowledge of his own mind also regularly experiences). The causal train is: scientist asks > subject acts inwardly > brain activity is observed > then the subject reports the solution to the puzzle. The actual brain activity is surrounded by four self-conscious subjective acts, and it is only our preconceived paradigm that makes us isolate the brain activity as if it is causally independent. The fourth act is the scientist's subjective act of interpretation of the meaning of the experiment.

1) scientist asks

2) subject acts inwardly

3) brain activity is observed

4) subject reports a solution to the puzzle

5) scientist interprets the meaning of the experiment

Clearly the observed brain activity is caused by the inner activity of the puzzle solving subject, and therefor the observed brain activity is a consequence of, not the cause of, this inner puzzle-solving act. What is actually being observed, once we free ourselves of the constraints of the paradigm, is a spiritual act which needs a material brain to act in a material world.

The research subject can't hear the voice of the scientist asking for his cooperation, without the physical ear, nor can the research subject report the solution to the puzzle without the material apparatus of the voice box. If, for example, we wired the scientists up as well, we would see the whole sequence of events quite clearly. But every time there was observable brain activity, there is prior to that the spiritual activity (thinking) of the participants in the experiment.

Yes, I know, there are lots of brain activity going on without the self-conscious intervention of the thinking subject, but all that just goes to prove the observation of soul healers in the centuries prior to the full materialization of scientific thinking, when Freud and others re-discovered the existence of the sub-conscious and unconscious elements of human inner life (something know to ancient mind sciences for centuries). The self-conscious subject has to be coaxed into sufficient self observation (talk therapy) in order to be able to report, what has otherwise been hidden from the I, or self-consciousness.

If this process of self examination is aided by the modern mind sciences rooted in deep inner disciplines, then it is possible to go even further in the direction of needed discoveries that can shed a great deal of light on the soul health of many. What the Freudians etc. discovered was just the surface of a plane of existence already well known to Alchemists, and others, for centuries. The sub-conscious and unconscious aspects of human inner life are already a well explored territory.

If this understanding is then integrated with all the remarkable research on brain physiology and chemistry, a whole unknown world of soul healing can result, such that ECT and overly powerful drugs then become completely unnecessary. The scientists of the material world have done a great work, which is only limited in its application by the restrictions imposed by the no longer workable paradigm of strict scientific materialism (all is matter, there is no spirit).

Let us come at this once more, this time with respect to depression, instead of hearing voices. What do the deep explorers of our shared human inwardness already know about depression?

What is the basic phenomena of depression? It is a paralysis of the will, and this a varying degrees. The deeper the mal-ease, the more immobile the patient. Some would take to their beds and never leave, if not otherwise treated.

The mind sciences of the Occident (as opposed to those of the Orient - who are differently oriented in terms of goals) have long recognized what is to be called: the doctrine of the temperaments (the choleric, the phlegmatic, the sanguine and the melancholic). These are quite apt objective observations of general human characteristics, and can be quite useful in their application. Depending on the temperament the course taken by depression will be different. A choleric might ignore it until some crisis ensues, while the melancholic will find self-satisfied glory in it, for it proves all his worst fears.

What is similar to all is the influence of the double or the shadow. There really is no understanding of the human being without appreciating not only soul and spirit, but also the dark side - the shadow. One writer (see Meditations on the Tarot, Arcanum XV The Devil), speaks in quite practical terms of the tempter, the prosecutor and of egregores.

Egregores are older (and wiser) terms for what addicts know as "the monkey on my back". I have taken to abandoning that name (it is clearly too archaic), and substituting the idea of "wounds". We bear wounds in the soul (psyche), some of which fester in such a way that they overwhelm our conscious will. I point out the temperaments and the three-fold nature of the shadow simply to suggest that this way of thinking is as equally complex and rich as is the present day conventional view. Not only that, but what is being offered here is meant to supplement, not replace the conventional view.

I also mean to suggest that depression is complicated, and one has to in any event carefully observe and examine whoever has such a problem with attention to a lot of detail, for not only is everyone quite individual, as all soul healers appreciate, the situation is delicate, and the patient very vulnerable and unsure - they won't know what facts to share, and may often hide relevant phenomena for a variety of personal reasons.

If it is clear that the basic problem is a paralysis of the will, and a related experience of "life is too much", then we can be fairly sure that the shadow, in the form of the prosecutor is in play. In the soul, the ego (or spirit) is overwhelmed by the dark.

A major aspect of the problem is that we tend to think that this is an experience that should be eliminated - people, we often believe, ought to not suffer, but should be happy. A choleric, who can more easily ignore a deep case of the "blues", will look down upon a melancholic, who revels in this mood. Since our culture teaches no coherent inner disciplines (materialism doesn't recognize their need), people do not think that the ego can be taught how to manage their soul life out of their own inner will. Thinking the brain is the cause of all inner states, we don't really following those lines of thought that would lead us to appreciating other possibilities.

At a cultural age where some think the self-consciousness is an illusion, we will no doubt never consider that this very self-consciousness can become the master of its feeling life. Of course, all kinds of people engage in serious self-help or self-development disciplines, with success. Some people do manage, through such as the 12 Steps, to overcome addiction and alcoholism, using a discipline that sees the whole process as spiritual in nature. Our culture is full of examples where the I masters something of the inner life, unless you get in the mental health system, which isn't permitted (in general) to apply any other treatment modalities but medications.

I always found it the strangest kind of paradox, in the hospital where I worked for ten years, to go from the adult unit to the substance abuse unit, where two entirely different paradigms were at work. What was even stranger was to watch how those labeled *dual-diagnosis* were treated. A bi-polar addict was a odd creature indeed (you just have to read the treatment plans and the doctors intake interview, to see just how weird this can be). For the addict especially, the problem was very acute, for what most troubles them (their addiction) tends to require that they take no drugs at all. But if they are simultaneously described as bi-polar with an addiction, and mostly depressive (those with mania aren't so bothered by their so-called *mental* disease) there is a big problem.

How to you prescribe to an addict an upper to defeat their depression?

If we survey the field over the last 40 years, we will see how just at this juncture the profession itself created addictions to mood altering drugs. Have a mood disorder (that is have a soul state the culture defines as deviant), why lets give you a happy pill. Oh, sorry, you've become an addict to Valium now? Gosh, you sure are a wreck. (The system and the doctors are not responsible - right?)

To summarize:

The soul healer who undertakes a serious study of his own inwardness, following a modern mind science, will find their ability to help people greatly increased with every step they take in self knowledge and understanding.

Details can be found in my books: **the Way of the Fool**; and, **American Anthroposophy**. *the forces opposed to the self-development of the soul healer*

Social institutions acquire power, and their leaders gain wealth and prestige. Pharmaceutical corporations have a lot at stake in manufacturing drugs to "help" the mentally ill. Politicians like to be seen as "doing something". People in general don't want to be bothered by deviant behavior. Patients cry out for aid.

Like many people, the soul healer is confronted with a house of mirrors of choices. He can swim with the pack, or plot his own course. One way is easier, the other harder. Which way does Society need him to swim? If we define Society by its power structures, those structures will certainly need the soul healer to provide services that lets the powerful take action. In the Soviet Union, hospitalization for a "mental" illness was a political tool of a totalitarian State. Recently during the Bush II administration, psychologists were used to oversee torture and to help in its application.

As I pointed out above, the soul healer is in the center of a surrounding set of forces, and this fact then reveals something else. While we can urge that a whole society move in a certain direction, if we understand the practicalities of how social change actually arises we realize that such change occurs one individual at a time. It can't happen by fiat from Washington, but only organically out of individual free choices.

Think globally, act locally. Only the soul healer can give us the example and from there suggest what others can and ought to do. The coming revolution is personal and biographical. We do it from within our own lives. My novel **America Phoenix** begins with the following discussion, which is entirely relevant here and a good place to end (with a bit of Art):

"Synergy?" said Hex-man.

"Right, synergy" replied J.C. "Things happen together. The whole is greater than the sum of the parts. We tend to think that political and social change requires that we organize movements. Remember when we always talked about the "movement".

"Sort of, that was really before my time".

"Yea, right, okay. So anyway, synergy is about multiple things happening together to create something they can't accomplish alone. Its one of the main organizing principles living in the social organism. Just one, by the way, but for our purposes it will help to understand it.

"Yea, I get it. You and I, we do something together. Get better results than if we do it alone. Plus, other people, people we don't even know. They do stuff, and it interacts with our stuff synergistically. Is that a word?"

"I think so, but you get the basic idea. The thing is we can count on it. In fact we need to become highly aware of it. Think of us as trying to navigate the seas of history. In these seas are currents, and if we can ride some of the currents, stuff happens in a better way, than if we are trying to steer across them or against them. So we have to learn to make mental maps of the seas of social existence, and then find that place we want to work, and with whom - keeping in mind that we aren't alone and that others have similar goals and it all works together synergistically. "

"Okay, I get it I guess. But can you explain a little why this works, especially when people aren't really organized into mass movements?"

"Well, actually, mass movements are kind of dangerous. The more mass the less consciousness. We get mobs and violence. Small groups appreciating that each other exists do better. They concentrate more on what they really can do, and less on ideology. The phrase "think globally, act locally" understands this.

"Try it this way. Lots of people today want to decide for themselves what is true and what is right to do. Think of this impulse, a very common modern human impulse, as a kind of emerging social force in the evolution of human consciousness, or human nature as some might say. But everyone doesn't always agree about what is right, yes? Yet, what happens is that when a lot of people are struggling to do what is right, and not just hiding under the covers, you get a lot of right things being done in a lot of places. The way the social organism works, in its synergistic sense, is that all these right things add up to something more than the individuals can often imagine.

"Everyone has a place, the place right where they are. In that place they seek to do what Plato might have called the Good. This ideal of the Good is like a wonderful landscape, seen from many different directions. So each one of us, seeking to do the Good, helps bring this wonderful landscape more and more into real social existence. Each of us is like a kind of small sun, shining into the social organism our own striving for goodness."

"Okay, I can see that. But how do we know what the Good is?"

"Well, everyone has their own Way of course, but if I was to try to put the how of it into words, it has to do with when we think with our hearts and not just our heads. If we think just with our heads we get a kind of cold and calculating idea, generally one more selfish. But we need to think with our hearts, that is we need to think in a warmer way, more empathic, more caring of the other person, the thou. So we will the good and think with our hearts. Everyone can do that, don't you think. Or at least try."

"Yea, I get it. Don't need somebody to tell us what to do. We do our own thing, and if we will the good and think with our hearts, something happens all over the country or the world because of the synergy principle, something we can't imagine."

"Right, you got it Hex-man. Oh, one other thing. Ever see the movie Six Degrees of Separation?"

"No, what's it about?"

"Well, the story is kind of funny, but it has this idea behind the title. The idea is that between ourselves and any other person there are only six relationships. You know someone, and they know someone else, and so on for six relationships, until each of us is connected to any other person in the world by only six such relationships, or six degrees of separation."

"Crap. Can't be true. You think between me and the President are only six people separated? Shit, no way."

"I don't know, its just the idea. Maybe some math people invented the idea. But there is some truth.   We are connected in ways we don't see. You know me. I was in Vietnam, and I knew this CIA guy. Maybe now he works in Washington and his boss knows a Senator, and the Senator knows the President."

"Christ, that is weird."

"Yea, I know. But think about it in a different way, along the lines of what we have been doing with the synergy idea. These connections are real. We influence each other. You need something from me, or I need something from you, then these relationships become important. Things spread like splashes on a pond. Who knows what energy flows along the connections. "

~!~!~!~!~!~!~!~!~!~!~

The Father a Rest
**magical and mystical dark-matter physics
in the Age of Technological Chaos**

[printed book: https://www.lulu.com/en/us/shop/joel-wendt/the-father-at-rest/paperback/product-znpekm.html?page=1&pageSize=4 $9.98]

authors CV: http://ipwebdev.com/hermit/thetree.html

"A truly magical book. To read it is to remember mysteries lost sight of, which if understood and acted upon, lets each of us change our own world" Nino Baldachi, Air-Cadet extraordinaire

"Astral (star) travel, while sitting still, … there are no limits in the hyperspace of the mind." Johnathan Cornelius Madrid (J.C. for short) captain of the living self-evolving intergalactic vessel: Strange-Fire

"Hard times, harder choices" Teller-of-Stories, to Rider, in private …

Do the gods and goddesses have a sense of humor? Some sages assert that They laugh when we make plans. The evidence is clear. Most of what we want or expect from the Future never happens. Pretty much every day in our personal lives expectations fail. There is Mystery there, for those willing to chart a new course on forgotten seas of thought. The following is meant to\ point out powers we posses, as beings of spirit and soul. A gift from Them

Names and Naming

A rose by any other name is still a Rose. "The Slow Regard of Silent Things", advises shaman Patrick Rothfuss. All of us live in fields of material objects. All different, although in a prison the rooms can seem repetitious. Maybe we have a desk in an office … but are we free to select what we name our desk? Then there is the "freeway" madness … no wonder so many die from heart attacks.

"Silly", of one to name a desk – or a car, yes, … maybe. Silly is a word that used to mean "possessed by the sacred". A favorite coffee cup, with its sentimental value, is also an object-magique. A familiar secret hidden in the Idea/Lore of the talisman. When we can individualize our work spaces, the magic is already there. Listen to your personal "teller of stories" … meaning made up, in the own imagination.

Dreams are real. Dreaming is power. Each of us is a gate into the Dreaming. From one point of view there are eight gates to Faerie*, and they come pairs (again, read the shaman Patrick Rothfuss's "The Name of the Wind", from which I have shamelessly borrowed) *[I use the terms Faerie and the Fae, being a romantic, elsewhere and when, others write and speak of the Underworld, or the Lost Cities]

In the East, elemental Air, aka: Intellect. Waking&Sleeping* South, Fire, Will, Living&Dying West, Water, Feeling, Sanity&Madness North, Earth, Consciousness, Remembering & Forgetting

*[For example, when we are on the edge of going to sleep, and also waking up, that edge is where wishes and dreams gather to dance. In many aboriginal cultures, dreams are shared each morning, because they understand the spiritual power of the "intercourse" between us, and Them.]

What do Thunder&Lightening call Themselves? That flashing noisy light-bang, that we experience, is the way They Name Themselves. We live in what is already a magical world, for there is a direct spiritual connection between ourselves and all "other" natures. Subtle, and yet obvious.

Sensible Nature as Divine Speech? …. ***God creates the heavens and the Earth in six days, then rests on, blesses and sanctifies the seventh*** … Each ancient Earth Religion has a creation story … a story about a "maker".

In the way back, long ago, when before, … human beings did not need to believe in Gods and Goddesses, and gnomes and fauns, … we saw them, and spoke with them, in that true once upon a time.

Want some evidence? Read Owen Barfield's "Speaker's Meaning" and learn that during that Age the Great Myths have remembered, languages were young, and a young language is entirely literal. We give names to what is experienced.

Modern arts of film and television are filled today with memories of something "other". Marvel's twenty-film Avenger series. Eight Harry Potter movies. The X-Files and the Twilight Zone. Ghost chasers. Dreams of vampires and werewolves. Charmed lives. Wonders of travel to even the further reaches of the Expanse.

The whole world lives in seas of meaning. The world we see is not the worlds others see. Some poetic examples: "Albert in Fugue":] http://ipwebdev.com/hermit/Albertinfugue.html ["Rhubarb's Dilemma":
] https://thecollectiveimagination.com/2020/02/15/rhubarbs-dilemma/ [or, "A Miracle for Fences":] http://ipwebdev.com/hermit/Fences.html [

In the Dreamtime, it was understood that if there were beginnings, there also had to be endings. So the story tellers had to teach of time/change as endless Now upon Now, something forgotten to modern civilized folks.

In our memories – organized around linear time – the Third Millennium, since the Single-Now Physical Birth of Word/Life/Light – this third Echo began/begins with the usual wars, plagues, famines, and conquests.

What, for example, should be the "name" of the Covid-plague? Where does Climate Change fit in? Some interesting questions, from the mind of JMS (Babylon 5, and Crusade). Who are you? What do you want? Where are you going? Who do you serve? And, Who do you trust?

There are cogent reasons for suspecting we are riding tsunamis of future history, the result of which will be the dying and becoming of "Western" civilization.

Imagine a drop of water – in slow motion, falling and landing/making waves upon waves in the seas of change, rippling out from a Center. Now reverse the image, where the infinite periphery of waves collapses into a point, from which then rises as/the single drop flying upward and back into the Source … only to disappear from both time and space, … until – by choice – inward bound once more … falling earthward from a heavenly sky full of individuals sparks of existence.

Did He/She make us, or did we make Them/Her/Him? The "Maker" has many names, but is still the maker, whatever the name.

In modern materialistic unnatural science there are beliefs and theories, which makes such works also religious, not just scientific. The essential core idea of scientific materialism – matter only, no spirit – is designed to exclude any possibility of there being "spirit/sparks", as a cause-active in the world. Instead the Maker disappears on the other side of a tale about big bangs, and random chaotic evolutionary and developmental changes.

At the same time, "modern science", as a Way of Knowledge, is young, if we were to compare it to the centuries of life and development of the cultures of ancient Egypt, or of the Maya. In a certain sense, this youthful science, while laced with human genius on a staggering scale, is only half of the picture/meaning of our "plan*demic" Pandemonium Reboot. *[The real "Plan" is from the Mystery, and the apparent conjunction with games of earthly power and wealth an incidental by-product of the operation of the Arts-Karmic, and their essential guide: Justice.]

There is a Genius to History. While civilizations come and go, the urge for order always arises post-the debris of excessive dis-order. It turns out that "spirit" is as real as "matter", just as the ancients knew, … the following pages try to map out some of the crucial riddles and mysteries.

Odd though, … the irony that in some places today, a few thinkers assert that order can be observed arising from chaos. In the chaos of modern life, what Phoenix stirs in the ashes? At the exotic regions of modern physics, the riddle of what is consciousness spices the stew of change.

In this writing – you might be reading, … let us turn the matter-only prejudice aside, and simply look at the world, as it is: a Mystery filled everywhere with spirit, a world both visible and invisible dancing the Art of Now.

We look upon the wonders of the Goddess Natura, remark as to Their beauty, and don't quite finish the circuit, where it is our consciousness that sees. We are nature looking at Herself. Emerson wrote: "Nature is the incarnation of a thought, and turns to thought again as ice becomes water and then gas. The world is mind precipitated, and the volatile essence is forever escaping into the state of free thought."

Notes on Structure: Matter-only based "science" claims that mathematics rules. Only the quantitative and measurable matters. If we add "spirit", we get to include the qualitative and intuitive, which has a mathematics based upon arts-music and the higher Ideals of potential human becoming.

A couple of decades ago I was writing a never finished book: "Strange Fire: the Death and the Resurrection of Modern Civilization" http://ipwebdev.com/hermit/stgfr.html At a certain point I recognized that I didn't knot-know the own dark as much as I needed. It has now been twenty-five years, yet the original structure wants to be remembered, … … a kind of abstract musical form … I've added some small bits of change … and yes, as my eldest son pointed out, that as an actual musician, the real – concrete "scale" is different. A nice riddle lurking there …

There are eight individual Notes, and then in between each Note, the Interval, which is where the music begins. The idea is to notice order, yet leave a core place for the heart's wild.

"Note": is from the common rule of practice among monks and nuns; "Interval": is one of the seven "I am" statements in the Gospel of John; followed by one of the seven liberal arts, and that followed by the one of the seven stages of the passion of the Christ-Maker …

do: (matins/2a.m.)
do-re: "I am the true Vine" … rhetoric … washing the feet
re: (lauds/sunrise)
re-mi: "I am the Way, the Truth and the Life" … grammar … the scourging
mi: (prime/6a.m.)
mi-fa: "I am the Door" … logic … the crowning with thorns
fa: (terce/9a.m.)
fa-sol: "I am the Bread of Life" … astronomy … the carrying the cross
sol: (sext/miday)
sol-la: "I am the Good Shepherd" … geometry … the crucifixion
la: (none/3p.m.)
la-ti: "I am the Light of the World" … arithmetic … the death
ti: (vespers/sunset)
ti-do: "I am the Resurrection and the Life" … music … the resurrection
do: (compline/before retiring)

Seven days in a week. Seven chakras. Each day connected to a planet. Sun-day, Moon-day, Mars-day, Mercury-day, Jupiter-day, Venus-day, Saturn-day. The chakras are organized into three sets of three.

The first threeness is the three above the heart, the heart itself, and the three below the heart. The upper threeness, Crown, Eyebrow, and Throat, have the "third eye" in the middle. The lower threeness, Solar Plexus, Reproductive, and Base, has its middle as well. The upper middle (Eyebrow), and the lower middle (Reproductive) are linked (as an example of greater complexities), through the influence of the imagination.

This imagination of a love object takes place in the third eye, as it were, and is affected by the appetites in the reproductive, while the circuit of energies unfolds together in the arts of the sensual-physical, and the erotic-mental.

Threenesses worth repeating: spirit, soul, and, body. Or, thinking, feeling, and, willing.

The point of the observation of the above number-relations – as built around the idea of seven and three – is an essential riddle, for understanding a Qualitative form of mathematical physics that does not Deny the Father and the Son (the anti-Christ spirit, of the first two letters of John). Why essential? Because each of us are sons and daughters of the Divine Mystery. Our biography follows such maps, … maps which vary according to the most ancient religious ideas in the geographic places we are born and travel.

For example, there is a reason the ancient Mayan scribes/priests counted days. Among all the speaking/deeds of the Maker, this day-spiral, both maze and labyrinth, to which all humans are cursed or blessed, according to their own reflection, … all the same tells, over and over, the story of the One and the Many, the Sun of the Day, and the Moon-ruled sky of the Night.

Suppose, rather than assuming that reality is all based on "matter", without spirit, we instead assume that Reality Requires both spirit and matter. What if we just look at the same facts, and add to them observations of a spiritual dimension, … on purpose!?~?! What if we "imagine", for example, that between our Self – and every surface of sense experience – is elemental beings, not mindless things.

Names and Naming, remember …

Newton and Leibniz had an argument just about this. Newton's "atoms" were soulless things, and Leibniz was of the view that consciousness had to be everywhere, so his smallest entities he called: "monads", which/who possessed consciousness and will.

What we today call molecules of air, the ancients knew as elemental beings, which we in the cultural West call: sylphs. In the East, their highest elemental spirit (according to Rudolf Steiner) has this name: Vayu. RS also sez: their over-seeing Archangel is Raphael.

That wind that touches our faces is alive, and awake, and while not exactly free* in its elemental nature, yet all the same Faerie Dust – for the Fae-spirits of the winds and breezes feels through/with them … all touching us, just as we feel their touch. *[These elemental folk have sacrificed their potential freedom, to serve the needs of the whole.

https://thecollectiveimagination.com/2019/10/29/rudolf-steiner-on-elemental-beings-karma-ceremonial-magic/

Some time in the far future, if we humans learn, we just might became able – as makers – to gift them freedom, in honor of their prior services.]

When a tornado roars by, a whole sky-full of spirits are involved, … if ideas of predestination, and or karma and reincarnation, bother a reader or two … both fall away in the Now … For some life goes on. Others die. "There is no Fate but what we Make", sez Sarah Conner (Linda Hamilton) in the "Terminator" films.

"As Allah Wills" can be a cop-out, or a religious – artistic – scientific representation about life and its mysteries. Most of us are at war with the Now. At some point we have to Surrender. "Take a breath", sez the zen-trained cop, in the TV show: Life.

My life led me to many more questions than answers. This is one of the reasons I write. Letters on a page, hiding an idea in the mind of the reader. When I was with Him, as Matthew, He taught me to become a fisher of men. Yet, … what should be the lure?

The Simple Truth. "pragmatic moral psychology" http://ipwebdev.com/hermit/stgfr5.html

What if we imagine that the whole electrification of the world, and all the related technology, is based upon our unconscious use of magic, in order to what: … mimic the Maker?

We took the Maker's Creation apart, because we would some time in the future be as Makers ourselves. Like Now, for example.

Inside – what became the world of things, without beings – there were secrets, Goddess Natura's underskirts – the deeper mysteries, as it were. Hidden. A very attractive quest to adventure, as long as we remember: She Exists.

A necessary limit that, however. For Humanity to find Itself, the deep spirit had to be forgotten.

So, out of Love, She lets go, and the Goddess/Earth Religions faded away to first become dominated by the three patriarchal monotheisms, ultimately producing the singular religion of unnatural science.

Among the ancient Lore of humanity are books of "magic".

Our ancient cultures also tell tales of even more forgotten times, … for example, those memories born in the geographic regions of India, speak of atomic powers before the before.

Ships of air and fire. Wars in the Skies, and Lands.

All the same, the "power" that exists, which we call electromagnetism, is everywhere. Not just everywhere, also every-when. How?

After the Creation, the Maker rested from Their Labors. Saw the mystery, having set free so many individual sparks, yet knowing there might be too much chaos, too much magical and mystical spiritual life. Some fundamental ordering principle needs to appear, or the forces of uncontrolled life would consume all (see the movie: "Annihilation").

From One "I" becomes many I, or "We". Having choices that effect, "We" become effectively a total: "God", borne in the reach of our personal wills. This blessed curse is shared by all, and together, all hearts singing, "God" becomes "Love". Yet, the land of the Unknown and Unpredictable and Unformed deserves its due: "Chaos".

Aka: the law of iwegodlovechaos. Never parts. Always whole.

Again, … restraining Chaos needs order. Both concepts are an aspect of the law of the universal necessary pair. Up and Down. Right and Left. Besides Himself.

If we wish to know the Divine, scientifically, we need to make careful observations that others can themselves also do. Take the pair: Mathematical Physics, aka: stuff we named and counted as we took apart the Maker's Creation, meanwhile denying that They existed.

Still, ;;;; the mystery of the four fundamental forces that physics recognizes today: electromagnetism, gravity, and the weak and strong nuclear forces … remains.

A thought experiment wanders by … imagine that all electro-magnetic "phenomena" in the whole of reality is the One that begat, and then rested. When you turn on your desk lamp, … that power is Unity expressed in matter, to be later pulled out of where hidden, woven into new shapes, captured, tamed, and put to use.

The Father at Rest. Not Asleep.

Awake, … willing Self to be put to use. Anticipating not being remembered. A power so miraculous, at Rest it still Serves. In the Avenger movies, "Odin" seems dead at one point, yet it turns out He was not, … just resting and waiting. Real were the Beings named by men in the Norse Myths.

Ragnarok: the death of the gods, … is Now. Which Gods is an excellent question? Perhaps, … the Gods of the Ego, and of the Forge. A world overrun with ambitious folk hungering for wealth and power, so as to indulge in all their craven appetites. Each needing to own the bombs and the poisons, and the fear. Yet, … forgetting: She. Her favorite trickster groupies – Loki, Raven, and Coyote, always trying to impress the Empress, are less actually scary if we understand that They are vehicles for Now-to-Now Course Corrections. Trump. Putin. The Wizards of Oz in the "intelligence gathering business". Physicists playing self-absorbed mind games in the Loki fantasy: "quantum".

The Idea – of tiny, tiny, and endlessly tiny material things – crosses the veil, crosses the veil between the visible and invisible worlds. As a consequence, we lose sight of it, yet still worshiping "thingness", for to modern scientific speculations there is no "beingness" anywhere out there.

We have been led to believe we-only have a self-aware sentient intelligence that is invisible to others, except as lives in our deeds.

The atoms, the quantum realm, the mysterious interior of sun and earth, plants, stars – all assumed to have no self-awareness.

A vanity of no little power. All the same, … the Whole of so-called material reality does have an interior self-aware sentience. She/They watch us, and touch us daily.

No? It is all about "names", not just numbers. We need to remember how to name the world of experience, so as to again seek contact with the Fae, and the realms of Faerie – the Underworld, and the Lost Cities.

We ourselves are included as of the Fae. Immortal spirits, suffering the teachings of Their School of hard knocks and shared pain, … in an illusory* matter-only world. *[The Idea of Maya, or that sense experience is not real as against direct experience of the spirit, is ancient. The ancients did not get everything right. What is called Goethean Science is learning to Read the Book of Nature – sense reality as Speech, – not an illusion.]

The Principle of Unity Itself is already proven by the experiment of the two related particles that, while they can be separated in space, cannot be separated in Now.

Like you and me. You are with me, as I write. And, I am with you, as you read.

Seeking to "know" such a power, as is behind and beneath electromagnetism more intimately, requires the skill of mysticism. No surprise there. Imagining a world filled with spirit – many old friends we don't even know anymore, yet still there in spite of the fact that unnatural science gave them meaningless names – for the most part.

Mysticism can't be separated from the magical. Magical Lore is still remembered today. Personally I recommend the works of Franz Bardon, on the Hermetic Science of the Ancient

Egyptians. For mysticism, the book by Valentin Tomberg: Meditations on the Tarot, a Journey into Christian Hermeticism.

Notice this following ancient treasure map, one among many:
Prima Materia divides into celestial salt and celestial niter, each of which divides into the fixed elements earth and water, and the volatile elements air and fire, respectively. Earth and water begat salt. Water and Air begat Mercury, while air and fire begat sulphur.

Fire is the symbol for the human will. Air is the symbol for human intellect. Water is the symbol for human feeling. Earth is the symbol for human consciousness.

If you want to follow that kind of map, buy: "On Becoming an Alchemist – a guide for the modern magician", by Catherine MacCoun. She modestly says she weaves together both Tibetan and Christian Alchemy. Most everyone I know, who has read this, has read it more than once. For many it occupies the place we make for just before sleep reading. In some of my writing, I call this work "a gospel of soul".

There need not be any longer secrets, in the true arts and crafts by which the Father at Rest is "appropriated", … as a gift of knowledge. For example, I wrote a long article on the relationship between the four classical elements, fire/will, air/intellect/, water/feeling, and earth/consciousness, and the four fundamental forces / transformations of modern physics. https://thecollectiveimagination.com/2019/05/20/letters-about-magic/

The search for a Unified Field Theory of Everything is easily answered once we re-insert spirit where it always has been. I wrote of this, from the point of view of a spiritual social-science: "The Art of God: an actual theory of Everything"
http://ipwebdev.com/hermit/artofgod.html

Here we are doing the same, yet from a more evolved mathematical physics.

Let us take a peek at light and gravity phenomena … in their primary expression to our experience … remember, the sense world of appearances is speech.

If we are fortunate, we have a bed to sleep in, and running water, with a personal toilet. Gadgets electrical everywhere. Lights to turn off and on. Garbage removal. Companies that deliver stuff right to the door.

A smart phone is an Aladdin's lamp. And just as dangerous.

At night we lie down, and surrender to gravity, happy that we did not experience what Bob Marley sang of in Talking Blues: "Cold ground was my bed last night. Rock was my pillow."

In the morning, depending, opening the eyes to the light can feel like a pain. Yet, sunrise and sunset are always blessings. In a certain Way of cognitive knowing, the senses are also wounds of soul. The impression of strong light, or sounds, or smells … even our spirit can be wounded, and some of these life-traumas that go into the land of: and-this-too-shall-pass, still can permanently scar the soul. Just think of all the children growing up today, being made (unjustly) fearful of human contact, and touch.

Cosmic Magic is our individual Consciousness of one Now following after another, … our experience a sea of constant change … a symphony of Nows. Still the mystery of other, … is my experience what my bed-mates experience? Stop time/change? What vanity. It is what it is, literally.

The Hermetic Science of the ancient Egyptians pointed to "four" elements, will/Fire; air/Intellect; water/Feeling; and, earth/Consciousness. To our experience these can be known as a Whole, which Bardon called the: four-poled magnet. Another member of the quality three, yet in this case the "fourth" element is the union of the first three. Also, to experience, the mysteries of: spirit, soul, and body. Thinking, feeling, willing. Wholeness in threes. Simple riddles, for magical times.

When lying in bed, or sitting quietly in a chair, we can study ourselves, for all the secrets are right in front of us – aspects of experience. The ancient Persians used the metaphor of a charioteer, a chariot, and a horse. The thoughts, or mental structure, coupled with our favorite feelings, is the chariot. The horse is the power of emotion, which yet needs guidance from the charioteer. We – as spirit – are the fire of will(ing) that creates the chariot of our intellect's ideas (thinking/meaning) of the what-is, and guides and tames and directs the emotional-power (feeling).

That emotional power is also perceptual. Aspects can be scary. Consciously directed empathy can lead to deep understanding, yet – the intimacy – that's where it gets, as we say today: Real.

Dare I look at myself through the eyes of a lover? Practice by listening/talking with Grandmother Trees. http://ipwebdev.com/hermit/GrandmotherTree.html

the day begins …

Sitting up, standing, overcoming gravity, with some quick-starting of the intellect with caffeine. Breathing.

The sylph-air is just there. Breathing is just there. Is there spirit there/here? Try to stop breathing. You could do it, but then you are dead, and where's the fun in that?

In Bardon's works on magic the first and most important task is to learn how to do: conscious full-body pore-breathing. Has health benefits. https://thecollectiveimagination.com/2020/03/23/the-magic-of-breathing-as-a-possible-aide-for-an-individual-with-the-flu/

Many people justly fear for theirs, and others – including the Planet's – future. Let me just observe in passing that the true meaning/name of "gravity" is an effect of the Love of the Holy Mother ~!~ Earth Mother; just as "breathing" is an effect of the Love of the Son.

*[The Moody Blues song: "One Step into the Light" has these lines: https://www.youtube.com/watch?v=hprKBU9btN8&ab_channel=illuminatedEntity

> One step into the light
> One step away from night
> It's the hardest step you're gonna take
> The ship to take you there
> Is waiting at the head
> Of the stairs that lead up through your opening mind
>
> Above the dark despair
> Shines a light that we can share
> Close your eyes and look up in between your brows
> Then slowly breathing in
> Feel the LIFE FORCE streaming in
> Hold it there, then send it back to him
>
> All the old things are returning
> Cosmic circles ever turning
> All the truth we've been yearning for
> Life is our saviour, saviour, saviour, save your soul
>
> The river of LIVING BREATH
> Is flowing through the SUN
> He was there before the earth began
> The world will drag on you
> Use his love to pull you through
> Find the mission of YOUR LIFE and start to BE
>
> All the old things are returning
> Cosmic circles ever turning
> All the truth we've been yearning for
> Life is our saviour, saviour, saviour, save your soul

> There's one thing I can do
> Play my Mellotron for you
> Try to blow away your city blues
> Your dreams are not unfound
> Get your feet back on the ground
> The TRUTH will set us FREE, we cannot lose
> We cannot lose, we just have to CHOOSE

By the way, the Moody Blues saw coming, what we today experience. If you want esoteric Christian rock 'n roll, these are the folk.

The Earth Mother aspect is the dangerous and wild one. Our first lessons harsh: run too fast, fall down, go boom. When a civilization goes too fast, same fall, different doom.

She is the Source of Rogue Weather, the Four Horseman of the Apocalypse, and the Gate of Death. What we notice – with our soul-less numbers, and experience in ever increasing "weather" calamities – is hand-writing on the wall of even greater coming "earth-transformations".

Each of us dies, and each of us meets our Maker in our own ways and Nows. Keep in mind these rules: everyone is the right person, in the right place, at the right time. Our biographies have similarity, but each spark faces life choices expressed in their personal and unique style. Just take a look at TikTok to see the variety.

We are in a descending cycle, in the sense of the value of our ideas regarding linear time. Change-massive is clearly appearing, from Trump to Covid to WTF is next!!! Aliens??? The Whole Sphere of the living Creation is flowering on a staggering scale.

There is a lot of background noise, mostly. Each persons' individual day, as pointed out above, is both maze and labyrinth. Our days are like that walkway on the floor of the Chartres Cathedral, yet that art only expresses a spiritual idea. Our individual labyrinth is different each&every basic cycle of night and day. Subtle differences for a prisoner, outrageous ones for soldiers in battle.

The maze is the mind's management exercise, for the puzzles not solved "yesterday", still seeming to lurk "tomorrow", meanwhile distracting from today's weaving of Nows.

Mind and Maze and Life and Labyrinth, a mystery celebrated in the fable-film: "Groundhog Day". Suppose that while walking to work you introduce some spontaneity in actions. This can be as simple as picking up some garbage, giving an extra thanks for this or that common courtesy, or moving an object from its place, trying to feel if it would be happier, here or there.

The brightest flowers are acts of kindness.

When our investigations of electrical and magnetic phenomena began a few centuries ago, it was necessary for something on the order of rites of ceremonial magic to arise. From the world of spirit we were led to this knowledge, in the same way we were helped to til the land, and build ships of seas of both water and air.

A workable concept, on a macro scale, is to call it the Ahrimanic Enchantment. Ahriman is not so much evil, as some sages imagine, but is rather one name of the God of Number. Science loves numbers. Many such wizards of the laboratory – wondering after matter's secrets – ran from religion, and were uncertain about art.

Although … Newton was an alchemist. Kepler an astrologer. Faraday a mystic. Keely and Tesla magicians.

Numbers – quantities – were easy names, … meanwhile the quality – of the smell of a rose, not being possible to name or measure, except in the vanities of poets, – falls away.

Germs and Atoms spring forth from this Number God's Forehead, ideas of the parts to the exclusion of the Whole.

Ceremonial Magic, with Sigils; and, electro-magnetic circuits with Signs for operations. Positive and negative powers integrated. Fire/will and Water/feeling shaping planets of elemental beings. Google: magic-sigil images, and then circuit -symbols images. Observe and compare.

Given the foundational nature of the material truths of the Father at Rest, though not asleep, a wide zodiac of communities of spiritual beings had to be organized into the various functions, like capacitors and switches, all dependent upon a materials science that can't yet imagine the Being of Tin.

These sigils and symbols were/are evocations of the relevant spiritual entities, the sigils more positive in nature, are built of curves and circles, while the symbols are more negative, straight lines and limitations.

If unconscious magical/mystical skills created the modern electrified world, what might conscious magical/mystical skills accomplish in the Next Nows?

If we generate a civilization that honors the interior nature of the Whole of the Creation, will we gain exactly how to heal many wounds, including the debris of atomic and chemical machines of death. In Faerie, among the Fae, the real alchemists wait. Their secrets can only appear as gifts, evolved in authentic and mutual courtship and love.

If we truly want a: *magical and mystical dark-matter physics, in the Age of Technological Chaos* – the path to that future is through the gateways of the past, the ancient earth religions remembered&honored.

In certain realms of Faerie, live the Gods we Now favor, previously mentioned. The Gods of the Ego, and the Gods of the Forge. We sing: i AM a maker too.

In the coming now-realms of reappearance of the Fae, and Faerie, knowledge magical and mystical is essential. The Mother decrees that individuals deserve a level playing field, for these new/forgotten gifts of the spirit.

All the same, while books such as this one have value, a far more important act is attending to our own adventures.

Why?

There will be Other-names (such as Brahma, Vishnu, Shiva) in different regions of the Earth-Sphere, yet via the Christian-style metaphorical language so far evoked in this book, it is fair to say that the whole sequence of incarnations of our individual sparks in matter, numbering seventy times seven (there's those pesky sevens again), taken together are the Holy Grail.

To make that journey more fun, apparently we don't have to have our particular biographies in order of linear time. Bill and Ted's Excellent Adventures.

Psychic gifts – as in invisible arts-forgotten – are of the wild. She grants them. A woman's intuition. A wondrous thought we receive while walking. The sense of "wrongness", often not trusted – because our cultures lost the knowledge of how to "know" Faerie and the Fae. Deep knowledge is now returning everywhere, yet fully awake to the real value of the Ideal of Science, as a Way of Knowledge.

Be your own scientist of your own intuition. Follow it. There is magic everyday, everywhere. We've been taught to call this: it-is-what-it-is-magic – coincidences and random events. The ancients studied the organism of existence, and learned to read the comings and goings of fortune and failure in the stars. Acquire and read, Saint Germain's "Practical Astrology", the only text fully rooted in the ancient Egyptian system, which makes/discovers a unity of astrology, tarot, and numerology.

In point of fact, all human beings on the planet are on the form of Path-Way we call:

shamanism. Paths of enlightenment and initiation are real, but only shamanism opens the heart's mind to the secrets of the True Dark, the Heart of Faerie, Her.

Steiner spoke of the return of the Moon. Not bad poetic notation for the Age of Chaos we now enter, from which new civilizations will be born. Their main feature … the wild gifts of magic and mysticism. The return of knowing how to commune-with Nature, rather than seek dominion-over.

Each region of earth has spiritual significance. Stone remembers. When we stand in Awe of Stonehenge, and the Sphinx and the Pyramids, … in awe of medicine wheels, and ancient stone drawings and carvings everywhere/when … then we are at one with those Fae, whose religion is humanity.

A stone knows the real name is the being and the being is the name: Gravity, Breath, Light, Self.

In the handwriting on the wall – the what's next over the event-horizon of Nows – is: social/political/economic/technological, and psychological, chaos. The warning is the current world-wide plague, and the endless and rising frequency of Rogue Weather.

The Pandemonium we are experiencing is Her, in Her Guise as Divine Providence, giving the whole world a time-out, to reflect.

Our artists are observant: the "Matrix" movies justly seen as a more than apt metaphor for our world. How about "Lost"? Or, "the Big Lebowski". Super-Heroes and super-powered people, fighting a world of endless evils, death, and, corruption.

There be dreams of wild powers. A wish that dragons* be real, as is magic in the Game of Thrones. *["Dragon Riders – the human being in maturity" http://ipwebdev.com/hermit/dragon-riders.html]

As shamans, we will find that we are often down in the dark of life. In the caves and water courses, of an underworld of inner and outer hungers and terrors, yet, … if we pause and take note, and also take a breath, arts magical can conquer any inner fault lines, … the ego can forge its own meaning of existence.

Consider the "prisoner", especially given that there was one sage who suggested: "we are all doing time". If we think about it.

Who is more in prison? Magic arts would be for the "prisoner" to understand the jailer's dilemma, for the truth they both know is that the jailer is the true prisoner. Obsessed with control. Demanding. A guard-stone that may not disappear, given that it is the thought that counts, in the land of money talks.

"Be like a rock in a waterfall" said "Born in Tibet".

All religions are real, even materialistic science. Yet, … there is always more to know, yes? Do we know everything? Which is larger, the golf ball of our own knowledge, or the Jupiter sized wisdom of what we don't know? If we take something from the sphere of didn't yet know, and move it into the realm of what we already thought we knew, isn't it entirely possible we will change/adjust our past way of knowing, in favor of something obviously better. Or, pointedly, … are we ready to learn?

There is this secret, open, obvious, and not seen, … it is of a romance between the Idea of 1, the numeric symbol of unity and the en-soph, the zero, the numeric symbol of a power beyond human ken.

so much we do not, and never may, know … The New Law, of iwegodlovechaos, was discussed in this poem. "Lazy Bear's Spirit Song" http://ipwebdev.com/hermit/lbsss.html

Nearly five decades have past since that was written, and understanding evolves quite naturally, into this higher teaching: lawlovesurrender. The Hebrews taught us the idea of God's Law. The Christians taught us the idea of God's Love. Islam teaches us of the idea of God's Surrender. Not three religions, one. Details here:
https://thecollectiveimagination.com/2019/11/08/tiger-saucy-tells-of-some-overlooked-features-of-the-true-story-of-religions/

We have – over the course of the preceding marks of pen upon page – been introduced to Ideas as Beings, whose Home invites the return of the prodigal sons and daughters … grand themes for a magical time, … A surprising answer to the questions that gave us the Drake Equation, and the Fermi Paradox.

If the starry firmament is physical three-dimensional space, just as we experience in this tiny tiny Earth locus of a vastness almost incomprehensible … the Drake Equation posits that if all those lights are planets, suns, galaxies, and other wonders, … in all that "huge", there must exist civilizations more advanced than are we. The Fermi Paradox agrees, yet … still, where are they, why haven't they contacted us?

What if the starry firmament is not physical? Not three-dimensional. A real "shimmering". I wrote one of those long, well footnoted, papers on these riddles: "The Misconception of Cosmic Space as Appears in the Ideas of Modern Astronomy.
" http://ipwebdev.com/hermit/space.html

Folk who dream of going into "Outer Space", seeking the intelligence and adventures there, will find the reality much closer, in the direct experience of seeking to commune-with Faerie and the Fae.

Science is not all wrong, just out of balance. Knowledge of the truth rests on the three legged stool: Science, Art, and, Religion. Reason, Imagination, Devotion. Truth, Beauty, Goodness.

While I have been trying to keep making sense, we both know little of what is said/written here should be taken on my word, alone, or otherwise. All the same, I have been thinking about this stuff for decades, and the links tell the story of many years of research. Each link a kind of complex footnote, themselves footnoted as well.

Want to know the stars? The kingdom of heaven is inside you. Inside/outside, a primal unity. Steiner believed that the split between thought and experience was due to the presence of the "I". That "I" experience is everywhere. All that manifests contains this presence. Still, experience is The Mystery Unlimited, so a change of pace is now called forth:

Fresh karma is always stinky, too sweet, too sour, brimstone and rain for the sorrow. Fresh tears always — want to fix climate? … get along with each other better. Still, out of ashes, miracles. A night's sleep. Indoor plumbing. A new sunrise. Even the company of birds, with spiders and moonlight on wishes becoming. Karma is not always "dark".

Wild horses help armies, if asked rightly. We know governments and corporations (not much of distinction that) try to Use psychically gifted people. In the TV show: "Stranger Things", children are abused to force enhanced powers. One of them, number 11, blows open a gate between Faerie and the "normal" world.

Gate? Hidden gate? The Veil. The Threshold. They called "it" the shimmering" in the movie Annihilation.

Every time an authentic crop circle has appeared, the Fae were dancing their joys and sorrows. Same with UFOs.

As the material world condensed into ever more complexity (see the table of elements), the resulting occupation of "nearly spaceless space", reached a limit. The Father's Life at stake, in a kind of Way.

Matter is His rest bed, having reached the limit of even the imaginations of the divine clowns, 42 Baker Street in La La Land, University of Sirius. The condensation process reached a limit as to the coherence needed to maintain order.

Matter spontaneously then began to fall apart, dancing alpha and beta Fae, caught in the act of swooning from exhaustion. This long-term living process (if we recall the fundamental law of unity), tending into the primal chaos decay of Matter, is an "effect" everywhere in the mineral realm of the planet.

Degenerating Matter. Uranium. Radium. Like Wily Coyote chasing the Road Runner, scientists try to use any possible available potential energy to make bombs and rockets.

Seems that if you gather enough of the uranium, where it was distributed but essentially inert, and then alchemically distill the powder, separating the brighter bits from the duller ones, wizards chasing wonders, recognizing that in this world knowledge becomes a weapon.

An atomic bomb blows a hole in the threshold between the material and non-material world, from one point of view. We take the most fully dense material, so dense it is falling apart, and concentrate it, with the last step, needing to achieve critical "mass", involving a complicated shaped charge that would blow inward, and increase instantaneously the level of density in that point-center.

Just because we didn't believe anymore, … the child still must play with the primordial clay on the way to learning to make something new.

Certain races of Fae, knowing holes were to be blown in the Veil, made ready. Some of these we might call masters of matter, via thought. The magical fact is that if one transverses from the non-material into the realm of the material, having a material body helps.

Among the UFO lore is a thought that there might be four primary races, among many minor ones. Recall the four elements, in the elemental kingdom, which is where "matter" appears, and is maintained by the littlest Fae: Fire Beings, Air Beings, Water Beings, Earth Beings?

Beings so real and intense in nature, that when we meet Their Guardians we become paralyzed with fear. One day, decades ago, while on LSD I evoked this Being, me being intoxicated, immature, and incautious: Aschmunadai.

As he came toward me out of the unknown, with sounds and roars and flashing lights, he grew larger and larger is size, and I ran away as fast as was possible. In Franz Bardon's book: "The Practice of Magical Evocation", this Being was described as: one of the original intelligences of the Zone girdling the Earth.

That book, in downloadable pdf form, can found on the Internet. Often for free. Also his other two books: "Initiation into Hermetics", and "The Key to the True Quabbalah".

More will be said in coming materials, which detail the Journey Into the Dark.

Often occult sources mislead – many fakiers, felt, yet unseen, as fiction meets this latent – and forgotten – Underworld, identifying it as a source of horrors. Monsters and fears appear. Young people running scared, getting to know each other, fighting and winning against the dark.

From H. P. Lovecraft to Stephen King, battles against the unknown dark are common. Not always do heroes survive. Harry Potter takes the whole magic tale to new heights and depths. Game of Thrones gives us dragon riders and madness.

From what dark source these stories? What kind of mind "sees" this Way? Artistic jedi-speak gives us: "I've got a bad feeling about this". "Reach out with your feelings Luke". Sometimes "Staying Alive", dancing, is the best we can do.

Carl Sagan was worried about a Demon Haunted World. He observed the swerve of the New Age folk toward magic, mysticism, and the return of the Goddess Religions. Wicca work is everywhere today, and not so much a joke as it used to be.

Yet, Sagan was right to worry that "beliefs", of this kind, might drown the scientific light that was shinning into the world. If we see his worry as a prayer, we can say: You have been answered. Both the science of knowing – the Anthroposophy of Rudolf Steiner, and the Goethean Science of his many gifted students, as well as the Hermetic Science of Franz Bardon, … all are firmly organized around the ideals of scientific inquiry.

It is safe to say today, that sciences of the spirit (of which this work is a sample) exist, … these sciences take scientific materialism and add in "spirit" through philosophical and scientific rigor. Dare we think/imagine, that the Son lives even now in the World of Thought, where the search for truth, beauty, and goodness is rewarded, allowing the healing of the disunity of science and religion, on a bridge between the two – built with art?
https://thecollectiveimagination.com/2019/10/29/tiger-saucy-writes-an-open-letter-to-greta-thunberg /

Next, … real "demons": Corporations are people? A "plan"demic?

Linear years ago, there came to be "stock" companies. If one wanted to adventure a ship searching for wealth, a company could be formed, and shares sold to investors, all understanding the risk that the ship, and cargo, and crew, could be lost at sea.

A lot of money was lost, or – since a lot of money was gained – lets say money "shifted" its locus of control. Moving money, lending money, borrowing money, generated the institution: a bank. Which/Who made money by managing certain necessary aspects of the circulation of money. Money about to be put today entirely at the whim of ones and zeros.

Banks also became stock companies. Meanwhile, the wealth and power formerly dominated by aristocrats of blood, and their wanton appetites, … that too began to shift its locus, or center.

As kings and queens became weaker and weaker, minor lords and common people acquired then greater power, and seekers after wealth found it prudent to – as much as possible – "manage" the legislative (law-Making) process.

In their own self-interest, holders of the necessary investment contracts, and executives and board members of stock companies, began to try to get the legislative process to free them from legal responsibility for their decisions.

Money talked. The corporation now became a complex legal wall between stock holders, executives, and board members. For the most part, … if a corporation committed crimes, those who made the decisions were often safe. In fact, their primary legal duty was to benefit the share holder, and unpleasant consequences to workers, consumers, and the environment, were acceptable ways to "make" money.

In fact, company officers were subject to suits, if the case could be made that these folks had not done their due-diligence of maximizing profits.

As these companies grew larger, mostly by eating others, there came to be a kind of jungle of individual corporation-cultures, a Way of Doing Business, that was unique to each organization. Not all banks are the same. Nor are all pharmaceutical businesses, either.

Those employees who grow in value to such cultures often do that at the loss of conscience. Empathy for the workers or consumers, or worries about pollution and side-effects, are not in the business "model". If it was "legal" was the only question. Not whether it was, or was not, moral.

Of course, the religion of unnatural science made such harms easier to accept, by failing to include the qualitative sciences with the quantitative, arriving at the Enchantment that "nature" was without being and intelligence.

From the stand point of Faerie, and the knowledgeable Fae, this "culture" became a kind of artificial spiritual being, generated by the combined love for and acceptance of it – the company, on one hand, and the social forces that sought to drive the moral out of the workers, lie to the consumers, and by-pass as many legal restraints as possible.

The sages, of the middle Ages, called such a created "creature" an egragore. Most people have little (as to scale, not effect) ones, such as drug and alcohol addictions. For large institutions these creatures of shadow were likened to the human double … a complicated field of spiritual understanding, see: "The Mystery of Evil in the Light of the Sermon on the Mount" http://ipwebdev.com/hermit/mysteryofevil.html

Here's The Question, which will generate fresh wine for new skins … in the law: ***If a corporation can be a person before the law, then certainly a Planet can be a person before the law.***

I have a law firm dedicated to this task, which involves the creation of an annual spiritual Rite, where on each Earth Day environmental lawsuits are filed, with that question as the core "idea". The point of this action is to publicize the question, so that the real nature of this Mystery appears where it most belongs: in the Court of Public Opinion. A shot across the bow, of the dangerous consequences of a spirit-less science. https://thecollectiveimagination.com/shamans-law-firm/

Beware the corporation-ruled news: They are a circus, a show, a mind-link to disasters, mazes, and labyrinth dancing … karma in action and then what?

So much awful, all over the world. Why does the Mystery allow the rape and sale of children, for example? Millions of fathers, tho' mostly mothers, are fleeing where they have been living … running away from the horrors inflicted by terrorists, or drug lords, or dictators, or soulless corporations – in some places little villages are caught between the appetites of all four "demons".

As part of my "education" as a shaman, I was in meditative prayer one morning, and the subject of my own flaws presented itself. Knot-knowledge of the own dark, if resisted, can manifest as depression. Luke, in Star Wars V, in the underground trial among caves and roots, meets Darth Vader, knocks him to the ground, … the mask comes off, and Luke is staring his own face.

In Star Wars VIII, Rey falls into water (the symbol of primal feeling), rises into a cave, discovering a double mirror-reflection, going off into infinity in two directions, however she turns.

https://thecollectiveimagination.com/2021/02/17/3008/ "Familiar Spirits, and the Education of a Shaman"

On this/that morning of meditative prayer – for me – a look hard. If I weighed myself by my conscience, I had been on many occasions quite wanting. By grace, though, not perfect yet.*
Still, that door once open revealed the Idea that "They" knew all. Nothing about me was hidden to Their Sphinx-like contemplations, Who loved all of us the same.
*["The Zen Potter": http://ipwebdev.com/hermit/zenpotter.html]

That Idea grew quickly into the form that all of the crap humanity does to itself was Known to Them – intimately. The pain of the perpetrator was as in need of nurturing as is the suffering of the victim. I was awed with this Idea that They knew and felt and forgave all, and yet what magic could be done with the what has been done, my heart asked … "what do You Do with our dark deeds?"

She said: "We Turn it into Love".

Said. Words. Presence. *"When I find myself in times of trouble, Mother Mary comes to me … Speaking words of wisdom, let it be … And in my hour of darkness she is standing right in front of me. Speaking words of wisdom, let it be".*

Intoxicated poets are touched by Fae spirits all the time. The heart's mind knows mystery, and trial. The flash flood of words, and sounds, … inspiration is a gate not easily closed.

Everyone gets "touched" in invisible places. Quiet sitting helps. One breath at a time. "Let it be". A few friends, some sticks and cans, a good beat – served with fine rhymes.

It took me about fourteen years to see just how They did that, in practice, in the social-political world. As part of my studies of the Now, noted above, I began to see that the fundamental act goes like this: Event (deeds that miss the mark*) is followed by Aftermath. The place remembers the balance, and the balance remembers the place … ceremony … right in front of us.

*[The word "sin", as used in the Gospels, is not an accurate translation of the actual Greek word, which is a term from archery, meaning: "miss the mark"]

An Event, such as a flood, displaces people, and breaks the habits of their lives. In the Aftermath, folk gather in high school gyms, growing relationships serving both those needing help, and those providing help. The presence of the Kindness of Strangers is from deeds in an individual's heart's mind. To accept and be grateful makes it a Eucharist, free of theology, yet filled with love.

Once we return to our understanding, that Divine Providence is a Living Mystery, we see then that the horrible disaster is healed. The dead are met at the Gate, by Him/Her, and Friends, while the living study the nature of need.

When Covid roared itself into the World, I now knew how to see Their Works of turning the anguish, from what misses the mark, into a work of art, literally unimaginable. We can't picture it. The seeing is the same organ that makes the choice of the heart's mind. Not a picture, a feeling.

Metaphorically imagine a large table, oddly shaped, almost like one of those maps where the sphere of the world is spread out onto a flat plane-like surface. The table is covered with riches, although not well shared. Tiny little sparks dance everywhere, living Life.

Part of that Life is how we understand the world, particularly in this age of great changes, that mark the beginning of the third millennium, or the first thousands of days of a new long count, or the end of the fourth world and the beginning of the fifth …

Then They, the Mystery of father, son, and holy ghost in plain sight, pulls the table cloth of scientific materialism out from under everything, like a stage magician, yet on a scale only Gods&Goddesses can carry out.

Yet, not quite. We are here not taking matter based science down … we are simply finishing its work, by growing/adding an additional dimension. See V. Bott's: "Anthroposophical Medicine: an extension of the arts of healing".

Scientific materialism, in that it infects our ideas of life, and death, and health, and illness, lacks understanding, because it doesn't know how to properly name, and or measure, such qualities of existence as: stress, sensitivity, the true state of the infamous "immune system", or the "will to live".

Of these riddles there is no escape, yet never give up, never surrender … or not … words are colors for the imagination, in verse – – – …

Art requires sentences-poetic = art/imagination. Physics requires meaning-exact = science/reason. The heart holds out for wonders = religion/devotion

If we turn conventional meaning-reality inside out, we change the world. The cause-spiritual, in this sense, is the own "I". We are makers of the meaning of our personal travels in life. We often can't make something happen, or unmake that they happened. Today's ironic view of the spirit of our time*, is this: It is what it is. *[In the '50's, this zeitgeist was captured by Alfred E. Neuman's "What, me worry". In the '70's, for a time, the zeitgeist was expressed by Zippy the Pinhead's: "Are we having fun yet?"]

If spirit is in anywhere, it is in everywhere & every-when. My daughter Doren is writing about a "sprite" that time-jumps back and forth between lives. Just where do we go, when we "sleep", and/or "dream"?

Just as materialism is a state of general consciousness, spirit is also a state of consciousness. This is not about changing reality, but discovering the true names of our experience. This act of naming being a sign of our divinity.

We are technically free to steal any other artists works of art, and self-medicate to our hearts content, with some great sex thrown in. Sometimes it is not so much the deed itself, but the consequences that is the problem. Each of us are survivors, with the power to let go materialism, and begin to look at, and through, the ground under our feet.

What is stuff? Any reason to believe the materialists know? a gospel of organic chemistry: "The Nature of Substance", by Dr. Rudolf Hauschka. How does stuff work? Again, any reason? a gospel of physics: "Man or Matter", by Ernst Lehrs. Barfield's "Poetic Diction", a gospel of the Imagination. MacCoun's previously mentioned: "On Becoming an Alchemist", a gospel of soul. My "The Way of the Fool", a gospel of the Second Coming, as well as: "The Art of God – an actual theory of Everything", a gospel of social/political life. Grohmann's two volume, "The Plant", a gospel of the green world. Tom Cowan's four volume works on medicine: "Human Heart, Cosmic Heart"; Vaccines, Autoimmunity and the Changing Nature of Childhood illnesses"; "Cancer and a New Biology of Water"; as well as the most recent: "The Contagion Myth" – a much needed gospel of the problems of illness and health. "Sensitive Chaos", by Schwenk, a gospel of living movement, generated from chaos in water and air. Steiner's "A Theory of Knowledge Implicit in Goethe's World Conception", a gospel of knowing. Shad's "Man and Mammals" a gospel of a biology of form.

These are just of few of modern books that have taken materialistic thinking, and woven into those Ideas, the obvious reality of spirit. As to the use of the term Gospel, … imagine that in thinking, we can engage in sacramental acts, such that we are not alone, and the Christ-maker is present in the thought/ethereal world to help guide us to the needed truths.

If you feel inclined to argue, getting to know the above works is a prerequisite to taking the Mystery of spirit and matter seriously

Meanwhile, what does all this human life-pain, and awful, and terrible, MEAN?!?!?

It is up to us individually to grow – those flowers of thought which we wish – in the garden of our own heart's mind. If you have trouble believing, in having hope, again watch some TikTok.

There exists a kind of world-wide language. Free of restraints due to local conditions. While attempts have, and are, … being made to take down such world consciousness connectivity as the Internet, where The Father at Rest, can be sought … nothing can be truly disconnected, least of all … us from us.

In the field of the culture of it-is-what-it-is, we have glorious artistic contributions to the "collective" imagination. There has been painted, Star Trek, and Star Wars, the latter bringing to us the Idea of the Force of Life. Movies, are based on the perception of archetypes. With subsidiary mystical asides like Arrival, Annihilation, and company. Even Disney, with its films Frozen One and Two, found time to speak of the four elements, as well as the causal fifth.

These arts are rich in metaphors, and … even better, riddles. Especially for those who have begun to understand what is being said here.

An aspect of reality is "metaphorical", in the sense that there is a place were reality lives in symbols and signs. Tradition calls it the astral world. The above films, along with others, are obviously rich with social commentary. Via these visual arts, the world talks to itself. A teenage acquaintance recently got me hooked on some Korean television.

Still, the Archetypes of the Collective Unconscious, as rediscovered by Jung and such, remain remnants of much older wisdoms. Wonderfully, the more modern Collective Imagination, in film and television, had pushed "correctness", and "appropriate" aside, riding in on arts even more dangerously real. Copious amounts of blood, more obscene than all that bad porn that is out there.

We are raising rather weird/strange/odd children, and from my vista in the caves filled with moonlight, these are very mystical times. Keep in the mind that the Idea of karma and reincarnation, implies that we descend into life with purpose. These remarkable young people came down in these Nows, because they have the strength and character to weather and master the coming social madness. Remarkable wishes for wild powers, by unusual people. A "weirding way" is pointed toward, by Frank Herbert's "Dune".

Heard a story once, about a guy who worked in the bowels of the University of California at Berkeley. Cleaned glassware. Handled potent garbage. Tunnels everywhere in between labs and buildings. Lights lighting the way. When this guy walked down the halls, the lights will flicker out when he passed, coming back on when he was farther away.

What is a "glitch", in technological terms? What happens when billions of human beings get very tired of the "way things are done"? In the wonderful "the Expanse", we are taught about the Idea of the "churn". The clashing of appetites and needs, constantly turning over social order, however hard the owners and bankers and politicians resist accepting the fact that revolution is the new now.

Divinity is Everywhere-when. We are not accidental animals in an uncaring Cosmos.

Among the Fae, somewhat akin to TV's "Sons of Anarchy", is this voluntary collective: sons and daughters of irony. The following was heard at one of their meetings:

"In the long long ago when before, might have been, the world was undifferentiated warmth, weightless, endless co-being. Then some idiot decided to go on strike. In the very center of the seething dancing mass, he stopped moving in time to the currents, and the resulting musical harmonies were radiated into becoming self-organizing notes. Some of the wise thought of this fool as a God, and gave Him the favored honorific: Son.

"All the same, nothing ever loses its connection to the fundamental unity, and each individual note was always also of the Whole, including the very creative idiot that choose to go against the aging and boring patterns ,,, "

In the Age of the Gods of the Ego (individualization), and the magicians of the Forge (making matter follow our lead), the memories of Saturn haunt our dreams …

Cleave the idiot said, hold each other in the shared warmth of the night, and remember who and what we always have been … even if it seems we are alone, the air we breathe, and growing garden of invisible friends is all the company we need …

Thoughts-spiritual are available, in moments of inner quiet. The Maker made it simple: Judge Not, Pray in Secret, and Ask, Seek, and Knock. The Kingdom of Heaven is Inside You.

Sometimes there is a collision between one style of thinking, and another. Observe, for a moment, this following described style, which is essentially derivative and secondary in its nature..

When we read text, and from that text "make" concepts about what the generator of the text meant … concepts that could be wrong in two ways.

One way is where we have not understood what the originator of the words spoken or written meant, such that the developed frame of reference is defective by our limits.

Another way is where the sources we read were themselves in error. If both conditions are present, the matter is even less reliable as "knowledge".

Another style, actually urged by Steiner, is to go directly to the experience of the percept – the perception, and let that experience generate the concept. This experience is not derivative, but can be flawed if our practice in this phenomenological art is "weak". The Sense-World as Speech. How hard do we listen.

When a writer/thinker mixes the derivative with the directly readable/perceptual, even if they are just high level abstractions (Ideas are perceptual, with care). the conceptual scaffolding can overwhelm the actual Idea-sculpture, which wants to emerge.

If there is a secret to the "churn", in our own mind, it is this: intoxicants are not always undesirable. Why do you think the Mother made all these medicines. Take a load off. Share the gifts, dancing and writing insane poetry. Forget. Thoughts should die, and we need to learn not to cling to them.

Is who you are – to yourself – dependent on what you imagine others think of you? Two mirrors, endlessly facing each "other". Consider this: "In It (the Word) was Life, and the Life was the Light of the World."

From where comes "light"? What is dark? What are dark forces, or dark matter?

The Word was the Speech of the Naming, from the Maker. It is a Living – Making, this Son … dance partner to the Living Making of the Mother principle. He, of the "I and the Father are One"; and, "No one gets to the Father except by me".

She, of the Many, the all surround everywhere/when. Our solar system dances to the music of Her Spheres. He Unity, She Every-part … a together mystery, not either/or … rather: both/and. Gravity is Her. She is point-centered. All physical objects have the quality we call a center of mass. If we shake the rug of the other ideas, the reason physics can't find the "god" particle, something imagined to be necessary because we notice a phenomena – we name the "mass" – which is measured, and therefore must exist. But we can't see it, … we can't see that "part", because the effect is of the Whole, the living pulsing Field of Life Existing.

One of the better ideas of physics is the idea of a "field". Play with some magnets, and you can feel a field. Advance our physical sciences enough, and we can imagine making a measurable invisible "force" field, … for an all-surround your spaceship.

Meanwhile, the Planet, playfully without effort, manages to offhandedly make a really excellent deflector shield. Only the right amounts – of the powers radiating inward, from sphere of the whole of the cosmos we call the stars – penetrate Her living/loving governance.

As She is Center, He is Periphery. An aspect of His Being is the Field of Life, which can seem centered in the Sun. All the same, following the "order" of the Father at Rest, the living unified field of "Life"(breath) begats* Light. In it was Life and the Life was the Light of the World.

*[See George Adams: "Space and the Light of Creation"]

We might try to imagine that the underlying electromagnetic field, which is measurable everywhere, retains its unity nature, being The Father at Rest. Taking a Nap. We might not want to wake the Maker of Makers up.

These spiritual "fields", of the Unified Field Theory riddle, have that illusive inside/outside conception. It is not easy to imagine inwardness to all the we experience, … an inwardness which is an analogue of our own sentient self-awareness. Still, one – inside and outside. Observe the Speech of Nature through the Senses, and the Speech of Thought, through the own heart's mind.

Lie on the grass, in a cool afternoon. Breath. Look. Someones are really there, looking down from the heavens, and – as well – up from the caves and dark places. There is no lack of unity, except in our mind via the Ahrimanic Enchantment.

The truth is out there. Believe.

Mother Nature keeps busy anyway, the knocking down, sweeping aside, rearranging, breaking the levies to get the needed nutrients to the right places, given that materialism is practiced dominion-over and disharmony on purpose. Event&Aftermath.

At the end of the original twenty film Marvel Avengers series, the heroes get to face a power, whose name is much like the Greek God of Death, that takes us gently and without pain: Thanos. The movie god-imagined is possessed* of the idea that suffering in the universe would be reduced if fully one-half of all sentient life was to disappear, which the film visually realized as us becoming dust, quietly, yet knowing this is the end. *["One must be able to confront an idea, and experience it, otherwise we will fall into its bondage" RS, The Philosophy of Freedom.]

There are human beings of that spirit ... who believe a lot of our earthly problems are solved if there are less people, a lot less people.

Certain additional elements in this Marvel-song – a chorus of many countless and unrecognized comic-book artists – included the Idea of "six infinity stones". They are given names, and don't we just love names:

The names of the Stones, and their place of momentary rest: Space/Thor, Reality/Collector, Power/Xandar, Time/Dr. Strange, Mind/Vision, and, Soul/Gramora. Always mysteries behind mysteries. Is a life of quest a natural state of Being Human?

The Infinity Stones, alone, without the Archetypes: Space. Reality. Power. Time. Mind. Soul. A six ... parts also a whole, to wonder – again – seven.

Should we ask the Fae about the "musical idea" of Six Infinity Stones*, we then are encouraged to find out these are related to Seven Intervals, born from Eight Notes. Do we have an instrument for weaving Intervals into Song? How many strings does the usual guitar have?

Aboriginal Drum Circles. Salsa Dancing. Jazz. Hip Hop. Rock 'n Roll. European

Classical&Opera. Reggae. Singing in the shower. Dancing like no one can see your … If not in the physical, at least in the heart's mind.

"What if God was One of Us?" https://www.youtube.com/watch?v=USR3bX_PtU4&ab_channel=bakkerbier

What if God was/is All of Us? We Are Groot.

One of the greatest film series is the movies about Godzilla. Over fifty to date. Born out of Japanese culture concerns, having been the recipient of two atom bombs, Godzilla is a Fae creature of immense size. The just progeny of our all too human hungers for power.

In the beginning, men in plastic/rubber suits, one of them seriously reptilian, duke it out in the middle of card-board models of downtown Tokyo. Mostly Japanese directors and actors. In our present moment (as of this writing) the franchise has huge computer generated image budgets, highly paid actors, big advertising campaigns, which tend to make a lot of money.

The tale has evolved. The number of "monsters" has exploded, many literally.

The latest involves an apparent conflict between two such screen giants: Godzilla, and King Kong. A reptile and an ape. How it turns out, I shall not divulge. In passing we can note that a couple of films ago, the Greek word "Titans", showed up, describing Godzilla's opponents.

That, and the co-idea that these stories are about "apex predators", who while powerful, can be allies. Still, if we let Godzilla be Godzilla, he takes care of the bad guys.

Frequently, over the course of all the films, there has been a child, whose innocence affects Godzilla, and they can even "touch". The movie just before Godzilla vs. King Kong, was called: Godzilla: King of the Monsters.

In that film Godzilla battled a lot of Titans. These battles invariably had to take place where masses of folks are in danger of being killed, which does happen. There are human heroes, who survive, … barely.

One creature, from the lore of Godzilla, is Mothra (a feminine spirit in the body of a huge furry butterfly), who helps Him in King of Monsters.
\
Films are stories. Story tellers with remarkable gifts. They set up conflict, and resolve it. The basic good and evil people are around. Bad people wanted to use the Titans etc. for their own purposes.

We do exist in a time of Titans. Inhuman powers, parasites and destroyers, the egregorial demonic Multinational Corporation. Each of them driving to become one, or perhaps the single one … apex predator.

It can seem as if humanity is powerless, except in this/our Tale too, there is a God-zilla, dancing with Mothra … aka: the mystery of the mother and the son.

To the rich materialists, the truth is a problem. The Mystery is Real. So they want to brand religion as a monster, because they fear it. For similar reasons, the institutional religions – in the sense of their titan-like powers in the world – are fighting over (and blowing up) the middle-East, the cradle of Western Civilization … these will be defeated by a King, with the Help of His Mother, … a king whose power is the truth. A king that lives in every heart's mind.

We breath thoughts in thinking, given that we are also a many, as is the whole of the thought world – all valid in their own nature, even the most terrible. Poetry, angry or otherwise. We have to master, for our own benefit, how to wisely release steam, yet sometimes a punch in the nose is needed to wake someone else up.

Our time … Real people. Real cities. Not actors and cardboard artistry. I am, we are: both Godzilla, and Mothra, in the micro world of our experience. Christ-love-light, with Mother-nurtured freedom.

The basic insight is: take care of the needs of the moment, that are within your reach, and leave the big picture, to the Big Picture folks. Trust yourself. They do. Faith means trusting Them back.

Oh, yes, … dark energy and dark matter? Him. The living invisible cosmic periphery, which creates space from Life, and then light.

We live poised between Him and Her, interpenetrating fields of levity and gravity. We also live in the fractal glory of one of the greatest adventures in centuries. We get to co-participate in the transformation of a remarkable – yet dying into its own new becoming – social-political structure.

We are the makers of the content of the meaning of existence. Your own imagination is the passport to a world filled with magical and mystical encounters, in the face of Titanic powers, raging through the world via our undisciplined appetites. We have met the enemy, and he is us.

Yes, there are demonic institutions, run by Titans of Industry, who are now faced with the existential drama of Gods&Goddesses, and the Afterlife being real.

The metaphor-astral presence of the Son-god-zilla is also known as the Lord, or – as I prefer, the Artist of Karma. To the ancients, there was deep wisdom in this: "as above, so below; and, as below, so above, … for the miracle of the one."

We are the microcosm (small universe), an exact analogue of the macrocosm (great universe).

Earth is the center of meaning of the whole Cosmos. It is where the Cosmos journeys to evolve into unexpectedness. Each of us is a Temple for this Rite, and are personally responsible* for the "thoughts", and we/I should be warned – as we are by dramatic art, … there will be consequences.

*[What we call "mental" illness used to be known as a spiritual illness. Many of these folk are tortured by invisible powers, often because they have what some used to call: "the sight". The normal veil/threshold/shimmering between the I and World, is weaker. Hallucinations are often real events, they are just not perceivable by scientific materialism. I wrote a long article: Healing the Insanity of Psychiatric Medicines and Practices.
http://ipwebdev.com/hermit/mental.html

Communion-With – or – Dominion-Over?

Each of us also has trouble with some of our thoughts. Just as we – ourselves – are dangerous thoughts of the divine mystery. Our freedom of choice is the Beast from the Abyss of the Unknown and Uncreated.

Our mind is an exact analogue of that mystical reality. Our thoughts are our progeny. We are father/mother/son makers of thoughts.

Just like we, in the Mind of God on occasion rebel, so our thoughts rebel. Inner conflict. Take a couple of deep breaths, stretch and dance a bit. They – Mother/Son – are with us/you … that close. Still some of our thoughts hide from their maker, just as do we. The Koran has a beautiful phrase: "the sneaking whisperer, from among the Djinn and mankind."

Love is all we need. All along the watch tower …

a never-ending story … self written, directed, and acted, using the material found at hand, in order to make – of our personal life – art … and yes, coloring outside the lines is essential …

Imagine a drop of water in slow motion, falling and landing/making waves upon waves in the seas of change, rippling out from a Center. Now reverse the image, where the infinite periphery of waves collapses into a point, from which then rises as/the single drop flying upward and back into the Source … only to disappear from both time and space, … until inward bound once more ... falling earthward from a heaven/sky full of individuals sparks of existence.

Supplemental Implications of the Self-change of Personal World View proposed here

Sometimes we want, justly, to change the world. Who doesn't want wealth and money and power and friendship and challenge and good drugs and no more war, or death or evil or meanness ... an endless supply of wants, shared among over seven billion people. There's that seven again.

In case the reader is struggling, ... as the ancient Egyptians knew, "enumeration" (numbering) was a power. If we moderns are to invent a qualitative Way ... then what?

Ursula K. LeGuin wrote a book: "The Dispossessed". In it she imagines a mathematical physicist, who strives to unite into a Whole, a physics of the sequential, with a physics of the simultaneous. We are doing that here by noticing the qualitative value of such fundamental Ideas as unity and many. As well as the ideas of music, sequences of musical notation, joined vertically with chords, via "the ten forms of change"*.

*[For details, the novel: "The Memory of Whiteness: a scientific romance" by Kim Stanley Robinson, an elaborate imaginative incursion into the relationships between music and physics.

"A music leads the mind through the starry night, and the brain must expand to contain the flight, like a tree growing branches at the speed of light"

All of living Reality (i.e. the Whole Universe) is layered in tones. The word vibrations is too weak, too airy-fairy actually. Life as savage poetry comes closer, in a qualitative sense of values needed for individual survival.

The Mystery of of Source and Sink

In kinship with the Above, the Macrocosm, we – the microcosm – also have the qualities of the mother and the son. In seed form, blossoming new each life, sometimes sunflower, other times a faerie ring of toadstools. Sun light, and moon light. One and Many.

The snake eating its own tale, endlessly. Yet, each weaving/devouring new – never the same. Tortured by winds we cannot control, in both the outer and inner worlds. Still, storms pause, winds abate, and the sun, at least for a moment, shines into our hearts.

There are two books far more important than this one, and come free of charge. The book of our personal biography, and the book of our own soul/mind. Both are right in front of us. In the Now from which we cannot escape, which includes our many-selves, from whom we also cannot escape.

We are our own teacher. Other's can inspire, but ultimately the content of the own mind is ours to cultivate, through our own thinking/refection. She and He, as Divine Providence, and the Artist of Karma, guide us, via unexpected events of fortune and failure. Life is a series of choices. Many not easy at all. What is forged in these trials?

What we learn from these personal experiences is up to us. The hard part is to trust what comes to us out of the unforeseeable future.

Sometimes, with real cause, we War against the Now. So many jailers trying to imprison our spark. Harder to see, and therefore all the more important, is just what aspects of the prison characteristics of our life are ones for which we need to accept responsibility.

Life is our basic teacher. Secondarily ourselves, as we work out the riddles and surprises. The vehicle for that "working out" is our own mind. Our brain is not our mind: "I am not my brain, the map is not the territory" http://ipwebdev.com/hermit/brain.html
"Sacramental Thinking" http://ipwebdev.com/hermit/SacramentalThinking33x.html

Sometimes opportunity knocks and we refuse to see it. Mostly out of fear of change, and the momentum of habit. There is a movie called: Chac, which is instructive (the title is the name of Central American, Southern Mexico, rain God).

A village is suffering a severe drought. Their "shaman" drinks and eats a lot, but his prayers, masks, and rattle shaking, produce no rain. Desperate, the village fathers decide to go into the mountains nearby and consult with a powerful sorcerer* that lives there.
*[https://thecollectiveimagination.com/canto-one-the-village-at-the-foot-of-the-mountain/]

He considers their concerns and takes several of them, including a boy who tries to tag along unnoticed, on a journey of a several days, seeking – the sorcerer says, the Mother of Waters.

At one point they spend the night by very a large lake, filled with fish, and its many shores and inlets dotted with reeds. At another moment, he leads the group in a perilous – up to your knees -walk across a river, just above its huge falls.

He has shown them places – with waters – to which to move the village, but the idea of doing that – of going to the water, rather than trying to force the water to come to them, – that idea does not arise. They have to see it without his prompting, but do not.

There is more to that story. For our purposes here, this idea: If something is wanting, maybe working at fixing it yourself might be better than tangling with a sorcerer, and the unexpected consequences of that.

The rule of Providence is this: If you really need something, its right there in front of you, … only unseen because you expect it to be packaged in a particular way, and don't notice the actual wrapping. Can be a needed object, a needed friend, a needed book, a needed job.

Future health for all relies on leaving the overgrown cities, back to the farms, and thence, once more, into the wild places. Walk Your Way. [Nomadland]

As to the Fae and Faerie … we have a want to see. Magical creatures out of ancient lore. How do we solve the riddle of knowing, without seeing? Is seeing needed to believe?

Just consider the Way we now believe in the age of unnatural science. Science is at war with religion, as well. Both religion and science believe in a lot of stuff they have never seen, except by acts of the mind. In fanciful quantum multi-verse how many times does God have to let Their-selves be crucified, before we will accept the glory of "This" existence itself.

Strange that, … the places we want to go so as to get away from where and when we already are. Sometimes folk choose madness, or suicide, their life too painful.

How much do we think we know, because we have been told this or that is the truth. In scientific materialism we swim in a sea of potential. Matter is real, in fact matter is more than Real, when you open your heart to Its Spirit.

It matters to me, for Matter to be, and that I, to Matter, do matter. Matter is a manifestation of the Great Mind at Rest. The "aftermath" is up to us.

When I look future-ward these days, I see increasing chaos, infrastructure collapse, and selfish and craven folk making it hard for the 99.999 %.

A world-wide cultural revolution enables us to out-think the demonic. We do it together. We become a source of seeing the world, recognizing that our choices have real meaning. We need more parties, and less protests. More risk taking in getting to know those – who were once named enemy – as just another human being.

People need to be able to move from dangerous places. Raising children requires this. Financial and political powers divide the plenty of the Earth into regions with borders. The same way a flood breaks levees, waves of people needing to move will break borders.

Social forces of order will try to inhibit the already present and increasing social chaos. China, for example, took a big risk quick-developing as an effectively capitalistic State, …

now their leaders want to increase control, when wisdom favors going with the flow of increasing dis-order&dis-ease.

The spark of spirit will not cooperate. Truths, such as live in this little booklet, defy borders as well.

Ancient Lore has it that a once great civilization, Atlantis, became ruled by evil two-hearted leaders*.

The Mother and the Son have no qualms about sweeping the sphere of life clean of illness producing activities. There are limits, and She keeps telling us this. This is being written when the Western United States of America is undergoing the highest temperatures, and worst fires, ever – in June and July of 2021.

*[http://ipwebdev.com/hermit/hppcy.html "From the Beginning of Life to the Day of Purification": (some of the) Teachings, History & Prophecies of the Hopi People http://ipwebdev.com/hermit/eldbr.html "The Mystery of the True White Brother"]

According to John the Baptist, the One coming after him, will baptize us in Fire and Holy Breath. Our time is what that looks like. The Fire is the circumstances of outer life, and Holy

Breath is the circumstances of inner life. Two books, that could not be more personal.

When Atlantis fell, there were two great migrations. One to the East, and into Europe and then Asia, and other to the West, and into the Americas. The Flood some folk called it.

There was also a less visible left-behind effect. Many of the Atlaneans were sea faring folks, both seas of waters, and seas of air. A few modern archaeologists have discovered that all over the world, in places far far removed from each other, there appeared in many places similar symbols. What connected these widely separated peoples?

If modern leaders could be counted upon to act sanely, this transformation through chaos might be done with little pain. All the same, habits die hard, so the Fire and Holy Breath will not – in the beginning – produce order.

In the Dreaming, I encounter. Of Atlantis I have been taught this: there were actually three groups, which are also two. Very specific leaders led folk all the way across Europe, into Asia, near the Gobi Desert. Other leaders, led folks into the Americas. One group East, the other West.

Both of these migrations involved leaders/priests that understood the importance of geography, in a spiritual sense. Names too can be important, as we've observed. I like these words/name, for those who migrate and settle: Earth Rangers.

They care for the Spirit of Place, and the Harmony of Community.

There are also the Travelers. These folk visit one or another of the various communities of Earth Rangers, and spread the stories of each to the others. A weaving of parts into wholes.

Right now, in the whole world, the cities are failing. We used to live closer to the land, more at one with "it" than can be imagined by those today, who in the city can easily find themselves cut off from the Earth, not yet consciously knowing their sorrow or anguish. Orphaned, having to work to get money to buy food in order to live and have life … in a world of plenty.

The modern Earth Ranger spirit is already present in all those places where people garden in cities. Our labor should be to make food, and serve the social needs of the whole. Instead we serve a social-machine, a demonic egregorial inhuman consciousness, … aka: the multinational corporation.

The School of Hard Knocks and Shared Pain does have rules. Doesn't make any difference how much money, power, things, status, whatever … many Ego has wants that will never be satisfied. Yet, if we have sought some wisdom, the Mystery does not create an "anything/condition" Event, without daily life being a garden we can Aftermath-cultivate anyway.

The mainstream News can create a false picture of life on the earth. Wars, plague, dangerous drug lords and priests. On any given day, most of the seven billion were not traveling life at warp-speed. Even a refuge camp has routine. The body controlled, but not the heart's mind.

All has purpose and use. The hard part is how much of our personal choices are we willing to recognize as a cause of our own suffering. What is the purpose or use of those choices, and appetites?

In the social it is ultimately ideas that count the most. The most powerful idea in the social is personal freedom, autonomy, and responsibility. At the same time, we live in the consequences of centuries of pursuing an understanding of reality, without any scientific concept of spirit.

This is the age of biology.* Our mechanical technologies can't make the living, only the living can make more living. In one sense there exists a kind of war-like collision between the purely technical sciences, and the biological sciences.
*[Visit the Bioneers website: https://bioneers.org/ "Revolution from the Heart of Nature"]

Once we re-ensoul the world (it already has soul, we just have been given the right to choose when and where to come home) our whole outlook changes. This can be done one person at a time. When even the "tech" is respected for having "being", we will learn to marry the science of matter, to the science of spirit, in the right way.

Take little steps … the world of the Real is not different, it just gets returned to a long forgotten meaning … magic and tech, biological and otherwise … life as a game of mystery unbound.

The biggest migrations, during the coming warming into Winter, will be from cities, out into the Land. Farms for some, the wilds for others.

She loves and trusts us, as does He. Will we love and trust Them?

Some basic goals

Find your tribe. You already might have one, and facing trials in community personifies: many hands make light work. Oh! Talk to the Little People. They are busy, and themselves well ordered, even the fire-folk. But wait, how do I see them?, a reader might ask.

By their effects. Dropping stuff that breaks, and consider the "sound" a scream of wonder. If you bang a door to hard, and the noise is loud? You wash your hands, and all water is living enchantment. Sing songs of praise when food dancing.

Pick up a made "thing". Imagine its manifestation, through all the iterations of molding and organizing – making purpose, that mystic lamp again. Our minds impress the world, with ships and planes and factories and little stuff.

All the parts of modern tech come from earth elements, transformed. These are getting scarce. Be ready to live without the internet, yet at the same time find a way to save for posterity all humans have so far accomplished, playing in the fields of the Lord.

I dream of hand-cranked laptops. And DVD's of all the culture, wisdom, knowledge, stupid, artistic, maddening, stuff of dancing ones and zeros, hard at play, being exchanged world wide so that all can know our Ways and Legends, and woes and worries.
What survives a dark age of collapse? Grit. Endurance. Friendship.

In Clint Eastwood's film: Pale Rider, a girl, whose village and family are being terrorized by bullies, prays for aid. A Fae spectre appears, bringing rough justice. In Revelations, certainly an artistic warning of some weight, the pale rider – of the four horseman – is death.

Still, what cannot be killed: faith, hope, and, charity … are ours to give and receive in the Eucharist of Communion-With.

~!~!~!~!~!~!~!~!~!~0

Shaman's Guide to the Covid Mystery

Before writing this paper, I did a search of the recent Deepening Anthroposophy PDF for the following terms: Cowan, Stress, Sensitivity, Touch, Will to Live, Immune System, Proliferation, Rainbow, Rate of deaths, and Hauschka. There were no hits. Why those terms are important will be explained below.

All the same, it is entirely possible that such matters were discussed in the many live links in the PDF. I admire all the work the various writers have done, to support their points of view. At the age of 81, I don't have the patience, or the time, to read all those papers and studies. If I have missed seeing that material there, which I am providing here, I apologize.

"Shaman" is a curious term, given the many people naming themselves in that fashion, such as the fellow who claimed this during the January 6th attack on the Capital building in Washington DC. In an "esoteric" sense, a true shaman (in the way I mean it) is as an individual who has the same spiritual quality as what Enlightenment means in the social East, and Initiation in the social Center. In this case we are referring to the true West, the Americas, where the seeker of the truth must investigate his own darker nature, as part of their education/learning.

My qualifications can be found at my article: "Familiar Spirits and the Education of a Shaman". (1) Essentially this type of Shaman is in regular contact with the Mother, as an aspect of what might be called an Earth Religion. Such religions are everywhere in our world, being normal for indigenous and aboriginal peoples. In Hermetic Science this kind of Way is called a Moon Wisdom.

Steiner taught us the New Sun Wisdom. As to the Mother, She has the whole world in His hands.

I am not vaccinated, nor have I ever been "tested". In fact, I have not had a "flu" vaccine in twenty years, except about six years ago, when my primary care physician urged me to take that year's version, immediatly then given in her office. That night I had the worst case of "chills" I had ever had. I did not sleep.

My view of this experience is that the Wisdom of the Body (the so-called immune system) was attacking this foreign matter and eliminating it. The "chills" are the long muscles in the arms and legs vibrating in order to create, and direct, more "heat" from the warmth body to use to repel this invasion. When I told my doctor, she assured me that there was no live virus in the vaccine. Still, what was in the vaccine the Wisdom of the Body did not like? "So it goes", to quote Kurt Vonnegut.

When the Covid riddle first appeared in my Facebook feed, there was a video in circulation, which title used the word: "Plandemic". What I found fascinating was that not only did links to this video quickly disappear, but that there followed an enormous number of posts attacking the author's character and qualifications.

Eventually I found the video, and the one point she made, that was perhaps so troubling to her opponents, was that it was all about the "patents".

In the first post to my blog, on this Covid pandemic, I wondered why people trusted Big Pharma, Politicians, and the Media, given that neither institution had much use for the truth. I also pointed out that (having a law degree, with the high A in Evidence), once (and if) we put Dr. Fauci and others on the stand, in a Court of Law, subject to cross examination and impeachment, they won't get past this test of their credibility.

About three decades ago, while I was reading a lot of Steiner, I twice read his lectures: "Spiritual Science and Medicine". Mostly I was learning about polar aspects of the soul and physical life, that manifest in a threefold way, such as thinking, feeling, and willing. Included are his concepts about "form", which is the ideas of nerve-sense system, heart-lung rhythmic system, and metabolic-limb system. These polaric systems seemed to me to be also features of a living social organism: Cultural Sphere, Political-Legal Sphere, and Economic Sphere.

My main phenomenological studies, beginning at that time in my life, were into the social-political life of humanity.

Relevant to the Covid riddle were his remarks about the "contagion" idea, regarding tiny tiny entities that were being observed in conventional medicine. I will paraphrase: Imagine traveling through an area filled with contented cows, feasting on the verdant grains everywhere present. The illogical thinking was that the cows caused the fields of tasty matter, when this was clearly not the case. If we apply this to the "proliferation" of micro-organisms in the body, the same mistake in cognition appears. The "bugs" are just another symptom, not the cause.

In my own thinking over the years, it became clear that "illness" is something that affects the whole system, not just the parts. This condition of imbalance in the whole then has areas of special weakness, and those are where the "proliferation" takes place.

The reason, I pointed above to the search term "Rainbow", is the book: "The Invisible Rainbow", which is about the causal relation between electronic pollution and illness. In the first seventy pages of that book, the author does a review of the scientific studies that appeared in the aftermath of the 1918 "flu" pandemic. There were, at the time, five "centers of outbreak", that were too far apart, and too simultaneous, such that the idea then of a contagious organism didn't really work.

There was, however, a shared fact for all five centers, that involved in each case the recent construction of high energy radar facilities in those areas.

Keep in mind that the alleged center of our Covid outbreak was Wuhan China. This is a city with a large elderly population, many of which were smokers, and at the time of the alleged outbreak the area had just become saturated with 5G cell towers. Smokers have lung problems, which is then a weak arena, where micro-organism can the proliferate.

When you add in the current Chinese totalitarian usage of massive observations of their people, via cameras, Wifi and other electrical/technical instruments, they were living in a sea of electronic radiation. Not only that, but these people know they are being observed, which certainly has to be a factor in increasing "Stress" (another term in my search).

Modern medicine is highly materialistic – all is matter there is no spirit. When you go to a regular doctor (yes, anthroposophical medicine is different, but few people have access) you get tested, and quantitative measures are used. From a spiritual point of view, there are aspects which are recognized as factors in illness, which are qualitative, and because they can't be measured it is hard for the materialist way of seeing to take them into account.

In my thinking, there are four known qualitative factors: "Stress"; Sensitivity"; "Will to Live"; and the real nature of the "immune" system (more properly named the Wisdom of the Body, which is why I did a search for those terms as well.

My friends, and acquaintances, when I tried to share my views as to how the pandemic unfolded – these asked a crucial question: Why are people dying, if not from a contagious disease?

To my experience the "flu" is a very strong elimination process. We sweat, we cough, we barf, we poop, and we have fever dreams (there is a psychological element). It is essentially a Wisdom of the Body process, which is trying to throw off toxins of various kinds. With the arrival of industrial civilization, we began to poison the planet, and ourselves. Poison in the air (acid rain); the water (pollution); the land (mono-agriculture possess, with their elimination of the microorganisms essential for our food to be alive; and, in our medicines (side-effects).

Additional psychological processes are Stress in the work place, and in the way we educate children. What is most horrible is the theft of the dreams of the future, normal to the young. I can remember, during the Cold War, made to duck and cover under our desks. Where is hope in the future, while waiting for the Atomic Bomb to drop? Today children are made to feel fear of touch, of close proximity, while at the same time undergoing "active shooter" drills in school … more stress.

The reason I did a search for Cowan, was that Tom Cowan is our age's Einstein of medicine. Yes, real physics, in a spiritual sense, goes beyond Einstein, but I am using that metaphor to speak to the deep change that occurred from Newtonian physics to Einstein's works.

Tom was, for a time, an anthroposophical doctor, but when certain standard remedies did not work, he had to think his way past that observed limitation. In the beginning of his book: "Human Heart, Cosmic Heart" he points to Steiner's three most important things for the evolution of humanity: 1) that people stop working for money; 2) that people realize there is no difference between sensory and motor nerves, and 3) that the heart is not a pump.

In the beginning of that book Tom reveals modern scientific work about how liquid moving through a tube creates a fourth state of liquids, which exists between the moving liquid and the walls of the tube. This fourth state is minuscule, yet strongly ionized, and that is the condition/force that creates movement. Keep in mind that the blood circulates before the heart is formed, as a means of regulating the flow.

He also wrote: "Vaccines, Autoimmunity, and the Changing Nature of Childhood Illnesses", "Cancer and the New Biology of Water", and during Covid: "The Myth of Contagion", which underwent a title change to: "The Truth about Contagion – exploring theories about how diseases spread".

When the first version of the latter was published, folk at the Nature Institute in upstate New York were asked to comment. They were troubled, and wrote an article, which I later criticized. (2) Essentially the Nature Institute was pointing to work with an electron microscope that seemed to contradict what Tom had written in the first iteration of his book on Contagion.

This is why I searched for the term "Hauschka". His book: "The Nature of Substance" points to some remarkable perceptions, born in a phenomenological approach, that did not seem to be known/recognized by the Nature Institute, which seems mostly working with what biological form teaches in a Goethean sense. An electron microscope puts us in the field of physics' phenomena.

In that book Hauschka makes a remarkable observation. When we attack water with electricity, or strong chemicals, we get two classical elements, oxygen and hydrogen.* To him, we have killed something living, and the molecules are essentially "corpse" material.
*[There are also light and heat phenomena, which are an effect of the release of elemental beings, from their work in "substances".]

In my thinking on the ideas of molecules and atoms, it seemed me that an atom is a corpse of a corpse, in these terms. Steiner tried to get us to see the idea of an atom as a problem ... the Idea.

In Nature, the elements of the periodic table generally do not appear outside of some complex "molecules" (carbohydrates and such). Nature creates wholes, not the parts materialistic science believes are the basis of material reality. Even such metals as gold never appear in a pure form. When we get to the "physics" practices at Cern, we get corpses of corpses of corpses. The molecule is a corpse, the atom is a secondary corpse, and the electron is a tertiary corpse.

An electron microscope is using a corpse to observe a corpse. The "images" are computer enhanced fictions. The "pictures" generated do not really see what we think they see. Like the pictures of the stars in astronomy, there are a whole level of assumptions, which have not been empirically validated.

Some readers of this will be justly curious about how I am able to speak of such matters. Go here (3) and here (4). The latter is a lengthy discourse on the relationship of the four classical elements of antiquity (fire, air, water, and earth), and the four fundamental transformations of modern physics (electromagnetism, gravity, and the weak and strong nuclear forces). This includes a discussion of the Loki sponsored Heisenberg Uncertainty Principle, and its mad stepchild: Quantum Mechanics.

SAY WHAT !?!?! Here's the tale: Physics ran into a riddle. If their instruments looked at particles, the looking effected the seeing. They could measure location, but not velocity. Or velocity, but not location. Instead of recognizing that that phenomena reflected a limit to their instruments, they decide to believe it represented a condition of Nature. Einstein's reaction was: "God does not play dice with the universe."(5) It took an MIT graduate engineer (a kind of thinking much different from that needed to invent theories), to disassemble the errant cognition ... "God Does Not Play Dice", by David Shiang. (6)

Even Steiner understood, that when you get to material manifestation you are dealing with elemental beings, not things – i.e. Salamanders (Fire); Sylphs (Air); Undines (Water); and Gnomes (Earth). (7)

Materialistic medicine recognizes "Stress" as a fight/or flight mechanism, which dumps adrenaline and other enzymes into the body. Human beings are stressed at work, and at home, and while traveling between the two. Multiple times a day then, these energy igniters appear in the physical body.

"Sensitivity" is a kind of individualized factor. When electricity was first being played with, The Invisible Rainbow describes people going to parties, forming a circle holding hands, through which an electrical "current" is then run. When some folk started fainting and having nose bleeds, the practice was abandoned. Another sensitivity is the "gluten" allergy, which is due to the Roundup weed poison being applied to wheat, just before it is harvested – if the wheat is "dying" it makes it easier for a machine to cut it.

I also did a search for the term "Touch", which had not appeared in the PDF. "Touch" is well known for its physical and psychological healing qualities. One sage I read on the Internet, suggested that five hugs a day would be helpful for people with "symptoms" for "long Covid".

The "Will to Live" is also well known. I personally, about three years ago, during a serious illness wanted to die – I was in a hospital at the time, and in this state the Mother appeared to me. I asked Her, would She take me if I wanted, and She said yes. The ball was then in my court, and I realized I was not finished loving my Lady, and decline Her offer.

This experience led me to a deeper understanding of the crisis that appeared in elder care facilities. Many such not only had serious chronic illnesses, in many instances their minds had gone walk-about – dementia. We were keeping the physical body alive, which at the same time ties the soul/spirit to the material. When they got flu symptoms, including fevers, they would approach the threshold to the afterlife, and consciously, or instinctively, surrender to the offered release from suffering.

In intensive care facilities, the patients are covered over with protective material, as are the doctors and nurses. Touch is then lost. Given the prevalence of breathing difficulties in the Covid Experience, they were dying of suffocation, which is how Christ died on the Cross.

Rudolf Steiner has told us, that all of humanity is crossing the threshold in our age.

My spirit had two other perceptions of curiosities, in the social Covid phenomena. One was the Rate of Deaths (another search term). A few calculations reveal that the death rate in 1918 was 36 times that of today. In a sense, we were going through this Event, in a better fashion due to advances in medicine over the intervening decades. Media never played it that way.

Another observation I made was that surely the stress of World War I had an effect on peoples immune systems. Today, Americans have had to endure the failure of our political life, the Trump presidency, and other such follies. During the "epidemic", more stress, while people were locked down, and had to wait in long lines to be tested, and then get vaccines.

All of the above Ideas have led me to recognizing the Covid Mystery as a massive semiconscious Spiritual Rite of Initiation.

  (1) https://thecollectiveimagination.com/2021/02/17/3008/
  (2) https://thecollectiveimagination.com/2021/06/01/dear-the-nature-institute-folk/

(3) https://thecollectiveimagination.com/some-of-joel-wendts-writings-on-the-science-of-the-future/
(4) https://thecollectiveimagination.com/2019/05/20/letters-about-magic/
(5) https://www.livescience.com/65697-einstein-letters-quantum-physics.html
(6) https://www.amazon.com/God-Does-Not-Play-Dice/dp/0980237300/ref=tmm_pap_swatch_0?_encoding=UTF8&qid=1557063687&sr=1-1
(7) https://thecollectiveimagination.com/2019/10/29/rudolf-steiner-on-elemental-beings-karma-ceremonial-magic/

~!~!~!~!~!~!~!~!~!~~

Medicine's Einstein

(Tom Cowan, doctor and healer … https://www.chelseagreen.com/writer/thomas-cowan-md/ https://drtomcowan.com/

This is not an academic paper, but a collection of personal experiences, coupled with my own scientific research. I am, however, not a specialist in science, but a generalist [see note 1]. As with Goethe, I also believe understanding context is essential.

Many people have heard of Einstein. Some of those will think of him as a great mind in the field of Mathematical Theoretical Physics. Very few will know that for decades after he published his early works, on special and general relativity (2) – which effectively made great advancements over the ideas of Issac Newton – the English scientific establishment refused to acknowledge that work …

"Einstein's theory of General Relativity is the benchmark example for empirical success and mathematical elegance in theoretical physics." (3) I bring forward this idea of " … empirical success and mathematical elegance", to apply it to the way Dr. Cowan has come to know the world of health and illness.

… to continue: It didn't help that Einstein was also German, and a Jew by birth. Nevertheless, the English physicist Sir Arthur Eddington recognized Einstein's genius, and they became friends (a TV movie was made – 4). Since the following essay has to deal with ideas in the fields of natural science, it is important to note that around 1920, scientists were saying: "We are learning more and more about less and less." (5) Or, in my words: the number of tiny details is increasing, while the meaning of the whole is being lost.

Tom Cowan is as far ahead in medical science, as Einstein was ahead of Newton. As a consequence, America's medical establishment (which has to include the corporations that make a lot of money from illness) makes war against him. If one Google's Tom, one will find a lot of trash talk.

https://en.wikipedia.org/wiki/Thomas_Cowan_(alternative_medicine_practitioner)

All the same, he is a leading light in the Covid Mystery, basically proving (science, remember), that the present day ideas regarding illness, contagion, and vaccines, are in error.

For stating such anti-establishment ideas in public, his license to practice was attacked, which is true all over the world of those who fought against the "Official Narrative" of the meaning of the pandemic. He then voluntarily surrendered his license. A link below will bring the reader to his writings and his web-presence (6).

I've been acquainted with Tom for over three decades, mostly due to the fact that a woman doctor (Kelly) I lived with for five years, was originally in practice with Tom, in Keene, NH.

Both were, at that time, practicing Anthroposophical Medicine. To do this medical art, one must not only graduate from medical school, and become licensed to practice these healing arts, one must also study the medical teachings of Rudolf Steiner, as well as "apprentice" with an experienced anthroposophical doctor.

Kelly went through med school in a time few women went to med school. She became board certified in internal medicine, and began to practice family care. After about 15 years, she observed that nutrition was a crucial aspect of illness and healing, a subject not dealt with at all in medical school at that time. Looking for folks paying attention to that, she found her way to Anthroposophical Medicine.

When I first met her, she was in practice with Tom, and she became my first anthroposophical doctor. Time passed, and Kelly and I ended up living together for five years. Just one of her stories: At a certain point in her practice, she worked out that she needed 2.5 (she has a very precise mind) office workers just to handle insurance, which greatly effected costs of diagnosis and treatment.

Finding this more and more unworkable – after many years, she said tearful goodbyes to her patients, took a break, and studied doctors, who did a kind of simple-care where the patient could show up at the door, be seen that day, and was expected to pay in cash. The fees were not huge, and could be adjusted according to means. Recently the medical regulation establishment took her license away in California. So far, she has been able to fend off the same mindset as regards her license to practice in Massachusetts, and her ways of healing continue to evolve.

Her main struggle these days is to protect the rights of parents to make medical choices. A long legal struggle to avoid masks, and forced vaccinations.

She told me she occasionally fought with Tom, over medical questions, and thought he was a bit smug. It was not too much later that Tom went on his own, no longer practicing pure "Anthroposophical" Medicine (several of the traditional remedies failed empirically, to his observation).

Before I met Kelly socially, I was at Tom's house, where a meeting was being held by his first wife, regarding the Kucinich campaign for President. At one point he walked through the living room, from his office to the kitchen, saying "Do you know why people are fat?", and on returning: "Its because they are starving". Later I understood that the idea here is that there is no nutrition in their food, and the brain keeps demanding the body be fed. A little later, passing through again: "Do you know what the biggest cause of death is in America?", returning: "Its the doctor".

My view, on present reflection, is that a mind/spirit of Tom's nature lives in a world we barely see. He can't help but be who he is (see biographical details in all his books), for example, after getting a BA degree in Zoology, he did Peace Corp in Africa, teaching gardening at an elementary school in Swaziland. There he met "Chris", who introduced Tom to Rudolf Steiner. Tom writes: "Anthroposophical Medicine at least tries to answer the real questions"

"Smug", or … a genius, driven by social riddles, that spends the rest of his life becoming a doctor, and is never satisfied – knows he does not have all the answers, yet is always certain of the path of the quest. Not just that … he walks the walk … such as, all the work that is involved in finding ways to avoid the toxins lurking everywhere, … he practices everything he teaches.

Some of the details are amazing. There is a kind of purified water: Quinton Isotropic Seawater, which for cancer patients contains all the needed minerals, plus it is "structured water". What's that? Reading Tom is always a learning experience. Supplements, as needed, he gives his family.

Tom's first book, which I bought for myself and then occasionally gave away as gifts: ""The Four-fold (****) Path to Healing", subtitle: "Working with the Laws of Nutrition, Therapeutics, Movement and Meditation in the Art of Medicine." (with Sally Fallon and Jaimen McMillan) (over 400 pages). Published in 2004. Rudolf Steiner is mentioned several times in the Introduction.

(****) [Nutrition – Healing the Physical Body; Therapeutics – Healing the Life Force Body; Movement – Healing the Emotional Body; and Meditation – Healing the Mental Body.]

Sally Fallon published her co-work in greater detail in: "Nourishing Traditions", "The Cookbook that Challenges Politically Correct Nutrition and the Diet Dictators" (over 670 pages) in 2007. She refers to Steiner on pages, 190, 369, 419, and 540. Jaimen McMillan – the movement teacher, has a website (7)

....

We've all seen the official Food Pyramid, which since I was a child has gone through a lot of changes. Tom's book starts with a Fat Pyramid, page 16. Sally's book points out that before present day industrial farming, people ate straight from their gardens, and raised their own animals. They knew a lot of wisdom about what to and when to plant, what to eat, and how to preserve it. Kelly is into making her own yogurt, fermented vegetables, and chicken broth. Sally's book is full of recipes, and practical advice. Imagine the loving teacher you never got in school, who will lead you to wisdom, about your health and the food you eat.

Tom (beginning in Africa), as well as Sally and Kelly, have became aware of Weston A. Price (8). He was a dentist in the 1920's, who traveled the world looking for the folk with the healthiest teeth. Why was that? In his work, his patients had horrible teeth. The link is to a website on his work. A main discovery was that these rather happy peoples universally ate a lot of animal fats, and tended to not being "skinny".

In Tom's above book, for example, he describes how it is a healthy development for what women might call their middle-age spread (9). Fundamentally, the body is far smarter than are we, and it is a territory that teaches.

Rudolf Steiner, in his works on medicine (some of which this generalist has read – such as the 20 lecture cycle to doctors: "Spiritual Science and Medicine"), points out that medical science first studied the cadaver, the body of a human being no longer living. As a consequence, the basic "ideas" in medicine took a path where they were built up from observations of death, rather than life. A potent example of science's knowing more and more about less and less.

Here I want to take another needed contextual side trip, about official medical "science". The root science of our age does not see anything but matter, no spirit allowed. The doctor is trained to see the patient as a complicated machine. Over the years of my own life, I spent several years working in mental hospitals (10). Their working model is that the material brain is the seat of consciousness, and that we can "develop" medicines that – often too forcefully (11) – effect the physical material, and thus resolve the "psychological illness". They do not heal, they just modify behavior to a socially acceptable level.

Imagine a science where spirit, and soul matter as much as the purely material. As to "medicine", Tom is the leading and cutting (dismantling the past) edge, and he knows we are not at the end of our need to know the truth of what it means to be "human". The science of seeking for knowledge is never "settled".

In my article about my experiences with the "mentally" ill, I called what was going on, when testing was being done for experimental medicines, a "horror show". I am next going to refer to a couple of relevant "horror" shows, in the world of socially dominated profitable medicine. I don't want to be believed, but where there is smoke, there is usually fire.

There is this tale: the sugar industry knew that sugar was a serious cause of disease, and as well, … all those bad teeth. So, they created a massive publicity campaign to have fats blamed, instead of sugar. Butter, for example, quickly converts to energy and water – not weight gain. Of course, which butter today is a riddle: biodynamic, organic, well fed animals, or since Fats are Bad, how about fake butter.

Then there is some research I did on my own.

I heard a rumor, that the idea of health dangers from "secondary" smoke, was not actually based on empirical science. Sure, the smoker has a problem, but they are taking the full load into the lungs, on a regular basis – keep in mind that Big Tobacco stood in front of Congress and swore on a stack of bibles that they did not know nicotine was addictive.

Curious, I started a Google search on the science for secondary smoke. What I initially found was layers and layers of articles, basically referring to each other as the source of the science. Google, of course, lists according to frequency of source citation. By the way, why don't folks exposed to secondary smoke become addicted?

I spent an afternoon, going to the next page, and then the next page, perhaps a hundred times, when I ran into this story. The origin of the idea of the problem of secondary smoke was a passionate anti-smoker, who made up the idea to frighten people into quitting. He was the original "authority", and all the rest of the following citations treated his idea as a scientific fact.

Once in awhile – during this search – I ran into tests on rats, but rats are not humans, and any person no longer asleep realizes that science today is full of "doubtful" research. Much is not per-reviewed, and the sample size is often too small – "publish or perish" is a warning sign of hurried research. My older brother had a PhD in microbiology, and he called the process of exaggerating the conclusions of an experiment: "globalizing". The experimental data is the only true result, … describing "what it all means" is never empirically justified.

Tom's next book that I read was "Human Heart, Cosmic Heart" "A doctor's quest to understand, treat, and Prevent Cardiovascular Disease." Published in 2016, 160 pages, with an index, and a bibliography that shames any dilettante.

Chapter headings: 1. Doubting Thomas, 2. Circulation, 3. The Misery Index, 4. The Geometry of the Heart, 5. Defining the Questions, 6. What Doesn't Cause Heart Attacks, 7. What Does Cause Heart Attacks, 8. Stepping Forth, 9. Treating the Heart, 10. The Cosmic Heart, 11. A Heart of Gold. 12. What's Love Got to Do with It?

In the beginning of the book he refers to Steiner this way: "… I first encountered Rudolf Steiner's idea that the three most important things for the future evolution of humanity are: 1) that people stop working for money, 2) that people realize there is no difference between sensory and motor nerves, and 3) that the heart is not a pump.".

Tom then goes on to show that the heart is not a pump, using – in part, … I summarize: Modern research on the nature of liquids, where it has been discovered that water has four states, not just three, reveals that this fourth state is highly ionized, and appears in between a moving liquid and the walls of the "tube", where this "ionization" [12] is causing the movement. The blood circulates in the human being, before the heart is formed, and the heart then arises as a regulator of the already flowing substance. All of this is covered in detail, in Chapter 2. Circulation.

It is written for the patient. I was into my second reading, when I ended up in the hospital with a "heart" event. It gave me the strength to understand that the doctors were trapped in a set of conceptions that limited their ability to treat. In two hospital visits, I more than once had the painful experience that doctors do not listen well – they already know more than the patient.

Go to any ER, and you get put into a box of assumptions that can often be wrong ("The biggest cause of death in America is the doctor").

Then, in 2018, he published: "Vaccines, Autoimmunity, and the Changing Nature of Childhood Illness." Over 170 pages, indexed and sourced, and again readable by a patient and in this case particularly, the parent of a patient. "Part I: The Origins of Autoimmunity; Part II: Vaccine Fallacies: Three Case Studies; and Part III: Treatment and Recovery.

To complete this three-work masterpiece, in 2019: "Cancer and the New Biology of Water" "Why the war on cancer has failed, and what that means for more effective prevention and treatment." 190 pages, index and sources, again not only for the patient, but as with all three, full of practical advice. "Part I: A New Understanding of Cancer; Part II Potential Therapies; and Part III: Practical Steps Forward for Individuals.

Then came the Covid Mystery, that gave the world a time out (13).

He wrote, and then published (with Sally Fallon Morell): "The Contagion Myth", "Why Viruses (including "Coronavirus") Are Not the Cause of Disease (I bought it). Since almost everyone was swept away by the Official Narrative, the word "myth" drew a lot of unwanted attention, even from "anthroposophists"(14), so some changes were made to the title, and now we can read:

"The Truth about Contagion" "Exploring Theories about How Disease Spreads". (190 + pages, end notes for each chapter, and an index). Part I: Exploring the Germ Theory of Disease, 1. Contagion 2. Electricity and Disease, 3. Pandemics, 4. From Aids to Covid, 5. Testing Scam, 6. Exosomes, 7. Resonance, Part II: What Causes Disease. 8. Water, 9. Food, 10. Toxins. 11. Mind, Body, and the Role of Fear. Part III: Choices. 12. Questioning Covid, 13. A Vaccine for Covid-19, 14. 5G and the Future of Humanity. Epilogue.

In a very real sense, there is nothing more dangerous to industrial medicine than an educated patient. Kelly's style of treatment was to place the doctor and the patient on the same "social" level. She teaches, and the well informed patient chooses.

Notes:
(1) https://thecollectiveimagination.com/some-of-joel-wendts-writings-on-the-science-of-the-future/
(2) https://en.wikipedia.org/wiki/Theory_of_relativity
(3) this quote is the opening line of an article predicting Einstein's work would eventually fail: https://arxiv.org/abs/1203.3827 Written by Niayesh Afshordi, it is titled: "Where will Einstein fail? Lessons for gravity and cosmology".
(4) https://www.imdb.com/title/tt0995036/
(5) https://quoteinvestigator.com/2017/10/25/more/
(6) https://drtomcowan.com/ His books are also available on Amazon. Tom's five books, plus Nourishing Traditions: $122.30 – hardcover and paper back; in Kindle – $108.99. It is a small price to pay, for such an amazing "library" on health and illness.
(7) https://www.westonaprice.org/#gsc.tab/=0
(8) https://www.spacialdynamics.com/jaimen-mcmillan
(9) In a discussion of "osteoporosis", he writes that women are a group that needs "liberation from the alienation – often but not always, imposed by men – of an unrealistic image of their own bodies, liberation from the tyranny of trying to force their bodies into assuming a shape different from that which it naturally wants to assume" page 241.
(10) http://ipwebdev.com/mental.html
(11) Kelly explained to me that high dilution homeopathic medicines were like a butterfly kiss – helping the body instead of forcing it to do something, so that "numbers" are in the right ranges. Sensitive people end up with "side-effects".
(12) The "anthroposophical" communities had a lot of issues, as regards how to treat and act in the "pandemic". Someone sent a copy of the book on the Contagion Myth to the "Nature Institute", a place where a lot of wonderful work is being done on form in biology. They argued against what Tom was saying about Covid, especially as regards the ideas of what was contagion. I disagreed with their work, and wrote an article for my blog. It includes a link to what the Nature Institute folks wrote. https://thecollectiveimagination.com/2021/06/01/dear-the-nature-institute-folk/
(13) Faith – trust in the Divine Mystery – has led me to seeking to understand the meaning in such catastrophic events. Here is one way of seeing the situation: "Event and Aftermath – the

Creation of Love through Crisis." https://thecollectiveimagination.com/2022/12/26/event-and-aftermath-the-creation-of-love-through-crisis/

(14) I do research in what might be called: ideal (spiritual) high energy physics. This has been a work of over three decades, and culminated recently with "The Father at Rest – magical and mystical dark-matter physics in the Age of Technological Chaos." "Ionizing" is a feature of the underlying principle of Unity, at an electromagnetic
level. https://thecollectiveimagination.com/2021/07/15/the-father-at-rest/..

Curious Ephemera

musings on the Steiner Ideas of the Eighth Sphere and the Third Force by Joel A. Wendt [Recall the cover of this book, and the sigil of Aschmunadai … an original Intelligence of the Zone Girdling the Earth]

It is unfortunate, yet necessary, to admit that Rudolf Steiner did not know everything, and on occasion sometimes was completely wrong. If we do not do this, we are trapped in a Cave of our own limits and assumptions, where no new spiritual life can enter. Details will be provided as needed, and we will begin with the most important, which has to do with his relationship with the Holy Mother – Earth Mother.

In Stephen Clarke's remarkable work: the "Mexican Mysteries Re-Imagined"
– http://ipwebdev.com/hermit/Clarke5.html – he points out that what Steiner had to say about the Inner Earth was not just wrong, but lost. Stephen writes, after quoting Steiner's descriptions (1) of the Inner Earth: "Good grief; only the deviant or mentally disturbed would want to muck around in this; why bother?"

Steiner had begun those remarks with this statement: *"The occult science of all epochs says the following about the interior of the earth … "*. Stephen points to this statement as problematic in using the world "all". It only takes one true and different view to falsify that assertion, and in the article he provides it.

As I studied Stephen's ideas here, I made my own judgment, which was that Steiner's mistake was to go toward this Realm as a "spiritual researcher". That's egotistical, as those of us who have met Her are aware, for we have those encounters when we are the most naked, the most empty, and the most vulnerable – ourselves as powerless as a new born baby.

When we do not do this, the Realm is a mirror of our own follies. We see only what we bring, not what is actually there. As a consequence, much of Steiner's works have this quality of not really appreciating Her reality. Artists recognize these characteristics. In Star Wars V, Luke is being trained by Yoda, and has a battle underground (among rocks and direct and dangerous roots), where he meets Darth Vader, and kills him. When Luke takes off the mask, it is his (Luke's) face that he sees. In Star Wars VIII, Rey is being trained by Luke, on Luke's island retreat. She has a dream where she falls (or dives) into a pool of water, and then comes up in a rounded stone covered underground cave. As she turns around and looks about, she suddenly is faced with a mirror effect which catches both her front and her back. Which ever way she turns she sees endless mirages of her self.

In the Hermetic Science of the ancient Egyptians (magic), we begin with the Emerald Tablet, and an appreciation of the idea of the One and the Many. God is One, the Unity of All, yet manifested in infinite ways = the Many. Below in the notes is a version of the Emerald Tablet, translation by Issac Newton (2)

Tomberg, in his monumental "Meditations on the Tarot – a journey into Christian Hermeticism" points out that if we do not see the Divine in Its Magical and Mystical aspects, we have lost the heart of the matter, and he criticizes Steiner for not including those aspects of Reality in his works except in the smallest and most insignificant ways.

Human beings have a need for these pathways, and we find this phenomena in European anthroposophical circles via the modern fascination with Are Thoresen, and Judith vol Halle. Are is "magical" in his work, and Judith is "mystical" in hers. These are not flaws at all, by the way.

Both do not speak of having the meeting with the Lesser and Greater Guardians of the Threshold, which – frankly – is not necessary for everyone to experience, in order to manifest deep spiritual knowledge.

Are has an "atavistic" (gifts from prior lives) clairvoyance, which has its value in spite of Steiner's "indications" otherwise. Are's idea of "translocation", however, is a sign of his limits, because it assumes that there is no divine meaning in the effect – but rather something evil. His dream about Vidar has generated a lot of interest, and may be completely true (Steiner claims to have met this Spirit) … the problem is that such a spirit has no place in the Americas.

Judith, with her stigmata and not eating, travels deeply into the time of Christ, but when I ask her students on the Internet, what does she have to say about Christ today, they have no answer. Steiner, in his work: Pastoral Medicine, speaks of a relationship between madness and the mystical awareness of saints. His research is that these "effects" represent a kind of out of sorts relationship in the connections between the ethereal or life body, and the astral or desire body, or between the ethereal body and the physical body.

This stuff about atavistic, and out or sorts relationships of the different bodies, works for Steiner, because he is hopelessly idealistic. Clearly, the Divine Mystery cares about those who have these qualities of soul. They have their place in the world, however much Steiner judges them as lacking some necessary characteristics.

Next I am going to take up some ideas of Steiner's regarding the Eighth Sphere. At note (3) one will find many quotes …

Before I had studied the Eighth Sphere material, it was just vague references in various places. As a consequence I already had a personal relationship with certain ideas about cosmic order.

For example, it was clear to my experience that the Divine Mystery worked from outside of time and space, in the Eternal Now. Steiner writes: "… we do not live only in the fourth but also in this eighth sphere through the fact that our Divine Creators live in this sphere together with us.".

In Steiner's work is an interesting diagram, which also appears in Andrew Linnell's short essay on "Anthroposophy and the Eighth Sphere". [If you want a copy, here is his email address for asking to receive the pdf file: jandrewlinnell@gmail.com

Basically it is a set of circles, in a somewhat flattened U shape, and each circle refers to Steiner's vision of seven different incarnations of this "place" in the Cosmos: Saturn, Sun, Moon (curving down) Earth (center), Jupiter, Venus, Vulcan (curving up). Below the Earth circle is another, called: the Eighth Sphere.

Steiner had mentioned, in Occult Movements of the Nineteenth Century, that it is helpful to see these spheres as nested inside each other, with the Eighth Sphere the outer circle. We also need to recognize the circles are symbols for spheres.

He writes as well: " … we live within a sphere which belongs to the Form Spirits just as our earth belongs to us, but which, as the eighth sphere, permeates our earth and our organism with the exception of our head and all that is sense activity."

Already I am curious as to why in one instance he uses the terms "our Divine Creators", and in another "the Form Spirits". I get the bit about our head, etc, because for us to have freedom in thinking, we need to have an aspect where They do not rule … we do.

He sez: "Will man now remain simply an inseparable member in the great organism which mounts to its eighth sphere, the great organism of the Elohim, or will he develop to freedom and become independent? This question of whether men should become independent was decided through a most definite cosmic act."

He also sez: "If however the human being has connected himself too strongly with the forces of the senses, which should now detach themselves, if he is related to them and has not found the way to attach himself to what is to pass over to the next Globe, he will depart with the slag and become an inhabitant of this body of slag, in the same way as other beings are now inhabitants of the present moon."

My reaction to the term "slag" was to wonder … If Nature recycles everything, will the same redemptive process not apply to "slag"? In fact, my view of the Asuras is that this is exactly what they do – They recycle the human spirit that loses the ability to continue, an experience leading to such a spirit giving up on existence all together. Having personally had a moment where my stress had so exhausted me, that I not only wanted to die, I wanted not to be – I understand the woe. In that mood the Mother came to me, and initiated me into Her Realm.

He sez "… there is an Eighth Sphere to which everything goes that cannot make any connection with this continuous evolution. This already forms itself as predisposition in the devachanic state. When a human being uses the life on earth only to amass what is of service to himself alone, only to experience an intensification of his own egotistical self, this leads in Devachan into the condition of Avitchi. A person who cannot escape from his own separateness goes into Avitchi. All these Avitchi men will eventually become inhabitants of the Eighth Sphere".

This idea of "separateness" is interesting. Patrick Dixon in "America the Central Motif":

"For this 'all seeing eye' to become an all being I' it must set into the darkest, most separate place, die to itself as the seed in the soil, give itself to the deepest purpose of all, then by a mysterious alchemy, the Will of all shall surrender to the one, and there shall arise a type of human being who will perceive the Universe as being an Individual while they and other human beings are experienced as being universes within themselves."

In Franz Bardon's book "The Key to the True Quabbalah", he distinguishes what he calls the path of sainthood, from the path of individual perfection. The saint only obtains to that particular aspect of divinity they currently manifest. The perfect man becomes himself all that God is.

Steiner sez: "The asuras inhabit the moon and from there they work on the men whom they want to drag down into the eighth sphere and thereby tear away from progressive evolution and its goal — the Christ. All those who strive towards the eighth sphere will eventually live on a moon. AUM. One wards off bad influences when one says it in the right way; it connects man with the creating Godhead, the three Logoi."

Here we start to drift away from the Mother, who has a definite connection to the Moon Sphere. Not just Christ, but the Mother as well makes up the nature of the Divine Mystery. A misconception perhaps due to Steiner's failure to see Her properly.

Here we need to take a look at the concept of "good and evil". Steiner's works are permeated everywhere with that idea. Keep in mind that in the Philosophy of Spiritual Activity Steiner writes: "One must be able to confront an idea, and experience it, … otherwise one will fall into its bondage". Was Steiner in bondage to the idea of "good and evil"?

Once we realize the Mother is the Many, it follows that all that what Steiner describes as evil beings, such as Lucifer, Ahriman, Sorat, the Sun Demon, and the Asuras, are limited and guided in their work by She, who holds the whole world in His Hands. The logos-logic goes like this: If the evil ones could win, existence would already be over. Since that is not the case, if we seek for why, we find Her.

Bardon writes: "There is nothing unclean in the whole of the Creation." "Good and evil are human conceptions", not the fundamental Reality. Steiner even admits somewhere that various beings of the hierarchies went through a human stage. Which means facing the problem of good and evil?

He sez: "The unalloyed evil must be cast out of the stream of world evolution like dross. It will be relegated to the Eighth Sphere."

… and: "But a part of this remained behind and was excluded, because it was no longer of any use to mankind. That constitutes the eighth sphere, which is no longer of use to the development of man, but can be used by higher beings." (for what purpose? Seems to be missing.)

He sez: "If we direct our gaze beyond the sense-world, we shall no longer see the world only as known to the senses, but we shall also recognize Infinity."

Here we get to a very special aspect of Steiner's situation. He could point to the idea of Infinity, yet at this time "Projective Geometry" was little known. Steiner's pupil, George Adams Kaufmann, with help from Olive Whicher, unveiled for us what this geometry can say about space. These works, such as "Space and the Light of Creation", and "Physical and Ethereal Spaces" deal with the "Infinite".

Reading the latter gives us a "yoga" for the imagination, and aught to be the most basic book in the stream of Goethean Science. Of course, few anthroposophists study Goethean Science at all, much less "Physical and Ethereal Spaces".

When Steiner said that about the Infinite, he preceded those remarks with the comment that the sense world is Maya, an illusion. This ancient Eastern concept is not true. The sense world is Speech by the Word. As Goethe showed us, we learn from observing the phenomena, and "reading the book of Nature".

I wrote a long essay on Cosmic Space: "The Misconception of Cosmic Space, as appears in the ideas of modern astronomy". http://ipwebdev.com/hermit/space.html Parallax is based on Euclidean Geometry, and if we substitute Projective Geometry all our conceptions about Cosmic Space change. Steiner sez: "Think on it: how the point becomes a sphere and yet remains itself. Hast thou understood how the infinite sphere may be only a point, and then come again, for then the Infinite will shine forth for thee in the finite."

[a little exercise for the imagination: Picture a dimensionless "point", to which we add a short line. Conceive of the point as the center of a sphere, and the line as the sphere's radius. In the imagination elongate the radius line, and be aware of how the sphere grows in "size". Contract the line to zero length, and once more we have the only the "point". Now increase the line to the Infinite. As we do this, the arc of curvature of the sphere lessens, until the sphere disappears into what is called: the Plane at Infinity.

This is hard to picture, but projective geometry allows for this as a completely logical transformation. Now imagine that the real "space" we inhabit has this qualitative nature. What has happened is that the three dimensional world we believe exists, has metamorphosed into a two dimensional Plane. The physical has crossed over into the ethereal. When we look at the starry world, we see a kind of boundary condition, behind which exists the invisible infinite ethereal realm.

This is also the Realm of Levity, or the abode of the Christ: "In It (the Word) was Life, and the Life was the Light of the World. Note in passing that Adams "Space and the Light of Creation", has three chapters, the first of which is: "Radiation of Space". From the Realm of Levity, He creates "space", via the Living Light, and this also explains the mystery of dark matter and dark energy.

As Adams points out, Steiner also said: "we must become able to think the extensive intensely, and the intensive extensively".

More Steiner: "Blavatsky was misled by certain beings who had an interest in guiding her into putting Lucifer in the place of Christ, and this was to be achieved by introducing precisely the opposite of the truth of the eighth sphere and by maligning the Jahve God, representing him merely as the god of the lower nature. Thus did those cosmic powers who desired to advance materialism work even through what was called "theosophy.""

The Third Force

I did a search of the Archive for the Third Force, and it couldn't find it. It would put up third and force, but that just went on and on. Fortunately here is some relevant remarks by Georg Unger in his booklet "On Nuclear Energy and the Occult Atom".

First quoting Steiner: "If we throw that which lives in the Harmony of the Spheres still further downwards, as far as the Asuras, there arises a still more terrible force, which will not be able to be kept secret for long. One can only wish … that mankind will have nothing immoral left in it"

Then in Unger's text, there is a more elaborate version of this diagram:

warmth ether generates – in rising steps: light ether, then chemical number sound ether, then life meaning atomic ether

Warmth Ether – Gaseous Condition – Fluid Condition – Solid Condition

warmth ether also generates in falling steps, electricity lucifer, magnetism ahriman, and third force asuras Third Force

After which, Unger refers to a fallen, or evil, light ether, a fallen chemical ether, and a fallen life ether = possibly the Third Force. Later he writes "It is much more important that we can indicate certain things which are now at hand, and which we know and understand, for physics has entered the realm of a type of magic, dealing with the sub-sensible."

Unger goes on trying to explain the difference between sub-sensible appearances and the sub-natural. He is uncertain whether or not atomic energy is the Third Force, or just the tip of an iceberg. In re-reading this text, I am still unable to clearly think the differences between the sub-natural and the sub-sensible appearances. The nearest I can come is to see the sub-natural as the community of Beings behind Nature, of a certain sort, and the sub-sensible the materialistic conceptions of such as electricity, magnetism, and atomic physics.

The booklet is apparently still in print, and is available at the Rudolf Steiner Bookstore.

In other places, Steiner has said: electricity is coagulated thought.

Is it possible for someone to know more than Steiner, in particular instances?

Anthroposophists tend not to even think about this, but there is no Steiner without a huge supporting case of spiritual beings The so-called Akashic Record is not a library, but living cosmic beings (see for example: "Cosmic Memory"). Even Steiner points out that various hierarchies do not share the same goals.

Are the Beings that support Tomberg and Bardon the same as those who support Steiner?

Steiner said: "Jahve is connected in this mysterious way with the moon, as you will find explained also in Occult Science. From this statement you can estimate how materialistic it was to designate the moon as the eighth sphere, whereas it really is the force itself, the sphere, that attracts the moon."

Bardon remarks that his work is very much an effect supported by Divine Providence. In my biography, I dedicated myself to the 23rd Psalm: "The Lord is my shepherd, I shall not want." My whole biography is filled with events that involved this aspect of the Divine Mystery, an influence even Goethe acknowledged. Details on this are in a long essay here: https://thecollectiveimagination.com/2023/04/30/stillborn-a-review-of-the-book-fire-borne and here: https://thecollectiveimagination.com/2022/09/21/out-of-the-closet/

She – Divine Providence – led me to Bardon five years before She led me to Steiner. When that transition was initializing, Jahve visited me in the flesh, essentially blessing the union of those paths that would emerge in my own biography.

As I pointed out above, Steiner had a goofy relationship with the Mother, thinking Her Realm contained at its Core this: *9. The "earth-core." This is the substance through whose influence black magic arises in the world. The power of spiritual evil comes from this source."*.

When we add in his fascination with "good and evil", we can get a sense of the nature of the hierarchies that support his activities. As my life unfolded, my main "guides" were of the Mother's Realm.

Tomberg writes of the Realm of the False Holy Spirit, and asserts that human beings cannot cross it without Her support.

To return to the idea of the Third Force, … my intuition is that it has always been Magic. Laying that aside for the moment, let me share my work on "electricity".

I never liked the idea of electricity as "fallen" light. As a consequence I studied the phenomena, free of any assumptions one way or another. This link refers to those studies https://thecollectiveimagination.com/2023/02/14/some-reflections-on-the-truth-value-of-modern-theoretical-physics/ :

Along side those studies, given that my gift was clair-thinking, not clairvoyance, I began to seek to understand what Beings stood behind material phenomena. The manifested sense world was an "effect" produced by the Spirit, so what Spirit manifested such aspects as "gravity", "light", and "electricity", and such as the four fundamental forces or transformations recognized by modern physics: electromagnetism, gravity, and the weak and strong nuclear forces.

When these studies reached a certain qualitative confection, I saw/knew – with my clair-thinking – that electricity (which can't be separated from magnetism) was the Father at Rest.

Goethe had asserted that there had to be some ground, some power, which gave order, otherwise the life forces alone would produce chaos. Ernst Lehrs' "Man or Matter" describes electricity as providing to matter the property of "coherence", aka "order".

Thinking in pure Ideals led to my seeing that after the Creation, the Father rested, yet was not asleep. He is the One, of the One and the Many, and gives us the Unity of All things, which modern physics finds in the idea of quantum entanglement, where you can separate "particles" in space, but not in time.

Another modern phenomena is the apparent effect of an electromagnetic "field" to be able to harm living organisms. To my thinking, this "field" increases the level of order wherever it manifests. So we get reports of disease conditions, where people live near a high voltage power distribution system.

We also get an explanation for why 5G is so dangerous, and contributed to the "disease" conditions that arose in Wuhan China.

Let us next consider the problem Unger pointed out, suggesting that when we played with atomic energy, we were playing with the Third Force, although he saw these effects as the tip of an iceberg, … "It is much more important that we can indicate certain things which are now at hand, and which we know and understand, for physics has entered ***the realm of a type of magic***, dealing with the sub-sensible."

Radiant matter is molecules which have reached a limit of the macrocosmic process of densification. See George Blattmann's discussion of the table of elements in his wonderful work: "Radiant Matter – decay and consecration". These "molecules" fall apart spontaneously. .

An Atomic Bomb is made by going out into the world collecting yellow cake uranium. Uranium is naturally decaying – and has a very long half-life. https://en.wikipedia.org/wiki/Uranium

What we do is collect a lot of yellow cake, and refine it, by getting rid of the other substances, within which Nature has embedded these molecules. The normal decay rate is increased by this process of concentration, producing U-235. The decay process involves emitting "alpha" particles, and when we put a lot of it together, we get a lot of free roaming alpha particles, which have the effect of increasing the decay rate of the surrounding uranium molecules – the "chain reaction"

We create then a globe of this deadly stuff, surround it with explosive substances designed to implode rather the explode, and make bombs. From one way of seeing, these activities produce extraordinarily powerful anti-life forces.

As a consequence, the bomb tears a hole in the ethereal realm, and then from the astral world, otherwise invisible beings rush in: aka: UFOs, for these beings have to clothe themselves in matter to remain in our material realm. Unger's near magical tip of the iceberg.

Let us now add some of the Ideas out of the Hermetic Science (Magic) of the ancient Egyptians.

Unger does mention the existence of the ancient idea of the elements: fire, air, water, and earth, but dismisses it as not relevant. Bardon, however, in revealing the secrets of the **Tetragrammaton**, describe Fire as the symbol for Will, Air as the symbol for Intellect, Water as the symbol for Feeling, and all three of which unite in Earth, as the symbol for Consciousness.

These four are also aspects of what Steiner called the various incarnations of the Earth. Saturn is fire/will. Sun is air/intellect. Moon is water/feeling. While Earth is earth/consciousness.

Another central conception is the idea of the Macrocosm and the microcosm, which is that the human being is an exact analogue of the Majestic Whole. One consequence of this is that we have to see that within us lives all those "evil" beings, such as the Asuras, the Luciferic, the Ahrimanic, and the anti-Christ, or the Sun Demon (Sorat?) and so forth.

In Hermetic Science there are three kinds of processes. Negative processes, such as those which disassemble the matter in the food we eat. Positive processes where the dissolved matter is reconstituted into bodily substance. As well as Neutral processes, which have no effects, but are able to balance the other two.

Keep in mind the idea of "Wholeness". All the processes work together, in a musical-like symphonic harmony.

When I first encountered Steiner internet venues, there was a lot of blame for current conditions, placed on Lucifer, Ahriman, and the Asuras, as if they worked upon humanity from outside us. Yet, Steiner describes, in "Lucifer and Ahriman", at page 21: "…the very purpose of our Fifth Post-Atlantean epoch is that man should become increasingly conscious of what takes effect through him in earthly existence." … takes effect Through him …

As a consequence, in Facebook venues I have often asserted that to understand the luciferic and the ahrimanic, we need to observe these impulses in ourselves, and avoid speculating that we can observe these effects in the outer world. To call this or that phenomena (or person) as luciferic, ahrimanic, or asuric, is to not actually see the phenomena. Mostly we see some event or process we don't like, and then attribute that to Evil. Our antipathies, or sympathies for that matter, are not (in the main) perceptions, but rather just examples of our lack of ability to "Judge Not", as given in the Sermon on the Mount.

Bardon's books examine the various "powers" of the Creation, and give ways to become able to apply those by ones-self. The first one: "Initiation Into Hermetics – A Course of Instruction of Magic Theory and Practice" [IIH] trains the student through a series of ten steps, each step training the mental sphere, the psychic sphere, and the physical sphere.

The second, which is the first book of his that Providence led me to, is: "On the Practice of Ceremonial Evocation – Instructions for Invoking Spirit Beings from the Spheres surrounding us" [PCE]

The third is: "The Key to the True Quabbalah – the Quabbalist as a Sovereign in the Microcosm and the Macrocosm". [KTQ]

On a certain level all of these concern the understanding and application of Magic Powers, the term Magic being another name for Hermetic Science. In these works, in accord with the "Lore" of magical books, the texts themselves are manifestations of living Beings, and they have certain "secrets" that only a scholar of all three books will find.

Over the course of fifty years (1973 to 2023) I have read each of these several times, aka: I am a scholar of this material. In the books Bardon often has sentences that begin "the magician will … ", and rarely, but definitely, has sentences that refer to the "meditating scholar".

Each book begins with an introductory section, called in IIH (50 pages) and KTQ (60 pages): "Theory". In PCE, we begin with a long discussion, which is also essentially a theoretical and necessary introduction (140 pages – which can be scanned and then read only if interested.

After this beginning, are the "practices". What this means is that first we are given the ideas, and then how we can set out to prove the truth of the ideas.

It should be kept in mind that Magic is a Moon Wisdom, which is under the aegis of Divine Providence, aka: the Mother. In addition, the God Jahve is a central supervising and Creative Spirit.

Steiner sez there are seven Elohim, or Sun spirits. One of them, bound Himself to the elements of Earth, and when the Hebrews left Egypt He became their God.

One intuitive understanding I acquired was that part of the point of Bardon's works have to do with many individuals whose prior lives include some familiarity with Moon wisdoms. Providence leads them to these books, to enable them to work out their karma.

I also intuited this Idea, of there being three levels of Magic. Sorcery, Magic Proper, and Holy Magic. Sorcery involves a practice where a tradition of some sort, gives instructions as needed to pursue a particular result. These can be for healing, or such horrors as creating a curse. The practitioner follows a recipe, in order to achieve the desired result. People who practice these arts generally find themselves exhausted after this "work". This happens because the sorcerer's life forces are used by the evoked Being, in order to produce the result. The Being does not provide them.

In Magic Proper, the practitioner has undergone serious training, whether it is in the form of what lives in the Navajo ceremonies, or the Way described by Bardon in his books. Each "tradition" has its own cosmology and methods, yet it is ultimately the same level of Beings that co-participate. We should not exclude the rituals of the many religions, such as lives in the Mass practiced by the Catholics, or such beautiful rites as in the Tibetan sand paintings.

Holy Magic is prayer, which is a kind of petition for aid in either understanding or healing. The forces in this case come from the higher Beings Themselves. Tomberg's "Meditations on the Tarot – a journey into Christian Hermeticism" can be seen as a deep revelation of Holy Magic.

The path of the meditating scholar is the one that I follow, and one that I believe is most effective for whoever wants to learn and appreciate Hermetic Science. The ultimate teaching is that the Highest Power is Knowledge Itself.

For someone who wants to learn the most from Bardon, it is the introductory materials that need the most attention … that is: the fundamental Ideas.

A special level of education is the result, given that the rules/Ideas are the fundamental processes by which the Creation was accomplished. Such that for a Steiner fan, we don't just come to believe that the Spirits of Form did a certain task, but we learn "how" they did it – what are the fundamental laws.

There is nothing "supernatural" about these laws. They came into existence at the moment of the Creation, and in Hermetics we learn practices which enable us to know personally various "hows" ourselves, through what is called "the Key of the Elements".

The primary principle is the akasha or generative principle, and from this we get the Element Fire, which is the Will, and was how that Saturn Globe was generated. Next came the Element Air, which is the Intellect, and was how the Sun Globe was generated, yet retains a kind of memory of the former. The Moon Globe which is the Feeling life again keeping aspects of the prior Globe, and all these eventually are united in the creation of the Element Earth, or Consciousness.

In IIH, the first Step is the basis of everything else. Its principle task is to enable us to learn how to breathe in the Light, and what can be done with this practice. Steiner had something to say about this, and Andrew Linnell wrote this:

"The undeveloped counterbalance for the future was called by Rudolf Steiner Refined Breathing. There exists a relationship of thinking with breathing that is expressed in these words from Steiner: "The lung is an organ that also has forces of head formation within it, though to a lesser degree. The whole human organism has everywhere these same forces, but in varying intensities. … The head is an advanced respiratory organ. Having moved beyond the lung stage, it represses air breathing and, instead of taking in air, takes in etheric forces through the senses." (4)

Having practiced whole body pore-breathing of the light since the mid-1970's, my suspicion is that the work, on Refined Breathing being "practiced", is basically stuff people are making up. I even wrote an article on the efficacy for this practice, for people with the "flu", which was happening during the inauguration of the Covid Mystery. https://thecollectiveimagination.com/2020/03/23/the-magic-of-breathing-as-a-possible-aide-for-an-individual-with-the-flu/

Here I need to confess that I have a number of serious problems with Andrew's work, as well as the community he is a part of: The Center for Anthroposophical Endeavors https://cfae.us/

My reason is very simple. They will not let me join. I do understand the "reasons" as it were, which is that I am a gadfly. I don't think they understand the weakness of the idea of "Good and Evil", or the epistemology problems that arise from their not understanding the significance of The Philosophy of Spiritual Activity. The uncritical belief that Steiner never made mistakes, or his every word can be seen as the Truth, is one aspect. It creates a religion that has to be called: Steinerism. The need for this "anthroposophical" work to be open and scientific is ignored.

The way the Facebook page "Anthroposophy" defines what that term means (I can't join that group anymore), is completely false … in fact dangerously false. Someone new to this work, who reads that, will get an entirely wrong idea of what Anthroposophy is. The CFAE journal on the Mysteries of Technology does not allow for disagreement, which makes it completely unscientific. Every contributor has their own field of interest, and these views are not disturbed with questions.

This same group tends to think that Ahriman has yet to incarnate, and since he is already here, they end up blind as to what he has done.

They are, however, justly concerned over various trends in modern life, such as Trans-humanism, and the serious attacks on the living Atmosphere of the Life Sphere of the Planet.

This brings us to Bardon's second book, on Ceremonial Evocation.

Right now we have a dependency on Steiner for knowledge of that which the various hierarchies do. As to PCE (and the other texts), it is possible to get a pdf download, which enables us to search its extensive lists of various spirits of various spheres, who are experts in various subjects. The book provides, the sigil (the evocational sign), the name of the Being, its sphere and position in the Zodiac, has well its arena of expertise.

As with IIH, PCE has a trick or two up its magical sleeve, as it were. In the "theory" section, there is an elaborate discussion of the meaning and practical use of the Magic Circle. There are instructions for what to wear, how to design one's "temple", and make an elaborate circle, even on a silk cloth, with various sigils and so forth inscribed around the edge of the circle. After which, he states -suggestively – that the meditating scholar with find that the highest circle is in his hands. That is, sit in your asana posture (even in a chair), and make a circle of your thumbs and forefingers, or fold your fingers together, and imagine the circle going from that gesture, in a circle that moves up to the shoulders, and around the neck.. That suffices for evoking all the qualities the circle is to provide.

When meditating, it is also possible to see that the knees are the base of a triangle, whose upper point is just above the heart. It is into this triangle of our consciousness, that evoked beings can appear right in front of us.

Once we have identified a particular Being as one with the knowledge and capacities we seek, we evoke them as an aspect of our "meditation", and perhaps apply Holy Magic, and pray for their guidance in the pursuit of our riddles. We can even just ask for intuitive support, as we ourselves worry the questions, for example: How do I connect with the Thrones in the Atmosphere, so as to gain advice for what to do to heal that world of chem-trails and other assaults.

Instead of doing a search of the Steiner archive, we go directly to the Source Itself. A meditating scholar will want all three books, for much can be learned by becoming slightly familiar with what they offer, keeping in mind that the highest "power" is Knowledge. "Knowledge" is the main aspect of KTQ.

In this book we are introduced to the "letters" which are the fundamental powers of the Creation. So, Bardon writes: "Pronouncing the letters: 1. in the experimenting (training) room

… 2. in the whole universe … 3. in the body as an internal hollow space … 4. inductively (project) and deductively, i.e., materializing and dematerializing (condensing) it.

Each letter has a Color, a Sound Note, a Feeling, and a Region of the Body.

For example the "letter" "A": light blue; G; feeling of ease; lobes of the lung (individually) … or "S": purple red; G#; warmth; gall.

This four-fold "speech" produces the effect of the "letter" in the Creation. Once we can pronounce two letters together, we can get certain effects:

"**D-J** Someone who makes use of this letter combination may place himself, or others, into ecstasy – rapture – at any desired moment. Also mediums or people with medial gift may, by the help of this formula, be put into a somnambulistic state within a few moments.

Transferred to the astral body, this formula evokes strong sexual instincts in human beings and animals of both sexes.

If this formula is transferred into the material plane of human beings and animals, it will prevent infertility, either by direct use, or by embodying it eucharistically in food or drink."

In IIH, Step II, we learn to concentrate on various senses, first one, then two or more (up to five) at the same time (optical, auditory, sensory, olfactory, and taste). As a practical matter, I made a list of the "letters", and their qualities, plan to make just working with one letter and one quality as part of a short daily ritual; itself built around Step I. of IIH.0

Keep in might that to a higher Being, this kind of complex many faceted active is as simple as breathing is to us. We don't actually breath, but rather are breathed. Highest hierarchies have same effect on the ones below them.

Also in KTQ there is an interesting diagram and comment, which I will try to describe and somewhat reproduce. Its discussion is near the end of the book, under the title Formulas of the Elements. It is suggestive (a companion short cut to Step I. Of IIH, and the creation of a Circle in PCE?) of how to use applications of single "letters" . It begins with this paragraph:

"These offer various possibilities of use. One formula, for instance, is for the power over each element; another one for the control of the magnetic fluid, or the qualitative power over the elements; and yet another endows one with power over the beings that are in the elements."

For the diagram … one the left page is a table, whose upper level is the symbols of the elements. The symbol Fire is a triangle point upward. Air is the same, except it has a short horizontal life bisecting it. For Water the point or the triangle is downward, and the symbol for Earth is a repetition of the line gesture. It is useful to give some thought to these symbols, which are not arbitrary.

The Lore suggests that Fire and Water are the primary elements, and the Air and Earth are secondary.

On the opposite page is a pair of circles, where one is encouraged to think of the activity or pronouncing these letters as an inner gesture and an outer gesture. Again, it helps to meditate on the nature of the symbol, these too not bring arbitrary.

All three books begin with a different "colorful picture", which is symbolic of the object of the course of study, and a worthy image for meditation. For IIH and TKQ, the symbols are near the front. For PCE, the symbol is near where the hundreds of "sigils" are laid out.

As I worked with remembering the wondrous complexity and depth of these works, I realized that Bardon had to be the reincarnation Hermes Trismegistus.

For fun, and further enlightenment on the wisdom of the ancient Egyptians, I encourage folk to get St. Germain's "Practical Astrology" which is the only book I know of that combines astrology, numerology, and tarot, into a single system.

Summery Judgments

I don't trust Steiner's indications on the Eighth Sphere, given the obvious contradictions pointed to above. Namely the lack of a true sense of the Mother, and the confusion of good and evil, as expressed in such words as "slag", "drag down", and "fallen".

One of Steiner's concepts concerns the "return of the Moon", which he places in the future. We can think of this in connection with the material, or matter based world. The Earth (consciousness) Globe was preceded by the Moon (feeling) Globe, an aspect of which was removed to the inwardness of the Moon, and then will return after the Earth Globe, perhaps in the Jupiter Globe.

My experience is that "materiality" is a created condition, and dependent on certain very powerful Beings, some of whom are what left the Old Moon Globe and now are said to be returning in the future. "It matters to me, for Matter to be, and that I to Matter do matter."

There is nothing in the Creation that is not created and shaped by Love. There is nothing that Love cannot transmute, via the "Word" (pronounced according to the lawfulness observed in KTQ). Nothing is lost, and all are able to be Graced with Resurrection, by She who has the whole world in His Hands.

The true return of the Moon involves the reintegration of those Beings, who left because their powers were too great. This is an entirely spiritual (non-material) process, which is presently ongoing in our modern Civilization, revealed everywhere through the stories of magical abilities that are a staple of the arts of fiction, film, and television.

In a certain sense ancient magical abilities are reappearing in new ways, via the Collective Imagination. For example, in the wonderful TV series: Babylon Five, that last war is a war of psychic powers. In Stranger Things, the appearance of many such abilities are celebrated, midst the knowledge that governments and corporations try to weaponize these powerful capacities.

"The Secret of Moon-Acre" tells the tale of the return of the Moon after a long absence, and the main character, a young girl, discovers the pearls of wisdom that had been lost, and breaks the string that binds them in a necklace, so that they fall into the surrounding Nature, each one revealing the lost Wisdom, that Nature is self-aware and sentient … in our terms: the Many.

To unify the Eighth Sphere, and the Third Force, has been my purpose here. The oddity is that Hermetic Science has no analogue to that idea. As I puzzled over this, I came to see that a major problem was the concept of Time.

In the Eighth – VIII., Step of IIH, the central consideration is the Great Moment. In my own self studies I became aware that we human beings cannot yet escape the Now, or our own nature … which we clearly might not choose to do, even if we could.

In Ursula K. LeGuin's remarkable novel "The Dispossessed", the main character is a physicist trying to work out the relationship between sequential time, and simultaneous time.

With this background I would like to revisit the shallow U shape: Saturn, Sun, Moon, Earth, Jupiter, Venus, and Vulcan, with the Eighth Sphere just below the "present day" Earth Sphere.

An underlying concept here is linear time. There is a past and a future and a present. In Hermetic Science there is the Idea of the Great Moment, which can operate free of any linear aspects.

For example, picture our earth and its surface. Some eight billion human beings are unfolding their biographies in a succession of Nows. One image I use is that of a place filled with flowers, each biography an individual flower, and each unfolding – in terms of the Nows – in an upward gesture. One Now piled upon the next Now. The linear aspect is not the existential truth, but a necessary fiction, needed for a conceptual orientation. The real nature of the Eighth Sphere is the timeless and spaceless realm where the Mystery resides. The various "Globes" are in movement, one after the other, yet always encapsulated by the Great Moment.

In that ever present Present, magical laws exist, and as the Beings who hid from view inside the Moon during the Earth period, and are destined to return – in Spirit, with knowledge of how to use Hermetic Science (magic) – we will discover how to evoke these fundamental powers in dealing with the real nature of atomic-anti-life, and discover how to get to know the Beings behind the UFO and Crop Circle phenomena, thereby replacing Dominion-Over with Communion-With.

See the movie "Moonfall", for an artistic vision of this coming event. The Moon starts to leave its natural orbit, coming nearer and nearer with each revolution of the Earth. The heroes discover that the interior of the Moon has a community of Beings, whose powers come from their capture of a white-dwarf sun, and are in a battle with a dark power … an Artificial Intelligence.

They need our help to survive this battle.

And … very far from last and not least … a film clearly based on a vision of the meaning of the Return of the Moon: "Moontrap: Target Earth" A necessarily lengthy examination of this Mystery, which includes a discussion of how that film fits in with the works of Rudolf Steiner. http://ipwebdev.com/hermit/moon~%21~earth.html

Notes

(1) **Steiner, on the Inner Earth**

"The occult science of all epochs says the following about the interior of the earth…The topmost layer, the mineral mass, is related to the interior as an eggshell is to the egg. This topmost layer is called the Mineral Earth. Under it is a second layer, called the Fluid Earth; it consists of a substance to which there is nothing comparable on Earth. It is not really like any of the fluids we know, for all these have a mineral quality. This layer has specific characteristics: its substance begins to display certain spiritual qualities, which consist in the fact that as soon as it is brought into contact with something living, it strives to expel and destroy this life. The occultist is able to investigate this layer by pure concentration. The "Air Earth". This is a substance, which annuls feelings: for instance, if it is brought into contact with any pain, the pain is converted into pleasure, and vice versa. The original form of feeling is, so to speak extinguished, rather as the second layer extinguishes life. The "Water Earth", or "Form Earth". It produces in the material realm the effects that occur spiritually in Devachan. There, we have the negative pictures of physical things. In the "Form Earth" a cube of salt, for example, would be destroyed, but its negative would arise. The form is as it were changed into its opposite; all its qualities would pass out into its surroundings. The actual space occupied by the object is left empty. The "Fruit Earth." This substance is full of exuberant energy. Every little part of it grows out at once like a sponge; it gets larger and

larger and is held in place only by the upper layers. It is the underlying life which serves the forms of the layers above it. The "Fire Earth." Its substance is essentially feeling and will. It is sensitive to pain and would cry out if it were trodden on. It consists, as it were, entirely of passions. The "Earth-mirror" or "Earth-reflector". This layer gets its name from the fact that its substance, if one concentrates on it, changes all the characteristics of the earth into their opposites. If the seer disregards everything lying above it and gazes down directly into this layer, and if then, for example, he places something green before him, the green appears as red; every color appears as its complementary opposite. A polaric reflection arises, a reversal of the original. Sorrow would be changed by this substance into joy. The "Divisive" layer. If with developed power one concentrates on it, something very remarkable appears. For example, a plant held in the midst of this layer appears to be multiplied, and so with everything else. But the essential thing is that this layer disrupts the moral qualities also. Through the power it radiates to the Earth's surface, it is responsible for the fact that strife and disharmony exist there. In order to overcome this disruptive force, men must work together in harmony. That is precisely why this layer was laid down in the Earth – so that men should be enabled to develop harmony for themselves. The substance of everything evil is prepared and organized there. Quarrelsome people are so constituted that this layer has a particular influence on them. This has been known to everyone who has written out of a true knowledge of occultism. Dante in his Divine Comedy calls this layer the Cain-layer. It was here that the strife between the brothers Cain and Abel had its source. The substance of this layer is responsible for evil having come into the world. The "earth-core." This is the substance through whose influence black magic arises in the world. The power of spiritual evil comes from this source."[i]

2) Issac Newton's translation of the Emerald Tablet

is true without lying, certain and most true.
That which is below is like that which is above
and that which is above is like that is below
to do the miracles of one only thing
And as all things have been and arose from one by the mediation of one:
so all things have their birth from this one thing by adaptation.

The Sun is its father,
the moon its mother,
the wind hath carried it in its belly,
the earth is its nurse.
The father of all perfection in the whole world is here.
Its force or power is entire if it be converted into earth.

Separate thou the earth from the fire,
the subtle from the gross

sweetly with great industry.
It ascends from the earth to the heaven
and again it descends to the earth
and receives the force of things superior and inferior.
By this means you shall have the glory of the whole world
and thereby all obscurity shall fly from you.

Its force is above all force.
For it vanquishes every subtle thing and penetrates every solid thing.
So was ye world created.
From this are and do come admirable adaptations
where of the means is here in this.

Hence I am called Hermes Trismegist,
having the three parts of the philosophy of the whole world
That which I have said of the operation of the Sun is accomplished and ended.

(3) Steiner on the Eighth Sphere

– I went to Archives and searched for "Eighth Sphere", which is why I just copied and pasted, without the name of lecture or the book. The ideas are as "clear" as possible, yet also often confusing …

~!~ Thus, is I designate the sphere of which I have just spoken as the eighth sphere, we do not live only in the fourth but also in this eighth sphere through the fact that our Divine Creators live in this sphere together with us. If we now hold this eighth sphere in view, we find living there not only our Divine Creator Spirits, but also the Ahrimanic beings. Thus by living in the surroundings of the eighth sphere we live together with the Ahrimanic beings.

~!~ Focus your attention upon these two fundamental concepts which we have just gained; focus your attention upon the idea that we stand within two spheres: the sphere which we entered by passing through the Saturn, Sun and Moon evolution and being now within the Earth evolution which is the fourth evolutionary stage; then consider the fact that we live within a sphere which belongs to the Form Spirits just as our earth belongs to us, but which, as the eighth sphere, permeates our earth and our organism with the exception of our head and all that is sense activity.

~!~ Will man now remain simply an inseparable member in the great organism which mounts to its eighth sphere, the great organism of the Elohim, or will he develop to freedom and become independent? This question of whether men should become independent was decided through a most definite cosmic act.

~!~ If however the human being has connected himself too strongly with the forces of the senses, which should now detach themselves, if he is related to them and has not found the way to attach himself to what is to pass over to the next Globe, he will depart with the slag and become an inhabitant of this body of slag, in the same way as other beings are now inhabitants of the present moon. Here we have the concept of the Eighth Sphere. Mankind must go through Seven Spheres.

~!~ Old Saturn corresponds to the physical body Old Sun corresponds to the etheric body Old Moon corresponds to the astral body The Earth corresponds to the Ego Future Jupiter corresponds to the Manas Future Venus corresponds to the Buddhi Future Vulcan corresponds to the Atma Beside these there is an Eighth Sphere to which everything goes that cannot make any connection with this continuous evolution. This already forms itself as predisposition in the devachanic state. When a human being uses the life on earth only to amass what is of service to himself alone, only to experience an intensification of his own egotistical self, this leads in Devachan into the condition of Avitchi. A person who cannot escape from his own separateness goes into Avitchi. All these Avitchi men will eventually become inhabitants of the Eighth Sphere. The other human beings will be inhabitants of the continuing chain of evolution. It is from this concept that religions have formulated the doctrine of hell. When man returns from Devachan, the astral, etheric and physical forces arrange themselves around him according to twelve forces of karma which in Indian esotericism are called Nidanas: They are as follows: 1. avidja non-knowledge 2. sanskara the organising tendencies 3. vijnana* consciousness 4. nama-rupa names and form 5. shadayadana what the intellect makes of things 6. sparsha contact with existence 7. vedana feeling 8. trishna thirst for existence 9. upadana a sense of comfort in existence 10. bhava birth 11. jati* the urge towards birth 12. jaramarana *

~!~ The asuras inhabit the moon and from there they work on the men whom they want to drag down into the eighth sphere and thereby tear away from progressive evolution and its goal — the Christ. All those who strive towards the eighth sphere will eventually live on a moon. AUM. One wards off bad influences when one says it in the right way; it connects man with the creating Godhead, the three Logoi.

> ~!~ They did not follow Lucifer because something was introduced into the evolution of the earth by the higher gods that prevented them from becoming light enough to do so. As I have shown you, what is called the eighth sphere was introduced into earthly evolution in ancient times. As one of its aspects, the eighth sphere consists of man's acquiring such a preference for and attachment to his lower nature that Lucifer is not able to remove the higher nature from it.

> ~!~ Jahve is connected in this mysterious way with the moon, as you will find explained also in Occult Science. From this statement you can estimate how materialistic it was to designate the moon as the eighth sphere, whereas it really is the force itself, the sphere, that attracts the moon. In her misguided ways, Blavatsky

> developed special malice in her Secret Doctrine by maligning the Jahve God as a mere moon god.

> ~!~ Blavatsky was misled by certain beings who had an interest in guiding her into putting Lucifer in the place of Christ, and this was to be achieved by introducing precisely the opposite of the truth of the eighth sphere and by maligning the Jahve God, representing him merely as the god of the lower nature. Thus did those cosmic powers who desired to advance materialism work even through what was called "theosophy."

~!~ The heavenly bodies became, according to human ideas, mere bodies to be estimated according to their physical condition. In the Middle Ages people saw in connection with the stars what only the eyes can see — the sphere of Venus, the sphere of the Sun, the sphere of Mars and the other planets, up to the sphere of the fixed stars. Then came the eighth sphere like a solid blue wall behind. Later Copernicus appeared and broke down the idea that only that which is perceptible to the senses can be authoritative. He led the gaze of man out into cosmic space, and announced that what people had called the limitations of space, what they had placed there as the eighth sphere limiting everything in space — was in reality no limitation; it was Maya, or illusion; for an infinite number of worlds had been poured forth into cosmic space. That which was formerly considered to be the boundary of space was shown to be only the boundary of the sense-world of man, and if we direct our gaze beyond the sense-world, we shall no longer see the world only as known to the senses, but we shall also recognize Infinity. It completes the work begun for external science by Giordano Bruno and others in that it says: that which external science is able to perceive is Maya, or illusion. Just as formerly one looked to the "eighth sphere" and thought that space was thereby bounded, so contemporary human thought believes that man is shut in or enclosed between birth and death. Spiritual science, however, expands man's vision by directing his attention out and beyond the limits of birth and death.

> ~!~ Those who still remained of the Abel line were Sons of God, they remained akin to the divine. But they now had to guard themselves against entering the earthly sphere. And from this resulted what was to become the principle of asceticism among those who dedicated their lives to the service of God. It became a sin for such a dedicated one to have anything to do with those who had committed themselves to the affairs of earth.

> ~!~! Stated in scientific terms, they are held in check, unable to move backwards or forwards, between the earth and the Eighth Sphere at the point of latency, where the attraction of both is equal on all planes, until the "great day" or axidal coincidence, when they will be drawn irresistibly into the vortex of the latter.

> ~!~ That is the cosmic problem which is fundamental to Christianity. Something occurred at that time in occult spheres; it was the banishment of the enemies of

mankind which has its echo in the Saga of the Antichrist, who was put in chains but will make his appearance again, if not opposed once more by the Christian principle in its primal force.

~!~ At one time, people looked up to the "eighth sphere" and believed it to be the boundary of the universe.

~!~ To cite an example which has often been quoted by me, let us assume that we have to do with a virtuoso pianist and an excellent piano technician, both perfect in their sphere. First of all the technician has to build the piano and then hand it over to the pianist. If the latter is a good player he will use it appropriately and both are equally good. But should the technician go into the concert hall instead of the pianist and start hammering away he would then be in the wrong place.

~!~ The unalloyed evil must be cast out of the stream of world evolution like dross. It will be relegated to the eighth sphere.

~!~ But a part of this remained behind and was excluded, because it was no longer of any use to mankind. That constitutes the eighth sphere, which is no longer of use to the development of man, but can be used by higher beings.' (From previously unpublished notes). In the year 1915, Rudolf Steiner again went very thoroughly into the concept of the eighth sphere.
~!~!~!~!~!~!!!~!~

(4) From Andrew Linnell's "Anthroposophy and the Eighth Sphere"

It is a Rosicrucian gesture to live in the environment of one's times. To do so, we must find appropriate counterbalances. I will highlight some important counterbalances that apply to you as an individual but also to humanity in general. Anthroposophy and the Eighth Sphere 18 1. Christ Consciousness becomes one's archetype. Christ consciousness within is the key to constantly refinding the balance and for all transformations. "The great problem of our time is that people slide into the ahrimanic sphere without having the support of the Christ force. ... We can only become sure of ourselves as human beings if we walk the road created by the whole of technology, but do not let our lives be governed by the products of technology and grow to become able to behold the Christ-power that can become part of us to enable us to inwardly overcome those products of technology." 2. Spiritual Science is itself a primary counterbalance. For example, as we venture into subNature, so must we balance this by ascending into super-Nature. 3. Modern Life Practices: • Practice spirit awareness. • Eurythmy where in the movement we experience the etheric. • Daily 1-hour Walk outdoors (not on a tread mill). • Singing such as in a choir or speech formation. • Gardening – something more than merely looking at Nature, get your hands dirty. • Outdoor play (children need at least 2 hours/day) especially in the winter months. • 20-20-20 Rule. If you are often wo

If you are often working in front of a computer screen, then, for your eyes, every 20 minutes, look out a window at nature that is at least 20 meters away and look for at least 20 seconds before returning to your screen. 4. Refined Breathing, an as-yet undeveloped counterbalance that uses the breathing of the four ethers analogously to how yoga practices breathe air. The undeveloped counterbalance for the future was called by Rudolf Steiner Refined Breathing. There exists a relationship of thinking with breathing that is expressed in these words from Steiner: "The lung is an organ that also has forces of head formation within it, though to a lesser degree. The whole human organism has everywhere these same forces, but in varying intensities. … The head is an advanced respiratory organ. Having moved beyond the lung stage, it represses airbreathing and, instead of taking in air, takes in etheric forces through the senses." During the course of our evolution, the substance of our breathing has changed with changes in our bodily makeup. On Old Moon, we breathed fire instead of air. Just as today we breathe oxygen in and carbon dioxide out, on Old Moon we breathed fire in and cold out. "Just as no human today breathes fire, so future men will no longer inhale air. It will be Light. The development of Refined Breathing helps to prepare this for the sake of our evolution. Today, Refined Breathing is only an indication by Steiner. It needs a lot of work from us to bring it to the state of truly being the New Yoga. Today, we exhale vapor which our inner being has permeated. What is present in what we exhale is the spirit we've built up by our thoughts. This watery element has been placed there by one's etheric body. Why this is so important? Because the sum of our moral-imbued exhalations becomes the foundation materials for the forming of the environment and bodies of the beings upon the human-stage of Jupiter. A clairvoya r. A clairvoyant can see in one's exhalation the morality present within that Anthroposophy and the Eighth Sphere 19 person. What we exhale today contains the result of our inner work. In the future, all will be able to see another's morality in their breath. Unconsciously, we are already at work in the preparation of Jupiter. More and more, we need to make this conscious.

In summary, we are called upon to be pioneers, to be the preparers of the future. Ahriman and technology have roles that provide the resistance for us to build strength for our coming cosmic tasks. Bemoaning technology comes from spiritual weakness. Rather, we need to face Ahriman and technology with soul strength and find the appropriate counterbalances. Facing evil is a necessary part of our evolution. But, without Christ active within us, we are no match for the powers of Lucifer, Ahriman, and the Asuras. Anthroposophy is a path that leads one to discover that they are truly cosmic beings where earth has been provided to us by God for our development. Only out of spiritual science, aware of our evolution and the necessity of evil, can we find the needed counterbalances. As one, Rudolf Steiner offered this meditation:

AUM. One wards off bad influences when one says it in the right way; it connects man with the creating Godhead, the three Logoi. The evil beings who want to tear men away from the Godhead can't stand it. AUM must be spoken with the awareness:
    Primal Self from which everything came
    Primal Self to which everything returns:

Primal Self that lives in me
Towards you I strive.
Peace-peace-peace =
AUM. A is atma, U is buddhi, M is the wisdom that directs the higher self to AUM.
(From Esoteric Lessons, lesson 15, GA 266)

Ingram Content Group UK Ltd.
Milton Keynes UK
UKHW050636290623
424267UK00014B/287